W9-ALJ-731

Spiritual Health and
Wellness Council

Preaching the Letters without Dismissing the Law

Preaching the Letters without Dismissing the Law

A Lectionary Commentary

Ronald J. Allen
Clark M. Williamson

Westminster John Knox Press
LOUISVILLE • LONDON

© 2006 Ronald J. Allen and Clark M. Williamson

All rights reserved. No part of this book may be reproduced or transmitted in any form or by any means, electronic or mechanical, including photocopying, recording, or by any information storage or retrieval system, without permission in writing from the publisher. For information, address Westminster John Knox Press, 100 Witherspoon Street, Louisville, Kentucky 40202-1396.

Scripture quotations from the New Revised Standard Version of the Bible are copyright © 1989 by the Division of Christian Education of the National Council of the Churches of Christ in the U.S.A. and are used by permission.

Book design by Sharon Adams
Cover design by designpointinc.com
Cover illustration: Detailed view of Moses Receives the Tables of the Law, *Marc Chagall.*
© *2006 Artists Rights Society (ARS), New York/ADAGP, Paris.*
Photo Credit: Réunion des Musées Nationaux/Art Resource, NY

First edition
Published by Westminster John Knox Press
Louisville, Kentucky

This book is printed on acid-free paper that meets the American National Standards Institute Z39.48 standard. ∞

PRINTED IN THE UNITED STATES OF AMERICA

06 07 08 09 10 11 12 13 14 15—10 9 8 7 6 5 4 3 2 1

Library of Congress Cataloging-in-Publication Data

Allen, Ronald J. (Ronald James)
    Preaching the letters without dismissing the law : a lectionary commentary / Ronald J. Allen, Clark M. Williamson.—1st ed.
        p. cm.
    Includes bibliographical references (p.) and index.
    ISBN-13: 978-0-664-23001-2
    ISBN-10: 0-664-23001-6
    1. Bible. N.T. Epistles—Homiletical use. 2. Christianity and law. 3. Lectionary preaching. I. Williamson, Clark M. II. Title.

BS2635.54.A45 2006
251′.6—dc22   2005058467

This book is dedicated to Gerald and Marcia Goldstone,
longtime companions in the conversation between
Jews and Christians

Contents

Preface

This book is a sequel to our *Preaching the Gospels without Blaming the Jews: A Lectionary Commentary* (Louisville, KY: Westminster John Knox Press, 2004) that highlights how knowledge of first-century Judaism illumines the Epistles in the lectionary for preaching.

Until about thirty years ago, preachers largely interpreted first-century Judaism as rigid, legalistic, centered in works righteousness, and promoting empty ceremony to the exclusion of ethical living. Even today, preachers often state or imply that Christianity saves people from Judaism. However, as part of the increasing dialogue between Jewish and Christian communities in the wake of the Holocaust, scholars are discovering that the ancient Jewish community, like its contemporary descendents, placed great stress on grace and love and had a permeating concern for living every day in harmony with God's purposes. We discover at the same time that most of the communities to whom Paul and the other letter writers directed their Epistles were made up primarily of Gentiles. For reasons that vary from letter to letter, some of those Gentile converts were living in ways that were not consistent with the desires of the God of Israel for love, justice, and peace in the congregation and in the wider human family. Some Gentiles were in danger of returning to the Gentile life of idolatry, exploitation, injustice, and violence.

Far from attacking Judaism, the letter writers typically want Gentile converts to become *more* Jewish in their attitudes and behaviors. The ancient authors did not envision Christianity as a new religion to supersede Judaism. They did not, in fact, speak of "Christianity" but of "the church," a term that in Greek reflects a Jewish way of speaking about the congregation of

God. Several letter writers envisioned the church as a provision of the God of Israel for Gentiles in preparation for the apocalypse.

We call attention to continuities that preachers often fail to recognize between Judaism (its major themes, texts, practices, and assumptions) and the theology of Paul and the other letter writers. Where the letter writers appear to be criticizing Judaism, new scholarship contends that the authors of the Epistles are correcting *Gentile* misunderstanding and misuse of the law.

This volume joins a growing bookshelf of works that seek for the church to respect Judaism and Jewish people, and, where appropriate, to consider ways in which church and synagogue might explore aspects of identity and mission that we have in common, as well as to deal pastorally with differences. These matters are not simply items of political correctness. They arise from deep theological convictions. The God of Israel is also the God of the church who reveals through both communities God's unconditional love for all. We pray that this book will help preachers and congregations more deeply recognize and respond to the God who wills for all to live together in love.

Introduction

We begin with a word about anti-Judaism that has long been a dominant lens through which to interpret the Epistles, as it has been of the Gospels. Preachers have often read Paul, Paul's followers, and many other writers of the Second Testament through the lens of anti-Judaism. It has been commonplace in Christian scholarship to portray Paul as antagonistic towards Judaism. From this perspective Judaism is a rigid religion that is void of grace and one that, instead, teaches works-righteousness, legalism and leads to an enervating religious life in which one is constantly preoccupied with whether or not one has done enough to merit a place in salvation. According to this point of view, people need to reject Judaism and instead accept the grace of God through Jesus Christ and thereby join the church, the community of the saved. In this view, Christianity has superseded Judaism.

As examples of this viewpoint, consider the following remarks from two well-known scholars. William Barclay, a Scottish scholar whose *Daily Study Bible* has been one of the most widely used references among preachers and Bible-class teachers over the last fifty years, commented on Romans 4, "Here again, we have the root cleavage between Jewish legalism and Christian faith. The basic thought of the Jews was that a man must *earn* God's favor. The basic thought of Christianity is that all a man can do is take God at [God's] word and stake everything on the faith that God's promises are true."[1] Commenting on Galatians 3:19–22, Barclay asks, "What, then, is the consequence of the law?" The answer: "It is to drive everyone to seek grace, because it has proved man's helplessness."[2] For Barclay, grace is available only through confession of Jesus Christ. Ernst Käsemann, one of the most influential scholars of the last half of the twentieth century, wrote that as a "devout Jew" Paul "had been pursuing a righteousness of his own, only to find the pursuit rendered pointless when Christ revealed to him quite another righteousness as being God's will and salvation."[3] Devout Jews, Käsemann opined, engage in confusion: they misunderstand the call of God "as a summons to human achievement and therefore as a means to a righteousness of one's own." This is synonymous with sin and fails to acknowledge that the question "Who is God?" can "only be answered from the Cross of the risen Jesus." According to Käsemann's reading of both Judaism and Paul, Paul comprehends, as Judaism fails to, that righteousness can be ours solely on the condition that we receive it from God as a gift from Christ.[4]

Scholars and preachers have long labored in the vineyard of anti-Judaism in interpreting Paul. It would tax the reader's patience were we to give a full bevy of quotations illustrating the point. Let it suffice to say that this view has had a long shelf life and all-too-wide an influence on how Paul is preached and taught in congregations.

Over the past forty years, a major shift has begun in the way preachers and scholars understand both Paul and Judaism. Jewish scholars have long seen something that growing numbers of Christian scholars are also seeing: the view of Judaism in Paul's time as being works-righteous and legalistic and as confusing one's own righteousness with God's grace is a false representation. As one Jewish scholar, Lester Dean, observed, "When we Jews hear about Paul's description of Judaism as legalistic and based upon self-works, we are astounded. This is neither what we believe today, nor what is found in the Hebrew Scriptures, nor what is found from any sources at the time of Paul."[5] A closer look at the Judaism of antiquity (as at Judaism today) reveals a religion of a gracious and faithful God in which following the commandments is a way of saying "Yes" to God's grace and of committing oneself to live covenantal love and justice in community. The permeating tone of this religious life is expressed by the psalmist who says, "I delight in the way of your decrees as much as in all riches" (Ps. 119:14).

It is nothing short of scandalous that the kind of view represented by Barclay and Käsemann survived as long as it has in Christian interpretation. As long ago as 1914, the Jewish scholar C. G. Montefiore highlighted three major discrepancies between rabbinic Judaism and the religion that Christian scholars claimed that Paul rejected. First, rabbinic Judaism regarded the torah (way or path) as God's gracious gift to God's people, intended to teach them to live according to the "way of life" and not the "way of death." The essence of rabbinic Judaism is captured in the expression "the joy of the commandments" (*simhat Torah*). Second, repentance and God's forgiveness were common in rabbinic Judaism; all one has to do is "turn" (*shuv*) to God. Like the "gates of prayer," the "gates of repentance are always open. . . . Let a man repent but a very little, and God will forgive very much. For he delights in the exercise of forgiveness far more than in the exercise of punishment."[6] Third, Paul's theology was far gloomier than that of rabbinic Judaism, which never contended that Adam's one solitary transgression brought all people under the wrath of God. Rather, it claimed that God forgave Adam, thus making "the attribute of mercy take precedence over the attribute of judgment."[7] Montefiore concluded that Paul was not familiar with rabbinic Judaism. H. J. Schoeps said that Paul had a "fundamental misapprehension"[8] of Judaism. Scholars such as Montefiore believe that the viewpoint articulated by Käsemann accurately represented Paul but that Paul did not accurately understand Judaism. As we shall see, however, it was not Paul who was confused; it was his Christian interpreters. Had Paul indeed been opposed, as Matthew Black put it, to "Pharisaic 'scholasticism,'" Paul could at least once have said so.[9] But he does not. Therein hangs a tale.

Talking about Our Jewish Neighbors

The problem with the anti-Jewish reading of Paul is not only that it distorts and misinterprets Paul; it also distorts and misinterprets Judaism, a faith practiced by human beings with whom hearers of sermons and students in church school rub shoulders during the week. Are Christians supposed to believe of their neighbors what they hear in church? Should their attitudes toward these neighbors be shaped by condemnatory Christian preaching and teaching? Is there not a deadly conflict between, on the one hand, being urged to love our neighbors and, on the other, being told that these same neighbors persist in following an illusion, seeking their own righteousness, and turning their backs on the cross of Jesus, the only place where they can learn the truth about the God whom they mistakenly think they worship? It is morally risky to proclaim that the author of a considerable chunk of the Second Testament was implacably opposed to them. Should any responsible Christian have repeated this notion in Germany, after the Holocaust? Should we repeat it today? Can we not see where the long history of Christian anti-Jewish talk has led?

That's the deeper issue. Sociological studies of Christian prejudice strongly suggest that Christians learn anti-Jewish bigotry in church.[10] Apparently pleas to "love the neighbor" fail to outweigh the incessant drumbeat of negative images of the neighbor proclaimed as the Word of God.

As an alternative to what Jules Isaac (the Jewish and French historian whose family was killed by the Nazis) called "the teaching of contempt" for Jews and Judaism, a growing community of Christian scholars propose the "teaching of respect."[11] The most frequently repeated *mitzvoth* (commandment) in Scripture is "You shall love the stranger as yourself," a commandment occurring in various forms thirty-six times, as in, for example, "You shall not oppress a resident alien; you know the heart of an alien, for you were aliens in the land of Egypt" (Exod. 23:9). Christians should learn to "know the heart" of our Jewish neighbors in their difference from and strangeness to us. And Christians should not oppress them by means of our language, for which Christians need to take responsibility. Anti-Jewish language both reflects and reinforces age-old prejudices and sews the seeds of prejudice among younger people. Talking is the most ordinary and common thing we do; we are obligated by the gospel of God's loving grace not to malign our neighbors with our words.

A New Paradigm for Reading Paul[12]

In this brief introduction, we present only the barest outline of the new way of reading Paul and the post-Pauline letters. The details appear abundantly in the commentary on individual passages; there is no need to belabor them here. Introductory information on all epistle readings is provided in the readings on chapter one of each biblical book.

The new reading of Paul begins with the recognition that Paul did not regard the Jesus movement as a new religion (later called Christianity) whose purpose was to supersede Judaism. Indeed, under the influence of Jewish apocalyptic theology, Paul believed that the God of Israel was about to end the present evil age with a massive apocalypse and replace the present age with a new world in which all things conform in every way to God's purposes. Paul regarded the death and resurrection of Jesus as revealing that this great cosmic transformation was underway. The apostle believed that the apocalypse would be centered in the return of Jesus in glory to complete the transformation. In order to be faithful to the promises that God made to Sarah and Abraham, God made provision through Jesus Christ for the Gentiles to come into the community of the new age. The event of Jesus Christ demonstrated God's faithfulness by showing how and when God would renew the world, a process that included a means whereby Gentiles could be saved.

Some elements of Judaism (such as circumcision and the dietary customs) functioned as reminders of identity. In the midst of pagan cultures across two millennia, such practices helped Jewish people remember their identity as the community of the living God (in contrast to the idols), who were called to model how God wants all peoples to live. Their identity markers reminded them not to compromise with the values and ways of idolaters. Paul expected the apocalypse soon. Because the time was short, Gentile believers needed to repent from idol worship and from qualities of Gentile life that were self-serving and unjust, but they did not need the long-term identity markers that came with full initiation into Judaism. Gentile converts became a part of the church, which, for Paul, was a community both awaiting the eschaton and embodying many eschatological qualities in community life.

The Gentile believers were called to adopt some essential aspects of Judaism, such as honoring the God of Israel and living in love in community. The Gentile members did not have to manifest all qualities of Jewish life because believers expected the time to be very short between conversion and the second coming. Because the Gentiles were to enact some key Jewish values (but not all), one of our acquaintances has referred in conversation to the early Gentile church as "Judaism light." For their part, Jewish members in the church did not turn away from Judaism and toward Christ but instead looked on Christ as God's means of fulfilling the divine promises to renew the cosmos—promises that were now freely available to Gentiles.

Some Gentiles who converted to the God of Israel did what converts often do by overemphasizing qualities in the original group. As comments on pertinent passages will show (e.g., Proper 4 [9]/Year C, Proper 5 [10]/ Year C, and esp. Proper 6 [11]/Year C), these Gentiles misunderstood the purpose of the law by looking on it as *work* that Gentiles must perform in order to merit salvation. The apostle takes these Gentiles to task for misappropriating Jewish heritage.

A key element in this new paradigm is a fresh understanding of Paul's vocation. Paul understood and declared himself to be an apostle to the Gentiles: ". . . when God, who had set me apart before I was born and called me through his grace, was pleased to reveal his Son to me, so that I might proclaim him among the Gentiles. . . ." (Gal. 1:15–16). What traditional interpreters referred to as his "conversion," Paul refers to as his call to proclaim him among the Gentiles. Paul uses the language of prophets of Israel, such as Isaiah, who also were called to bear witness to Gentiles: "The Lord called me before I was born, while I was in my mother's womb he named me" (Isa. 49:1). Isaiah follows that remark by saying for God,

It is too light a thing that you should be my servant
   to raise up the tribes of Jacob
   and to restore the survivors of Israel;
I will give you as a light to the nations [Gentiles],
   that my salvation may reach to the ends of the earth.

                         (Isa. 49:6)

Jeremiah 1:5 speaks in the same manner.

Strikingly, the Acts accounts of Paul on the Damascus Road make the same point. The Lord said to Ananias: "Go, for he is an instrument whom I have chosen to bring my name before Gentiles" (Acts 9:15; see also 22:14–15 and 26:16–18). Paul did not convert in the sense of moving from Judaism to Christianity (any such separation of the two came much later).[13] He did convert in the sense of changing drastically from being a persecutor of the church to being an apostle to Gentiles.

Moreover, Paul reported, "James and Cephas and John . . . gave to Barnabas and me the right hand of fellowship, agreeing that we should go to the Gentiles and they to the circumcised" (Gal. 2:9). Paul was not authorized to preach among Jews and apparently did not (his own letters never report his doing so). Acts claims that Paul went to the synagogue wherever he preached, but Acts and Paul's letters are often difficult to reconcile with each other. Indeed, Acts does not even mention that Paul wrote letters! Paul's letters are explicitly addressed to Gentiles (Rom. 1: 5, 13; 15:9, 12, 16, 18, 27; 16:4; Gal. 1:16; 2:2, 8; 3:8; 3:14; 1 Thess. 2:16). Other letters make it clear in different ways, as when Paul says to the Corinthians, "When you were pagans, you were enticed and led astray to idols that could not speak" (12:2). He cautions the Philippians to "beware of those who mutilate the flesh" (3:2), a comment that makes sense only if directed to Gentiles. The letters often regarded as written later by members of the Pauline school also address Gentiles (Eph. 2:11; 3:1; Col. 1:27; 1 Tim. 2:7; 2 Tim. 4:17).

To put it differently, as we noted above, Paul did not write to Jews about their fidelity to the covenants and to torah. He wrote to Gentiles about Gentile problems. If he disagreed with his fellow Jews, that disagreement was not, contrary to the traditional view, about Judaism as such but "rather about a Jewish understanding of Gentiles."[14] Paul did not want his Gentile Jesus-followers to have to perform "works of the law," but this phrase is not found in Jewish literature. By it, Paul meant that Gentiles did not have to observe the food laws or undergo circumcision to be included in the people of God. These are the only commandments that Paul ever disputes, and he does so only as they apply to Gentiles. Rather it is God's faithfulness and Christ's faithfulness that "justifies" Gentiles (expressions such as "faith in God" in Paul are best rendered as "God's faithfulness," that is, as subjective and not objective genitives).

As it turns out, Paul never disparaged the Torah for Israel. Instead he was committed to affirming the equality of Gentiles with Jews in the church: God showed "faithfulness to Jews, mercy to Gentiles," a formula we meet more than once in his letters, as we will show. Only once does Paul refer to Jesus as "the messiah" (Rom. 9:5); typically for him "messiah" is the title that has become a name, as in "Jesus Christ." It seems much more important for Paul that Christ be understood as the one who confirmed God's promises to Abraham concerning the Gentiles: "In you all the families of the earth shall be blessed" (Gen. 12:3; see Rom. 4 and Gal. 3).

We should never forget that for Paul the church was a temporary shelter where Gentiles and Jews could briefly and safely be together awaiting the return of Jesus with the rule of God, when Jesus would bring "the glory about to be revealed to us" (Rom. 8:18), a salvation that "is nearer to us now than when we first believed" (Rom. 13:11). Paul's theology is apocalyptic throughout, and this apocalyptic theology is still evident in his last letter, Romans.

That point should give us some pause about Paul's arguments. Paul believed that he knew the timetable of God's economy and that the end of this present oppressive age would come quickly. We should not beat about the bush on this one—it did not. In his time, some could well have disagreed with Paul because they did not share his confidence in the sudden end of the old age. For Paul, that imminent closure meant that certain distinctive characteristics were unimportant, such as identity markers (i.e., circumcision and the dietary laws). Today, however, we have so-called "mainstream" churches that are insufficiently attentive to their distinctiveness and who are losing their sense of mission and identity and dribbling away into the surrounding culture.[15] Many congregations today would benefit from a heightened sense of identity.

Paradoxically, one service that Paul can perform for congregations today may well be to encourage them to think more deeply about the gospel of God's unconditional grace that freely justifies the ungodly—the good news that we are freed by God to love and loved by God into being free and that we are claimed by God to live lives that make it plain that God desires love and justice to be done for all. Paul calls us to pay attention to the heart of the matter—the good news of the promise and command of the gospel of Jesus Christ—and to let that shape our lives together for the sake of "all the Gentiles."

Paul also calls us to reconsider our relations with the people Israel. It is clear from his letters that the last thing he would be able to comprehend about today's church is that it is a Gentile affair with little if any relation to the people Israel and that it has an attenuated if nonexistent sense of being "fellow citizens" with Israel in God's all-inclusive economy of grace. He would be aghast. That should bother us. We offer this commentary as one of many efforts made by conscientious Christians to call and invite fellow Christians on a journey to rediscover ourselves and our Jewish neighbors by reacquainting ourselves with the Apostle to the Gentiles, who proclaimed God's faithfulness to Israel and God's mercy to us.

Letters and Documents after Paul

Seven letters indisputably came from Paul himself: Romans, 1 and 2 Corinthians, Galatians, Philippians, 1 Thessalonians, and Philemon. We share the conclusion of a large body of scholars that the following books, though attributed to Paul, were actually written not by the apostle but by his followers at a time after Paul: Ephesians, Colossians, 2 Thessalonians, 1 and 2 Timothy, and Titus. As we have already noted, while the letters written after Paul deal with somewhat different issues than do those in the seven letters of undisputed Pauline authorship, the other letters tend to presume understandings similar to those in Paul's own letters regarding the relationship between the God of Israel and Gentiles, and between Judaism and the early communities of Jesus' followers. A similar perspective is also behind the non-Pauline letters of 1 and 2 Peter. Many of these epistles presume issues that involve Gentiles who are leaving the worlds of the idols and coming to love and serve the God of Israel, who are struggling in the process, and who need encouragement to continue the faithful life. Many passages in these documents encourage Gentile believers to adopt some key characteristics of Judaism.

In comments on specific passages we also describe situations in other letters that seem to be addressed to congregations that appear to contain significant numbers of Jewish people who are loyal to Judaism and who believe that God is acting through Jesus Christ. These documents include James and Jude (apocalyptic in outlook), Hebrews (an early sermon), and the three letters of John (that were written from the perspective of Hellenistic Judaism).

The Revised Common Lectionary occasionally assigns a reading from the book of Revelation instead of an epistle. The last book of the canon is an apocalypse similar to many others from the same historical epoch. Not only does the book of Revelation not evaluate Judaism negatively, but it makes such thorough use of Jewish ideas and images that it cannot be understood without knowledge of the First Testament and other Jewish literature. The book of Revelation differs from other Jewish apocalypses in its claim that Jesus Christ is the one whereby God is effecting the end of the present evil age and the re-creation of the world as the realm of God in which all things work together for God's purposes.

Year A

First Sunday of Advent/Year A

Romans 13:11–14

Romans 12–15 deals with ethics, how Jesus' followers should live. It begins with an eschatological comment: "Do not be conformed to *this* world" [emphasis ours], the old one that is passing away, "but be transformed by the renewing of your minds" (12:2). So today's Advent reading begins by striking an eschatological note: "You know [that is, 'recognize,' *eidotes*] what time [*kairos*] it is" (13:11). The salvation of which Jesus Christ is the "first fruits" (Rom. 8:23; 11:16) "is nearer to us now than when we became believers" (13:11).

The lectionary places this reading in Advent to remind us that full salvation, the redemption of the world from what Paul has earlier called "the sufferings of this present time" (8:18), still lies in the future. On the day after Christmas evil will continue to stalk the world; thirty children per minute around the globe will still die of starvation; people will still be oppressed by war, famine, homelessness, and ambiguity in communal and political life; justice and peace will only have a tenuous hold in this "old, passing" world that is still with us. We are not to sentimentalize Advent and Christmas.

Nonetheless, according to Paul, we should recognize that we live in a *kairos*, a time that is singularly significant. We are familiar with the notion of a time when we are ready to do something for which we were not ready earlier, when the time is "ripe" to get married, to be responsible for children, to decide to enter the ministry. That is what *kairos* is like although on a larger scale—it is a time that is "opportune" (*opportunitas* is the Latin

1

equivalent of *kairos*). We, says Paul, live in such a time: the first fruits of salvation have been made actual in Jesus Christ; "the night is far gone"—the darkness of this old age of oppression, unspeakable brutality and war—and "the day is near."

With the eyes of faith we can recognize in the resurrection of Jesus Christ and the presence of the Spirit that the new age in which God will rule has dawned. The eyes of faith can see it *in spite of* the fact that it is far from obvious in the death-dealing ways of the world (Rom. 8:36: "We are being killed all the day long"). Christians are tempted to locate salvation in the past, to say that it has been accomplished in Jesus Christ, and to leave it at that. For Paul, we can say that, of course, but we cannot leave it there. Jesus as Messiah still has work to do—to bring the rule of God to earth when God's will shall be done by all, as we pray in the Lord's Prayer.

What this means for Paul is that we should change the way we live; we should "lay aside the works of darkness and put on the armor of light" (13:12). This is a more forceful expression than the translation makes clear—we are to "throw off," *apothometha*, the works of darkness. From eschatology, Paul draws an ethical implication. We live in a new day; we should act like it. The new day is a gift to us; acting appropriately is our response. We should live in the daylight, doing only deeds that we are willing for others to see. Paul then lists a representative sample of deeds to be thrown off—reveling, drunkenness, debauchery, licentiousness, quarreling, and jealousy. This is standardized rhetoric from the early church (compare Gal. 5:19–21). This list correlates readily with ancient descriptions of much that went on in Rome. Preachers should feel free to expand the list in ways appropriate to the present.

Instead, says Paul, we should "put on the Lord Jesus Christ" (13:14). We already have put on Jesus Christ in baptism, says Paul (Rom. 6:3); here we are asked to remember that and be intentional about it, to live in the renewed humanity of the new, dawning age. By doing the deeds of daylight we "mend the world" (*tikkun olam*); we wait actively, not passively, for the return of Jesus with God's rule.

Second Sunday of Advent/Year A

Romans 15:4–13

In this passage Paul appeals to Gentile Jesus-followers in Rome to "welcome one another . . . as Christ has welcomed" them (v. 7) and describes his ministry to Gentiles (15:1–33). He begins with a comment about the

Scriptures (*graphen*): "Whatever was written in former days was written for our instruction, so that by steadfastness and by the encouragement of the scriptures we might have hope" (v. 4), reassuring his Roman community that it can trust the Scriptures for "instruction."

The community in Rome needs to manifest "steadfastness" (*hypono-mone*, perseverance), and Paul seeks to fortify them with the remark that "by the encouragement of the scriptures we might have hope" (v. 4). "Courage" comes from the French *coeur* meaning heart. The Scriptures give us the heart to endure and to hope, a grand concept for Advent. Indeed God is "the God of steadfastness and encouragement" (v. 5), who gives us the heart to "live in harmony with one another" and "with one voice glorify the God and Father of our Lord Jesus Christ" (v. 6). Living in harmony within the community and in relations to outsiders has been the theme since 12:1.

In verses 7–13 Paul sets forth Jesus Christ as the type for our acceptance of one another: "Welcome one another, therefore, just as Christ has welcomed you, for the glory of God" (v. 7). Christ through the faithfulness of God made possible the entry of Gentiles into the family of God precisely in order that this inclusive glorification of God might occur. Whereas the previous passage found Paul discussing relations between the "weak" and the "strong" within the community, encouraging them to welcome each other and to refrain from passing judgment, here Paul speaks of the people Israel and the Gentiles. His intended audience for these remarks remains the Gentiles, as it has been throughout Romans (1:5, 13).

In verse 8 Paul proclaims that "Christ has become a servant of the circumcised on behalf of the truth[*fulness*] of God in order that he might confirm the promises [*epangelias*] given to the patriarchs." Note that Paul speaks of God's "confirming" the promises to Israel; in 2 Corinthians 1:20 he says of Christ that "in him every one of God's promises is a 'Yes.'" Paul says simply that Christ "confirms" God's promises to Israel; he never speaks of God's "fulfilling" them, perhaps because he did not think them empty. Note also that God deals with Jews on the basis of God's "faithfulness" or "truthfulness" (*hyper aletheias*). If God is not faithful to God's promises to Israel, can we trust God?

Verse 9 continues the thought that Christ became a servant to the people Israel "in order that the Gentiles might glorify God for his mercy." Note that God deals with Jews out of faithfulness and with Gentiles out of unadulterated mercy (*hyper eleous*). Paul thought of Gentiles as "sinners" (Rom. 1:18–32; Gal. 2:15) in need of God's mercy. Then, in verses

10–12 Paul quotes the Torah (v. 10), the Prophets (v. 12), and the Writings (v. 11), what Jews call the Tanakh (an anagram for Torah, Prophets, and Writings), that is, "the Scriptures," the only ones he knew.

Speaking for the LORD, Isaiah states Paul's advent theme

> "It is too light a thing that you should be my servant
>   to raise up the tribes of Jacob
>   and to restore the survivors of Israel;
> I will give you as a light to the nations,
>   that my salvation may reach to the end of the earth."
>
> (49:6)

It is this inclusive understanding of Israel's faith of which Paul is speaking in today's reading.

Yet Paul urges us to "abound in hope" (v. 13) for Christ's second coming; the rule or kingdom of God is not yet altogether here.

Third Sunday of Advent/Year A

James 5:7–10

Today's reading is James's plea to his readers to persevere "until the coming of the Lord" (v. 7). Interpreters often suggest that the reason for this request for "endurance" (v. 11) has to do with the travails of the end time that are usually associated with apocalyptic. That may well be true in James's case, but it is also true that in 5:1–6 he denounced the "rich people" who "kept back by fraud" the "wages of the laborers who mowed [their] fields," peasants whose "cries . . . have reached the ears of the Lord of hosts" (5:4). The defrauded laborers are likely members of James's community. Hence, there seem to be two reasons behind the call for patient endurance, not just one.

James urges his "beloved" to "be patient until the coming of the Lord" (v. 7). James had spoken of "the last days" in the prior paragraph (v. 3) when warning the rich about their immorality. Now he turns to speak affectionately to the "beloved" (*adelphoi*, "brothers" or "brothers and sisters" since he was committedly egalitarian), urging them to be patient. In the theological background is the patience of God ("a God merciful and gracious, full of patience," Ps. 86:15). God's patience with us enables us to be patient. The expression "the coming of the Lord" refers to the second coming of Jesus.

The latter part of verse 7 is a brief parable about the farmer who waits patiently "for the precious crop from the earth . . . until it receives the early and the late rains." The farmer waits patiently because the crop is "precious"; indeed, the life of his family depends on it. So, too, is the "coming of the Lord" precious. The early and late rains were an important weather phenomenon in the western edge of the Fertile Crescent. James's knowledge of these two rains could indicate that he was familiar with the land of Israel, a familiarity that is compatible with his closeness to the teachings of Jesus and the apparently early form of belief in Jesus that his letter reflects. As a result of the reforestation efforts in contemporary Israel, the two rains returned in the latter part of the twentieth century.

James urges his readers also to be patient (v. 8): "Strengthen your hearts, for the coming of the Lord is near." This is equivalent to asking them to stand secure in their faith, to remain stable amid their troubles, of whatever kind those may be. Typically in the Scriptures it is God who strengthens our hearts; the Holy Spirit is spoken of as the "comforter," who supplies us with strength (which is the meaning of "comfort"). Paul urges the Thessalonians, "Comfort your hearts and strengthen them in every good work and word" (2 Thess. 2:17).

Twice in today's reading, James discloses his belief that the second coming of Jesus is close at hand: it is "near" (v. 7) and "the Judge is standing at the doors!" (v. 9). James's stress is not on how long his readers have to wait but on the need for them to remain steadfast while they are waiting.

"Beloved, do not grumble against one another, so that you may not be judged" (v. 9). It does not take much to make many of us grumble; a thirty-minute wait at the airport security desk easily does the trick. We should note that James is not critical of grumbling as such, which need be nothing more than venting our feelings over frustration or difficulty. He is opposed to grumbling "against one another," targeting other members of the community as the objects of our complaints. Instead of holding them responsible for our problems, we should learn patience, as did the prophets (v. 10) and Job (v. 11). The Lord, who is coming soon, "is compassionate and merciful" (v. 11). So be patient.

Fourth Sunday of Advent/Year A

Romans 1:1–7

Today's reading should include Romans 1:8–17, all of which is the introduction to Paul's letter "to all God's beloved in Rome" (1:7). Paul is keenly aware that he is unknown, or perhaps unfavorably known, to the community of Jesus-followers in Rome, and that he has no authority among them. He says in 15:20, "I make it my ambition to proclaim the good news, not where Christ has already been named, so that I do not build on someone else's foundation." This is why he says in 1:11–12, "I am longing to see you so that I may share with you some spiritual gift to strengthen you— or rather so that we may be mutually encouraged by each other's faith, both yours and mine." Paul does not want to put off these Romans but to introduce himself and his mission to those whose "faith is proclaimed throughout the world" (1:8).

Paul refers to himself as "called to be an apostle, set apart for the gospel of God" (1:1), reminding us of his statement in Galatians 1:15: "But when God, who has set me apart before I was born and called me through his grace, was pleased to reveal his Son to me, so that I might proclaim him among the Gentiles." Paul's mission was that of an apostle to the Gentiles (obviously there were Gentile Christians in Rome whom Paul had not evangelized and, hence, apostles to the Gentiles other than Paul).

Therefore Paul also describes his audience in Rome as Gentiles when he speaks of having received the gift of apostleship from Jesus Christ "to bring about the obedience of faith among all the Gentiles for the sake of his name, *including yourselves* who are called to belong to Jesus Christ" (1:5–6; emphasis ours). Whatever the actual makeup of the Roman community of Jesus-followers and however much it may have been a mix of Jews and Gentiles, Paul's intended audience is the Gentile Jesus-followers in Rome. He wants to "reap some harvest among you as I have among the rest of the Gentiles" (1:13).

He underscores this point twice in chapter 15: first when he says, "For I tell you that Christ has become a servant of the circumcised on behalf of the truth of God in order that he might confirm the promises given to the patriarchs, and in order that the Gentiles might glorify God for his mercy" (15:8–9); and second when he explains, "I have written to you rather boldly by way of reminder, because of the grace given me by God to be a minister of Christ Jesus to the Gentiles . . . , so that the offering of the Gentiles may be acceptable, sanctified by the Holy Spirit" (15:15–16).

He wants to ensure that these Gentile believers not look down their noses at Jews who do not believe in Jesus Christ—telling them not to "boast" over such Jews but to "remember that it is not you that support the root, but the root that supports you." You Gentiles, he says, are the branches grafted into the olive tree of Israelite faith, "so do not become proud, but stand in awe" (11:17–20).

Paul describes the content of his gospel (*euangelion*) as the Son of God "who was descended from David according to the flesh and was declared to be Son of God with power according to the spirit of holiness by resurrection from the dead" (1:3–4). This seems to be a piece of older tradition with its adoptionist-sounding language.

Two facts are not to be overlooked: the first is that the Roman Empire frequently announced the good news (*euangelion*) of the crowning of a new emperor. The inscription from 9 BCE concerning Caesar Augustus is the best known: "The birthday of the god [Caesar Augustus] has been for the whole world the beginning of the gospel" (*euangelia*). The second is that the emperor was frequently called "son of God."

In his lifetime, Jesus of Nazareth proclaimed the good news of the "kingdom [rule] of God," affirming that only God is "king" and denying that the king (the title "Caesar" means "king") is God. Paul's bold proclamation of the good news of Jesus the Son of God equally denies the claim of Caesar to be son of God and to bring good news. Paul finds that claim bogus. In 1:18–32 he will describe the ungodliness and wickedness of the present and deny the promises of a "golden age" promised by the likes of Augustus and Nero (Nero was emperor when Paul wrote), a "golden age" to be brought in by military power, oppression, and brutality.

Christmas Day/Years A, B, and C

Proper 1

Titus 2:11–14

Both 2 Corinthians and Galatians mention Titus as a representative of Paul to congregations (2 Cor. 2:13; 7:6; 8:6; 12:18; Gal. 2:1, 3). The letter to Titus, probably pseudonymous (the majority scholarly view), presents itself as a letter from Paul to Titus, in Crete, charging him with two tasks: first, to "appoint elders [*presbuterous*] in every town" (1:5) so that, second, those elders could "preach with sound doctrine and . . . refute those who contradict it" (1:9). We note that in the paragraph describing Titus's commission (1:5–9), "bishop" (*episkopos*, v. 7) and "elder" are used interchangeably. There is to be one "in every town"; they are local pastors, not hierarchical bishops, and their task is "oversight" (the meaning of "bishop," overseer) of the community.

The teachings to be opposed seem to be various: "there are . . . many rebellious people, idle talkers and deceivers" (1:10). "Those of the circumcision" are singled out as among those who "must be silenced" (1:11). Yet they are also identified as "Cretans" (1:12), and the Cretan poet Epimenides is quoted: they "are always liars, vicious brutes, lazy gluttons." This is a piece of standard slander and subject to the question: Since Epimenides was himself a Cretan, was he lying?

Hence, those of the circumcision, promoting "Jewish myths" (1:14), may well not have been Jewish but may have been local citizens who taught something (the exact teachings are not described) with which the author disagrees. Women are to be submissive to their husbands (2:5; did the opponents urge them to speak up?), and slaves are to be "submissive to their masters and . . . not to talk back" (2:9). The very submission of slaves to their masters will "be an ornament to the doctrine of God our Savior" (1:10). Though Paul, in his authentic letters, said similar things (1 Cor. 7:21, 24), the tension between this attitude and the claim that "for freedom Christ has set us free . . . do not submit again to a yoke of slavery" (Gal. 5:1) is decidedly missing from Titus.

This is the literary context for today's reading, which turns to the topic of the "sound doctrine" that elders are to proclaim. Perhaps in spite of Titus's accommodation to Greco-Roman culture, the opening announcement is that "the grace of God [*charis tou theou*] has appeared, bringing salvation to all [*pasin*]" (2:11). Here we find another proclamation of universal salvation in the Pastorals (1 Tim. 2:4). It is remarkable how often this statement is overlooked by those who like to make the opposite theological claim. On Christmas Day, it is a herald of good news.

Grace, in the Pastorals, is emphatically transformative: it is to "train" us "to renounce impiety and worldly passions," and in the present age to "live lives that are self-controlled, upright, and godly" (2:12). We should not downplay what may seem stodgy moralism. War making is a worldly passion; we should resist it. And our character should manifest our deepest convictions. The "present age" is passing and we "wait for the . . . manifestation of the glory of . . . Jesus Christ" (2:13), that is, the eschaton. This is another good note for Christmas Day: Christmas is not the end of the adventure but a beginning. The rule of God is not yet here, a point on which the author and Jews would agree. Neither sees the world as yet fully redeemed.

The reading ends on a Jewish note (one reason to think that the opponents were not Jews): that Christ gave himself "that he might redeem us from all iniquity and purify [*katharise*, cleanse] for himself a people . . . zealous for good deeds [*kalon ergon*, good works]" (v. 14). Being pure and doing deeds of loving-kindness are quintessentially Jewish. Note that we do not do them to receive grace but because we have already received grace (2:11).

Christmas Day/Years A, B, and C

Proper 2

Titus 3:4–7

In the lectionary's other reading from Titus (2:11–14, Proper 1 for Christmas Day/Years A, B, and C), the text focused on the transformative grace of God bringing salvation to all people and transforming the people of God from living lives of "iniquity" and purifying "for himself [Jesus Christ] a people of his own who are zealous for good deeds" (2:14). Proper 2 continues this train of thought.

Because our reading begins with "But," indicating that it picks up in mid-thought, we should put it in its literary context. Paul (or the author writing in his name) begins chapter 3 by asking Titus to "remind them [the congregation in Crete; 1:5] to be subject to rulers [*archais*] and authorities" (3:1). This is in keeping with Paul's advice in Romans 13:1–7. The early church was keenly aware of Rome's readiness to come down hard on assemblies that were not, in its view, peaceable. Acts 18:2 reports that Aquila and Priscilla went to Corinth "because Claudius had ordered all Jews to leave Rome." Titus is concerned that the people stay out of trouble with Rome while they await "the manifestation of the glory of our great God and Savior, Jesus Christ" (2:13).

There follows in Titus a list of six virtues: Titus is to remind the Cretans "to be obedient, to be ready for every good work, to speak evil of no one, to avoid quarreling, to be gentle, and to show every courtesy to everyone" (3:2). Such lists were commonplace among Hellenistic moral philosophers and would have been readily comprehended by the Cretans. The list is a character ethic: this is the kind of person whom you are given and called to be—one who avoids evil, does deeds of loving-kindness, and is gentle.

Then Paul comments, "We ourselves were once foolish, disobedient, led astray, slaves to various passions and pleasures, passing our days in malice and envy, despicable, hating one another" (3:3). This is not a self-description to be taken literally; the author is speaking "in character," as we do when we say, "I wouldn't do that if I were you." Paul is here identifying with his Gentile audience by describing their former life prior to their encounter with the transforming grace of God.

"But," begins today's reading, "when the goodness [*chrestotes*] and loving kindness [*philanthropia*] of God our Savior appeared, he saved us" (3:4). "Loving kindness" is a standard Jewish way of speaking of God's faithfulness or steadfast love. When God's loving-kindness appeared, "he saved us, not because of any works of righteousness that we had done, but according to his mercy" (3:5). Romans 9 and 11 speak nine times of God's mercy: "So it depends not on human will or exertion, but on God who shows mercy [*eleos*]" (Rom. 9:16).

Faithfulness to Jews and mercy to Gentiles is Paul's usual message. Relations between Jews and Gentile followers of Jesus are not explicitly mentioned in Titus, but the Gentile background of the community is alluded to in 3:3 with its typical list of Gentile sins from which the community is now saved.

This salvation is the work of the Holy Spirit's renewing of us (3:5) and celebrated in baptism, "the water of rebirth." Here, too, God's grace takes the initiative. The Spirit is lavished on us through Christ "so that, having been justified by his grace, we might become heirs according to the hope of eternal life" (3:7). Justification is the beginning, not the end, of God's transformative grace and its efficacy upon us.

Christmas Day/Years A, B, and C

Proper 3

Hebrews 1:1–4, (5–12)

For our commentary on verses 1–4 of today's reading, please see Proper 22/Year B. This commentary will focus on verses 5–12.

The topic of verses 5–12 is the relationship of Jesus Christ to the angels. We do not know why this should have been of concern to the author of Hebrews, but he is obviously concerned that his readers get things figured out and so puts this matter at the very introduction to the text. In some parts of the early church there was an angel Christology in which Christ was construed as or associated with the other angels talked about by some Jews at the time (*1 En.* 39:10–13). Indeed the words *aggelos* and *euaggelos*, messenger and message, respectively, are clearly related. The likely possibility, then, is that Hebrews was concerned that Christ be seen as transcending the angels, not as just another one of them.

So, verse 5 asks, "For to which of the angels did God ever say, 'You are my son; today I have begotten you'?" Hebrews takes Psalm 2:7 as having been said by God to Christ; the psalm was a royal psalm celebrating the enthronement of a king of Israel and the king's relationship to God as God's son. Similarly, Hebrews quotes 2 Samuel 7:14 ("I will be a Father to him, and he shall be a son to me") and takes it as said by God of Christ. In its original context it was Nathan's prophecy to David about David's son. Hebrews's exegesis is, like that of numerous Jewish exegetes, playful and creative.

Verse 6 quotes God as saying of "the firstborn," "'Let all God's angels worship him.'" Hebrews always quotes the Septuagint (in some version of which there were several), and we have difficulty finding this exact quote today; it may be a paraphrase of Psalm 97:7: "All gods bow down before him." If so, originally God was the one before whom all "gods" were to bow down. Hebrews takes the text christologically, in the manner of exegesis at its time. Verse 7, a quote from Psalm 104:4, refers to the angels but not to Christ. It is not clear what it seeks to establish about Christ and the angels.

Verses 8 and 9 quote Psalm 45:6–7, initially a song of celebration at the marriage of a king of Israel; the psalm extols God, whose "throne endures forever and ever," who loves righteousness and hates wickedness, and (7b) who anoints the king "with the oil of gladness" on the occasion of the wedding. Hebrews takes Christ as the one whose throne endures forever and ever. That Hebrews so freely uses royal psalms to speak in the present about Christ is one indication of Hebrews's deep-rootedness in the Scriptures of Israel. His proof-texting was a form of exegesis also practiced by various Jewish groups at the time, sometimes to make points not particularly obvious in the text.

Verses 10–12 quote Psalm 102:25–27. Psalm 102 is a prayer to God from a person in anguish: "Do not hide your face from me in the day of my distress" (Ps. 102:2). The point of Hebrews's quoting of this passage is to contrast Christ with the angels who "will perish, but [he will] remain" (v. 11). Verse 12 continues, "Like clothing they will be changed. But you are the same, and your years will never end." This introduces an important theme in Hebrews: like Melchizedek who was "a priest forever," so Christ, unlike the angels, reigns eternally.

Beneath the issues of Hebrews's exegesis lies a theological point worth grasping: in worshiping Christ, we worship the One who is ultimate and nothing less.

First Sunday after Christmas Day/Year A

Hebrews 2:10–18

The thesis of today's reading in Hebrews is that "it was fitting that God . . . should make the pioneer of their salvation perfect through sufferings" (2:10). That Christ will become the "merciful and faithful high priest"

(v. 17) is what Hebrews wants to explain. Like some Hellenistic Jewish writers (see our comments on Christmas Day Proper 3/A, B, and C), Hebrews converts the story of liberation from bondage to slavery in Egypt into a story of freedom from bondage to death by making the journey to heaven. Aspects of that conversion are visible in today's reading.

Notice (v. 10) that it is God who engages in the enterprise of salvation. (By implication, any human beings who inflict suffering on Jesus are simply God's agents.) The sufferings of Jesus are the consequences of God's action in making him "perfect." The purpose of God's doing so is to bring "many children to glory" (v. 10). God's aim is that all God's children should attain the consummation of salvation and blessedness that is life in God. In order to do that, as Hebrews sees it, Christ must be the "pioneer" (*archegos*), that is, leader of them to salvation, and to be the pioneer he must be perfect.

Verse 11 claims that the sanctifier and the sanctified "all have one Father." The Greek does not have "Father" but says, somewhat mystifyingly, that the sanctifier and the sanctified "are of one all" (*henos pantes*), apparently meaning "one source." The NRSV interprets this as God in its translation "one Father." It could refer to Adam or Abraham. Given God's initiative in verse 10, however, the NRSV's interpretation seems appropriate. This makes clear that God's intent is that all humanity constitute the group whom Jesus "is not ashamed to call . . . brothers and sisters" (v. 11).

Verse 12 quotes Psalm 22:22: "I will tell of your name to my brothers and sisters; in the midst of the congregation I will praise you." Initially a prayer of a person in anguish, this verse is used to stress Christ's role in making known God's name and to encourage Hebrews's readers to hold fast to their congregation from which some have drifted away. Verse 13 cites two more biblical texts. The first, "I will put my trust in him," is most likely a Septuagint rendering of Isaiah 8:17: "I will hope in him," that is, in the Lord. Hebrews's next citation is Isaiah 8:18: "See, I and the children whom the Lord has given me. . . ." The message is that we are to trust in God and that Christ's brothers and sisters have been "given" to him by God.

Verse 14 is incarnational: because these brothers and sisters "share flesh and blood," so too must Christ in order that "through death he might destroy the one who has the power of death, that is, the devil." The theologically striking point here is that Christ "destroys" the devil. After Christ completes the work of salvation, the devil is no more! Verse 15 strikes the note of liberation: Christ frees "those who all their lives were held in slavery by the fear of death." Without reducing death to a figure of speech for a life curved in upon itself, Hebrews nonetheless makes an existential point: release is from the fear of death that prevents us from living an authentic life of love and service to the neighbor.

Verse 16 declares that Christ came to help not "angels, but the descendants [*spermatos*, "seed"] of Abraham." All human beings join the people Israel in being the "seed of Abraham." Because Christ became like us "in every respect" (v. 17), he is a "merciful and faithful high priest." Because he was tested, he can help "those who are being tested" (v. 18), as Hebrews's readers were and as, in various ways, we all are.

Second Sunday after Christmas Day/Years A, B, and C

Ephesians 1:3–14

Psalm 72:18 is a typical liturgical blessing (*berakah*) from the worship of Israel: "Blessed be the Lord, the God of Israel, who alone does wondrous things. Blessed be his glorious name forever; may his glory fill the whole earth. Amen and Amen." Ephesians 1:3–14 is one long *berakah*. Ephesians is influenced by liturgical language and is concerned with the ongoing viability of early Pauline congregations. It reflects the importance of liturgy and ritual for forming community identity.

Today's reading is in the indicative—it recites for the community of faith what God has done for us. The God and Father of Jesus Christ "has blessed us in Christ with every spiritual blessing in the heavenly places" (v. 3). "In Christ" means that God has blessed us by way of Christ, with the nuance that we are incorporated into Christ's body, the church (Eph. 4:12). "Spiritual blessings" refer primarily to the presence of the Holy Spirit with the community; they are the gifts of the Spirit before they are qualities of human life. "Heavenly places" is an ambiguous term in Ephesians; in 6:12 it refers to "the spiritual forces of evil in the heavenly places." Yet in verse 3 "heavenly places" refers to God's transcendence where Jesus sits at God's right hand (2:6).

"He chose us in Christ before the foundation of the world to be holy and blameless before him in love" (v. 4). Here Ephesians draws on Israelite understandings of election to remind the community of who they are—God's beloved, always close to God's heart, and elected to live lives characterized by love (*agape*). Ephesians 2:11–22 will remind its Gentile readers that their election confirms that of Israel, that through Christ they have been "brought near" to Israel. As a result, we Gentiles also were "destined for adoption [*huiothesia*] as his children through Jesus Christ" (v. 5). Israel's special relationship with God is now shared by Gentiles.

This happens (v. 6) "to the praise of his glorious grace." God acts out of grace, and we, in turn, praise God's glorious grace. The Greek reads, "To the praise of the glory of the grace [*charis*] of God with which he graced [*echaritosen*] us." God did this through "the Beloved" in whom we are also beloved. Verse 7 proclaims that "in him we have redemption [*apolytrosis*] through his blood." This term was used for escape from danger—from exile in Babylon and slavery in Egypt. Slaves in the community, numerous in the Roman Empire, no doubt heard the latter meaning as good news. Verses 7–8 declare the "riches of his grace, that he lavished on us." Rich, lavish, bottomless grace; boundless—enough for everybody; we do not need to hoard it.

Wisely, God "has made known to us the mystery of his will" (v. 9). The mystery of God's will made known in Christ has to do with the *kairos* in which the community lives: God's plan for the time when things are ready for the consummation of creation to occur in the eschaton. In "the fullness of time, [God will] gather up all things in him, things in heaven and things on earth" (v. 10), according to God's "plan" (*oikonomia*). *Oikonomia*, economy, alludes to the supervision of a house; here it means God's direction of the world, the carrying out of God's purposes.

Verses 11–13 deal with the "inheritance" that Gentiles have "also obtained" in Christ. We have been adopted by God "so that we . . . might live for the praise of his glory" (v. 12). We have "heard the word of truth . . . [of] salvation," and "were marked with the seal of the promised Holy Spirit" (v. 13). We Gentiles, too, have been marked as included in the people of God, marked by baptism and by the Spirit.

Epiphany of the Lord/Years A, B, and C

Ephesians 3:1–12

Today's reading follows the presentation of "Paul's" gospel to the "Gentiles" (2:11–22) and precedes the ethical section of the letter, which entreats its readers "to lead a life worthy of the calling to which [they] have been called" (4:1; Paul is in quotes because most scholars think that a second-generation student of Paul wrote Ephesians). It prepares believers for the moral exhortations to follow by making a case for Paul's authority to confront them with the demands of the gospel. Its topic is Paul's authority. In Greek, 3:1–12 is one long sentence; we will divide it into two paragraphs: verses 1–6 and verses 7–12.

Verses 1–6 describe Paul as being in prison "for the sake of you Gentiles [*ethnon*]" (v. 1); three times in today's reading (vv. 1, 6, 8) Ephesians makes it clear that the implied audience is Gentiles. That verse 1 says, "I Paul" also stresses that Paul's authority is being asserted. "Surely," says Ephesians, "you have already heard of the commission of God's grace that was given to me for you" (v. 2). Except for Romans, Paul's authentic letters are written to communities that he had founded; Ephesians is written to one (or some) who were not directly acquainted with him. The "commission" of God's grace is Paul's "stewardship" (*oikonomian*) of God's grace. Ephesians speaks of *oikonomia* also in 1:10 and 3:9; it is God's "plan" for the world. Ephesians 3:1–12 deals with Paul's role in moving that plan to realization. The "mystery" of God's plan was "made known to me by revelation" (*apokalypsis*): that is, the timing of Christ's enabling "the Gentiles . . . [to] become fellow heirs, members of the same body, and sharers in the promise in Christ Jesus through the gospel" (v. 6). What God had always promised, that in Abraham and Sarah and their descendants the Gentiles would be blessed, has in Christ started to be actualized.

"In former generations, this mystery [of the timing] was not made known to humankind," but it has been revealed to Paul (v. 3) and to Christ's "holy apostles and prophets" (v. 5), that is, early church prophets. Paul is becoming an authority figure. The content of his gospel, following the Greek, is that Gentiles are "joint-heirs, joint-sharers of the promise in Christ," and part of a "joint-body" with Jews (v. 6, authors' translation). Each noun has the prefix *syn*, meaning "with." We Gentiles are the "also-sharers" of the promise, not the only sharers. We should not enfeeble Ephesians's strong emphasis on this point.

Verses 7–12 turn again to "Paul" who has been a "servant [*diakonos*] according to the gift of God's grace." The later office of deacon is not intended here. Paul exercised his servant ministry by preaching: "This grace was given to me to bring [*evangelisasthai*] to the Gentiles" (v. 8). His role is "to make everyone see" God's plan (v. 9), to *enlighten* all about the "wisdom of God" (v. 10), even the "rulers and authorities in the heavenly places." Paul speaks to the universal church and even to the heavenly "rulers" (see 1:20–21) who vainly imagine themselves in control of the world and us.

All this coheres with God's "eternal purpose that he has carried out in Christ Jesus our Lord" (v. 11). In one sense, what happened in Christ was not new; it was always God's plan. In another, it was nonetheless a not-yet; God's revelation is always both an already and a not-yet. "We [Gentiles] have access to God" in Christ; prior to Christ Gentiles were "without God" (2:12). We have access "through faith in him" (3:12). "Faith in him," *pisteos autou*, can as well be translated "through his faithfulness" that evokes our faith. Such a translation better conveys the initiative of God's grace.

First Sunday after the Epiphany/Year A

Baptism of the Lord

Acts 10:34–43

Although the book of Acts is not a letter, the lectionary assigns Acts 10:34–44 to the place in the four readings for today that is normally occupied by a passage from a letter. One of the goals of the Gospel of Luke and the book of Acts is to help the reader recognize that the God of Israel ordained for Gentiles to come to the knowledge of God through Jesus Christ and to live in covenantal community with God and other believers in the church. In the larger picture, as informed by apocalypticism, Luke believes that Gentiles confessing the God of Israel is a sign of the last days of the present wicked world and of the imminence of the return of Jesus to finally and fully manifest the divine realm in which Jewish and Gentile peoples would live together in covenant.

According to Acts 1:8, the news of the present and coming transformation will be carried by witnesses from Jerusalem and Judea, through Samaria, to the ends of the earth (that is, to the Gentiles). Acts 2:1–36 paves the way for today's reading. On Pentecost, a large group of Jewish people in Jerusalem received the ecstatic experience of the Spirit. Under the influence of the Spirit, they began to speak other languages. Not only did individuals speak other languages, but they also heard in their own language (2:1–13). Peter demonstrated the essence of preaching by interpreting their experience. According to the apostle, what happened was a sign that the movement towards the eschaton was in its final stages. Peter quotes Joel 2:28–32 to show that God was breaking down the barriers among people in the old world and making them into a community of the new age (Acts 2:14–21). When Peter finished preaching, about three thousand people repented and prepared for the coming world with baptism.

The gospel witness passes through Samaria in 8:4–25. Beginning with 8:26, the witness turns towards the Gentile world and comes into clear focus with the call of Saul, a Jewish person, to preach to Gentiles (9:1–31). The first dramatic Gentile conversion (Cornelius) takes place at the hand of the Jewish apostle, Peter, thus reinforcing for the reader the continuity between the Jewish and Gentile communities of believers (10:1–33).

The scene in Acts 10:34–44 unfolds in much the same way as the events on Pentecost. After a dramatic experience, Peter interprets the event. The outpouring of grace on Cornelius demonstrates that God has no partiality but embraces and blesses all who reverence God and do what is right, an idea that was central to some Jewish groups (Acts 10:34–35; Deut. 10:17–18; 1 Kgs. 8:41–43; Sir. 35:15–16). According to Luke, Jesus Christ is the means through whom this impartiality is now leading to blessing among Gentiles as it spreads from Galilee through Judea. To be sure, a few Jewish people did not understand the significance of Jesus and were complicit in his death. Nevertheless, God caused Jesus to appear to the faithful disciples with whom Jesus ate and drank. Jesus commanded them to preach that the great day of the judgment of the living and the dead is coming, but that all who acknowledge Jesus as God's agent will pass through that judgment uncondemned (10:36–43).

In 10:44–48, the Gentiles receive the Spirit in the same way as did the Jewish community on Pentecost. Under the influence of the Spirit, Gentiles, who are normally idolaters, not only speak in tongues but also "extol" the God of Israel. Immediately, they are baptized. When Peter returns to Jerusalem, he reports to the apostles and other believers that the Gentiles are, indeed, fully vested members of the community of the new age, for they manifest the same signs as those of the Jerusalem community. Luke wants readers to understand, "God has given even to the Gentiles the repentance that leads to life" (11:1–18). For Luke the experience of the Gentiles is valid because it is consistent with that of the Jewish community. The Jewish experience authenticates the Gentile one. In a similar spirit, we learn in Acts 15:28–29 that baptism and the bestowal of the Spirit mean that the Gentiles need to become more Jewish in their outlook and behavior.

Second Sunday after the Epiphany/Year A

1 Corinthians 1:1–9

The Corinthian congregation, like the others founded by Paul, was made up primarily of Gentiles (1 Cor. 12:2) though some Jews were part of the community. In this letter the great apostle calls these Gentiles to leave behind their pagan orientations and calls both Gentile and Jewish people to live together in covenantal love, which demonstrates how God wants all people to live now and in the eschaton.

Paul's theology is influenced by Jewish apocalypticism—the belief that God is about to end the present evil age with an apocalypse and establish a new world (e.g., 1 Thess. 4:16–5:5; 1 Cor. 15:1–57). This motif is crucial for understanding 1 Corinthians, for the apocalypse includes a moment when God will judge all people and either welcome them into the new world or condemn them. According to Paul, the death and resurrection of Jesus reveal that the moment of transformation is near.

The apostle writes to prepare the Corinthians for the apocalyptic event. Paul wants them to be "blameless" on that day (1 Cor. 1:8) and not to perish (1 Cor. 1:18). He has heard that some Corinthians are living in ways that deny God's intentions—supporting social fragmentation, engaging in inappropriate expressions of sexuality, and not believing that history is headed towards an apocalyptic climax.

Paul begins 1 Corinthians with a standard indication of sender and recipient (equivalent to the salutation of today's letter, 1:1–2) and offers a brief blessing (1:3). A Jewish overtone is evident as Paul in 1:1 identifies himself as author in company with Sosthenes, a synagogue leader (Acts 18:17). According to Galatians 1:11–24, Paul presents himself as an apostle (one sent with a commission) from God to Gentiles.

Although the receivers are designated as "the church of God" (1:2), we need to remember that for Paul the church was not a separate institution that broke away from Judaism but a mission of the God of Israel to prepare Gentiles for the apocalypse. While the term "church" (*ekklesia*) generally means "called out" and was used of different public assemblies in antiquity, the Septuagint sometimes uses it to translate the Hebrew *qahal* or "congregation" in reference to Israel (e.g., Deut. 23:2; Lam. 1:10; Mic. 2:5; Sir. 24:2; 1 Macc. 4:59). We should not project the later separation between church and synagogue into the time of Paul but should recognize that the Corinthians would have heard positive resonance between the church and the Jewish communities. Indeed, we can even think of the early churches as Christian synagogues.

The theme of Corinthian identification with Judaism continues as Paul describes the church as those who are "sanctified in Christ Jesus" and as "saints" (1:2b). The terms "sanctify" and "saints" are from the word family of *hagios*, "holy," which the Septuagint uses of God (e.g., Josh. 24:19; Ps. 22:3; Isa. 40:25) and of the vocation of Israel (Exod. 19:6; Lev. 11:45; Isa. 62:12). To be holy is to be set apart. God is holy in the sense that God is one and is not beholden to other entities for the divine character, which is undivided love to bless all. God intends blessing for the whole world (Gen. 12:1–3). Israel and the church are set apart from the other peoples of the world in the sense of living according to the purposes of God so that all, especially Gentiles, may experience the divine blessing.

Paul adapts the usual Greek letter style by changing the word *chairein* ("greeting") found in the typical Greek letter to *charis*, ("grace"), an alteration that itself moves the letter in a Jewish direction inasmuch as the

Septuagint often uses *charis* to translate *hen*, which is often rendered in English as "grace" or "favor" and sometimes translates *hesed* (steadfast love, loving-kindness). These terms reveal essential aspects of the divine character in the First Testament (e.g., Exod. 34:6; Ps. 119:29; Wis. 3:9). Jewish people wish "peace" (*shalom*, relationships of support) to one another. Paul thus wants the church to know God and peace in the same way as the Jewish people.

Paul writes 1 Corinthians to help the congregation (synagogue) live in ways that prepare them for the apocalypse and that allow them to tell others of the opportunity to live the blessed life now and evermore. The impending apocalypse infuses this vocation with urgency.

For consideration of 1 Corinthians 1:4–9, please see the First Sunday of Advent/Year B.

Third Sunday after the Epiphany/Year A

1 Corinthians 1:10–18

In today's lection, Paul reveals the problem that prompts the writing of 1 Corinthians: people in the congregation have fractiously different approaches to their common life, a fractiousness that misrepresents the gospel and prevents the congregation from fulfilling its purpose. As the letter unfolds, readers learn that relationships among the Corinthians continue the denigrations of social class that are a part of the culture outside the church.

In 1:10, the apostle states the thesis of the letter: "that all of you be in agreement," have no divisions, and "be united in the same mind and the same purpose." Paul appeals "by the name of our Lord Jesus Christ," a phrase likely used at baptism. In 1 Corinthians 12:13, Paul interprets baptism as bringing people into "one body" whose various parts, while different, are to serve the common purpose. Baptism initiates people into eschatological community and empowers witness in the present to the coming realm (Rom. 6:3–14; Gal. 3:27–28) of love, justice, abundance, and other qualities of eschatological community. The Corinthians think and behave in ways that contradict the life into which baptism has initiated them.

Paul learned of the problems at Corinth by means of a report from a member of Chloe's household—a family member, employee, or slave (1:11). Chloe was likely an independent businesswoman or a widow of means.

Most scholars today think that the phrases in verse 12, "I belong to Paul . . . Apollos . . . Cephas . . . Christ," refer not to actual groups but are a rhetorical way of depicting the partisan quality of life in the congregation. In the Greek language, questions are typically formulated to suggest either a positive or negative answer. The questions in verse 13 are phrased to presuppose a negative response. "Has Christ been divided? Was Paul crucified for you? Or were any of you baptized into Christ?" The answer is no.

In verses 14–16, Paul does not downplay the importance of baptism per se. Indeed, it is foundational to his appeal to the Corinthians. Paul's point is that being immersed by a particular person does not result in loyalty to that person but brings one into a community whose purpose transcends partisan loyalties. This point is worth repeating today: Christians should not limit loyalty to individual pastors, groups, or causes but should be committed to the whole community of witness.

According to 1:17, Paul's particular calling is not to baptize but to preach the gospel, the turning of the ages that results in welcoming Gentiles into the eschatological community. Paul, however, does not preach with "eloquent wisdom" (*sophia logou*), a loaded phrase that does not simply refer to high-sounding ideas (e.g., philosophy) but in the first century was associated with persons in the upper class who sought status and public recognition through the use of sophisticated and impressive rhetoric. By contrast, Paul preaches "the cross"—shorthand for the death and resurrection of Jesus that signals that God is creating a new social world that ends the negative of this old age (including the repressive effects of the highly stratified class structure of the first century) and replaces them with a new social world.

This passage is both a challenge and problem for today's church. The challenge is for congregations, denominations, and Christian movements to live towards common purpose and community while respecting differences. The problems are how to identify faithful common purpose as well as delineate the limits of acceptable diversity in community.

Presentation of the Lord/Years A, B, and C

Hebrews 2:14–18

Please see the first Sunday after Christmas/Year A for commentary on this passage.

Fourth Sunday after the Epiphany/Year A

1 Corinthians 1:18–31

First Corinthians 1:17 introduced today's theme by contrasting "eloquent wisdom" (*sophia logou*) with Paul's preaching of "the cross" or the "the message of the cross" (*ho logos ho stauros*) (1:18), that is, the news that God is moving towards the apocalyptic conclusion of the current repressive world and the final manifestation of the divine realm. Paul now takes up the language of wisdom (*sophia*) and message (*logos*) to point the community to the true wisdom and message that come from God.

Readers are asked to turn to our remarks on the Third Sunday in Lent/Year B for discussion of 1 Corinthians 1:18–25. In today's commentary, we focus on 1:26–31.

In 1:18–25, having contended that "eloquent wisdom" is really foolishness that leads to perishing and that "the word of the cross" is divine wisdom that leads to salvation, Paul next asks the Corinthian congregation to recognize that they are living proof of the truth of Paul's claim about how God is at work. Most of the descriptions of the congregation in verse 26 are taken from ancient ways of speaking about people in the lower class: not powerful, not of noble birth. Those of "eloquent wisdom" enjoy high status now, but this community from the underside of power will be a part of the unending new world. Of course, the community did contain a few people from the upper class, as revealed in Paul's phrase "Not many of you. . . ." Such folk are welcome in the community of the new age when they recognize God's power in the word of the cross and give up trying to garner power through "eloquent wisdom."

Ancient society placed much more importance on shame and honor than North American culture does today. To be shamed was not simply to be embarrassed but to lose honor and respect and be disgraced. Furthermore, Jewish texts use the vocabulary of "shame" to say a community was condemned (Ps. 83:17; Jer. 17:13; Sir. 5:14; 2 Esd. 7:87). Thus Paul makes a strong negative evaluation when saying that God *shames* the strong who partake of "eloquent wisdom" (i.e., who are in the upper social strata).

Verse 28 presumes an apocalyptic frame. The death and resurrection (the things that are "low and despised") reveal that the "things that are" will pass away and in their place will be a renewed cosmos. Neither upper nor lower classes can effect such a transformation and, consequently, cannot engage in self-boasting.

This passage ends theocentrically. The God of Israel is the source of the life of the eschatological community. Paul describes the following acts of God through Jesus, all of which are continuous with how God is described as acting in Jewish tradition: (1) In the sense just discussed, Jesus imparts the wisdom of God; (2) Jesus reveals God's righteousness, that is, reveals God's will for all relationships to come to life with love, justice, and abundance; (3) Jesus sanctifies, that is, makes holy as discussed on the Second Sunday after the Epiphany/Year A; and (4) Jesus redeems. This term, borrowed from the slave market where it described buying slaves out of bondage, more generally refers to the final redemption (*1 En.* 51:2; cf. cognates in *Pss. Sol.* 3:6; 8:11; 17:3).

Many Christians and churches operate in larger North American culture via "eloquent wisdom," that is, by accumulating and using social power in the ways of the old age. Even more troubling, many people within the church reproduce the Corinthian problem by satisfying their egos and accumulating ecclesiastical power through their versions of "eloquent wisdom." To such impulses, this passage is an invitation to recognize that "God's weakness is stronger than human strength."

Fifth Sunday after the Epiphany/Year A

1 Corinthians 2:1–12, (13–16)

Paul now uses the characteristics of his own ministry to urge the Corinthian congregation to reinforce the ideas of 1:18–31. To a culture taken with high social status (represented by impressive rhetoric—the "eloquent wisdom" of 1 Cor. 1:17) and high social standing, the cross was most unimpressive. In a similar way, Paul's initial ministry in Corinth was uninspiring.

In antiquity rhetors spoke with "lofty words" and presented themselves with confidence and power. The apostle, however, began "proclaiming the mystery of God" in Corinth in an opposite style by speaking not "in lofty words or wisdom" but in weakness, fear, and trembling, with words that would seem implausible to people impressed by the old-age social system (1 Cor. 1:1b, 3–4). Paul's mode of presentation corresponded with the content of the message. For Paul, "Jesus Christ and him crucified" specifies the content of "the mystery" (2:1) and is an abbreviated way of speaking of the apocalyptic renewal of the cosmos that began with the cross and resurrection. Ministers might reflect (1) on the degree to which our modes of preaching participate in styles of communication and social values that are today's equivalent of the "eloquent wisdom" and (2) on the degree to which our patterns of preaching are shaped by the cross.

In 1 Corinthians 2:6–12, Paul reinforces the notion that the content of his preaching is authentic wisdom. The expression "this age" in Paul is negatory as it has in mind the current sinful age. The "rulers of this age" include both suprabeings—cosmic powers who seek to enslave the world—and the human beings who are their agents (such as the Romans who put Jesus to death).

In verses 7–10, Paul draws on an idea from apocalyptic theology that seems strange to many moderns: that before the creation of the world, God decided when the present era of history would end and would hide the time of apocalypse until that time is near. In 2:9, the apostle warrants this idea by citing a passage that conflates elements of Isaiah 64:4 and 52:15. The notion of mystery from 2:1 presumes much the same. The "mystery of God" is not a deep metaphysical puzzle but refers to the timing of the apocalypse, which is a "mystery" in the sense that the plan was hidden until God decided to reveal it.

However, God is now revealing the plan decreed before the ages by means of the Spirit (2:10–13). For Paul, the Holy Spirit is an agent of God that can communicate the knowledge of God. One reason Paul believes the word of the cross is that this word is confirmed through the experience of the Spirit. The awareness that comes through the Spirit is reliable because the Spirit "searches the depths of God" (2:10–11).

When Paul says, "We have not received the spirit of the world" (v. 12), he means that we should not subscribe to the values and behaviors of the present evil age. These qualities have an animating power, a spirit, similar to that of the Holy Spirit

Paul deftly negotiates a difficult issue of theological method. At one level he believes that the death and resurrection of Jesus are a part of the apocalyptic consummation because of the *experience* of the Spirit. Interpreting experience as a source of the knowledge of God can be notoriously difficult. How do we distinguish what is of God and what is not? Paul offers a helpful criterion: Experiential awareness may be of God when it is consistent with the wisdom that is revealed in the death and resurrection of Jesus and leads towards the regeneration of the cosmos.

Sixth Sunday after the Epiphany/Year A

1 Corinthians 3:1–9

The reading for today, like many of Paul's other writings, presupposes a contrast between the spirit (*pneuma*) and the flesh (*sarx*). For Paul this contrast is not between a superior nonmaterial dimension of life (spirit) and an inferior material one (flesh). Rather, spirit and flesh are two spheres of existence involving the whole of self, community, and cosmos. The pneumatic realm is animated by the Spirit, recognizes that history is moving toward the apocalyptic moment (as described in comments on previous lections in Epiphany A), seeks to live faithfully, and manifests qualities of the realm of God. The flesh, a characteristic mode of Gentile existence, is life apart from the awareness of God, including complicity in the fractiousness, repression, and violence of the present world that is passing away. Paul also refers to this mode as "behaving according to human inclinations" and being "merely human" (1 Cor. 3:3, 4). When the apocalypse comes, the fleshly realm will be destroyed, but in the meantime the two realms exist alongside one another with people living under one influence or the other.

In 3:1–4, Paul makes the crucial point that although the Corinthians have received the Spirit (2:6–16), their common life is still under the aegis of the flesh. Jealousies, quarrels, and other human inclinations continue, such as saying, "I belong to Paul." As we saw in connection with 1:10ff., the problem with such attitudes and actions is that they distract the church from being able to fulfill its purpose.

When saying, "I fed you with milk" (v. 2), the apostle uses the image of a mother who has nursed the Corinthians. This motherly behavior continues as Paul makes the judgment that the Corinthians are not "ready for solid food."

First Corinthians 3:5–9 introduces a theme that becomes ever more central in the letter: different people have different gifts for helping the congregation fulfill its common purpose. Differences among people in the congregation are not, in and of themselves, either positive or negative. Difference becomes negative when it is expressed in such a way as to undermine the purpose of the community and positive when it strengthens the mission of the congregation.

Paul "planted," that is, introduced the seed of the gospel to the largely Gentile constituency in Corinth. Apollos "watered," that is, instructed the Corinthians in how to think and live in the final days of the present. Apollos was a learned Jewish leader from Alexandria who played a role in Luke's narrative in Acts 18:24–19:1 and who was evidently well regarded in the congregation (cf. 3:22; 4:6; 16:12). Paul and Apollos are servants (*diakonoi*) of God's mission in Corinth.

The life of the church is to manifest the kind of unity of purpose within its different elements as exhibited by Paul and Apollos. Closer attention to Paul's Greek in 3:8 reveals that this passage makes an even more important point that resonates with one of the deepest themes in Jewish literature. Where the NRSV says that Paul and Apollos have a "common purpose," the Greek reads more simply that they "are one" (*hen eisin*), thus evoking the confession that God is one (Deut. 6:4). The church derives its oneness from the integrity of God, and the characteristics of its life are to witness to the same.

The distinction between spirit and flesh gives the preacher a helpful lens. Is the congregation oriented more towards life in the Spirit or in the flesh? How does the congregation need to grow in the Spirit, that is, to work through old-age-quality jealousies, quarrels, and divisions to move towards a common life that testifies to the rule of God?

Seventh Sunday after the Epiphany/Year A

1 Corinthians 3:10–11, 16–23

Continuing the motif developed in 1 Corinthians 3:1–9 of different congregants having different roles to help the church achieve its common purpose, Paul recollects laying the foundation while others build. When referring to the foundation as Jesus Christ, Paul means the complex of events from the death and resurrection to the apocalypse.

A number of writers in antiquity employed figures from the realm of construction to speak of people in community. In a spirit closely akin to Paul's use of the language of building in this chapter, several rabbis speak of teachers and students of torah as "builders" whose work is to create covenantal community by teaching and learning torah and the works that should issue from the faithful life in everyday relationships (*b. Ber.* 64a; *b. Shab.* 144a; *Fathers according to Rabbi Nathan* 24). The "grace of God that has been given to Paul" (1 Cor. 3:10) is to be missionary to the Gentiles, that is, helping Gentiles learn those qualities of life that are essential to their identity as a household of God.

In 1 Corinthians 3:12–15 Paul indicates that the day of judgment will disclose the quality of the work of each builder as buildings are put into the fire to determine whether they stand or burn (on fire as testing see Deut. 3:22; Amos 7:4; Mal. 3:2). The builders will receive a wage or suffer loss according to whether their buildings survive the judgment. Those who suffer loss may not face eternal condemnation but may be saved "through fire," that is, refined much like ore placed in the fire to burn away impurities and leave pure metal (3:15b; cf. Isa. 1:25–28; Ps. 66:12; Isa. 43:2; Zech. 13:9; Mal. 3:3–4).

The community needs to repair its divisions because it is "God's temple" and "God's Spirit dwells" in it (as in 2 Cor. 6:16). Paul does not suggest that the church replaces the temple at Jerusalem, and, in fact, he never criticizes that temple. For Gentiles, the church functions much like the temple in Jerusalem. Jewish theology recognizes that God does not reside only in the temple but is omnipresent (for example, 1 Kgs. 8:27; Ps. 139:7–11). The temple is a sign of God's presence and faithfulness. The temple and its rites represent liturgically God's presence in all phases of life in empowerment, forgiveness, and community building. The dwelling of the Spirit in the church means that by participating in the congregation, Gentiles can experience the same assurance, confidence, forgiveness, and sense of community as the Jewish community in the temple. However, quarrels and jealousies inhibit the life of the community from fulfilling this purpose. Paul uses strong language to urge the Corinthians to reshape their common life: "If anyone destroys God's temple, God will destroy that person" (1 Cor. 3:17).

He exhorts the Corinthians not to be deceived by mistaking what passes for wisdom in the present for real wisdom. If the recipients want true wisdom, they should adopt the theology of Paul, although that approach to life appears to be foolish to whose who do not share it (3:18). In 3:19–20, the apostle turns to Job 5:12–13 and Psalm 93:11 to point out that God can distinguish the truly wise from the foolish.

The truly wise do not boast about following a particular leader, for such partisanship inhibits the community from building itself into a temple. Instead, the people should recognize that "all things are yours"; in other words, from God's perspective, you are already in covenantal relationship with the people with whom you are in tension. For all things in the present (such as life and death) already belong to God, who is at work to bring them into eschatological harmony at the apocalypse (3:21–22).

Eighth Sunday after the Epiphany/Year A

1 Corinthians 4:1–5

By assigning only 1 Corinthians 4:1–5, the lectionary removes the passage from its explanatory context, which indicates Paul's reason for including this material in the letter: to encourage the congregation to become one in purpose. The apostle has just emphasized that all things belong to God and that, by implication, God seeks for all things to work together in mutuality in accord with the divine purposes of love and justice.

In 1 Corinthians 4:1–5, Paul uses the ministry of the apostles as an example of how the Corinthians should see the purposes of God, the congregation as community, and themselves in relation to one another. Because all things belong to God, the readers should think of the apostles as "servants of Christ and stewards of the mysteries of God" (1 Cor. 4:1). The expression "God's mysteries" is simply a plural for the similar concept in 1 Corinthians 2:1. Paul uses a word for "servants" here—*huperetas*—that refers to one whose service is not imposed (like that of a slave, *doulos*) but is willingly given and one who acts with the authority of the one served. The *huperetes*, servant, is a kind of executive assistant who carries out the owner's injunctions. In the Septuagint, monarchs are sometimes identified as "servants" of God (Wis. 6:4). The "steward" (*oikonomos*) is the chief servant in the household who manages the other servants and perhaps financial and legal affairs.

Although Paul delays direct mention of the apocalypse until verse 5, that scenario is in view as the apostle reminds the readers that stewards (*oikonomia*) are to be found "trustworthy" (*pistos*). The Greek term translated "trustworthy" is the same one that Paul used in 1:9 to describe God: "faithful" (*pistos*). Stewards are to be faithful witnesses to the divine love and call for right relationship in community in their limited spheres as God is in the cosmos.

The fractiousness in Corinth has evidently included criticism of Paul. Yet Paul says in verse 3a, "It is a very small thing that I should be judged by you or by any human court." Confidence in the gospel frees the apostle to think and act in accord with the gospel even though some of the Corinthians disapprove. Human approval is not ultimately significant to the apostle, nor should it be to leaders in the church today.

When Paul says in verse 3b that he does not judge himself, he does not mean that anything goes or that he does not engage in the critical self-reflection (with an eye towards monitoring faithfulness) that was standard practice among Pharisees. Such reflection should be a constituent of every life in communities of faith. Rather, the apostle voices the proper perspective of a servant whose work will ultimately be evaluated by the owner. To be sure, Paul is not aware of any charges against him in the divine court but does not assume that he is completely self-aware: "It is the Lord who judges me" (v. 4).

The Corinthians, therefore, should not presume to pronounce God's judgment on Paul (4:5). In language that the apocalyptic tradition uses to describe what takes place on the great day of judgment, Paul points out that when Jesus returns, "God will bring to light the things now hidden in darkness and will disclose the purposes of the heart." At that time, God will give appropriate commendation (or condemnation) to each person.

Rather than risk final condemnation from God, the apostle accepts the interim disapproval of the Corinthians. Ironically, the Corinthians object to the apostle because he faithfully calls them to life that would win them approval on the day of judgment. The Corinthians who condemn Paul only make the case for their own condemnation.

Ninth Sunday after the Epiphany/Year A

Romans 1:16–17; 3:22b–28, (29–31)

In the opening verse of today's reading, Paul begins with a strong statement of his confidence in the gospel; his "not ashamed" as a negative is stronger than a simple positive statement. Paul reassures his Gentile readers that they should trust the gospel that they have heard, in spite of the fact that this gospel has been rejected or ignored by the mass of the population among whom this small group of Jesus-followers lives.

The rest of the verse describes the reasons for Paul's willingness to rely on the gospel: "It is the power of God for salvation to everyone who has faith, to the Jew first and also to the Greek" (even to these Roman Gentiles). "Salvation" for Paul does not mean being saved from this world and taken up into heaven. Rather, it is the "righteousness [*dikaiosyne*] of God" (1:17) that is revealed in the gospel. Righteousness means setting things right. Martin Luther used the German term *Rechtfertigung*, a gerund, to refer to God's setting things right and to claim that God is a right-setting God. The gospel of Jesus Christ reveals that God will, in the apocalyptic finale when Jesus returns, set right all things, and, indeed, that this right-setting has already begun. God will particularly set right the relations between the people Israel and the Gentiles, making both children of Abraham who bless each other. "The righting of things," as Krister Stendahl puts it, "catches much of the sense. Putting things right, *all* things, not just the soul game, and not just the political situation, but all things—that is the meaning of *dikaiosyne*."[1]

When the apocalypse happens and Jesus returns, human beings will live lives that reflect God's faithfulness (God's "steadfast love," *hesed*), a faithfulness that will be reflected in their own lives: "The one who is righteous will live by faith" (1:17); the time will come, God's future that is ahead of us, when all will live by faith. This statement looks forward to God's right-setting of the entire world.

Romans 3:22b–26 claims that God's righteousness is now freely accessible by all believers: "All . . . are now justified by his grace as a gift, through the redemption that is in Christ Jesus" (3:24). "Now" is important—now, at this late moment in the apocalyptic time frame when everything is running headlong to devastation, God has acted in God's messiah to transform the human situation from one of hopelessness and injustice to one of hope in a time when all will be set right. God's righteousness has been manifest apart from the law, but the law and the prophets witness to it (3:21). Righteousness is now available through the faithfulness of Jesus Christ "for all who believe" (3:22). "All," *pantes*, occurs frequently in this part of Romans, stressing that Gentiles are included along with Jews in grace, as both are included in the solidarity of sin (Rom. 2:12).

All are "now justified by [God's] grace as a gift, through the redemption that is in Christ Jesus" (3:24), whose sacrifice is our atonement. This is not a sacrifice paid to God to secure God's mercy; God is the actor here. Jesus Christ is the Yom Kippur, the Day of Atonement of the whole world, in whom God bears and overcome the effects of sin. The God of Israel, whom Paul calls "God the Father," redeems all humanity.

Therefore, Paul proclaims in 3:27–31, neither Jew nor Gentile may boast. Jews may not boast because God's right-setting of all things did not come through the law but through God's gracious act and the faith that appropriates it. Nor may Gentiles boast because they have been graciously included—God is God of Gentiles *also*. Jesus-following Gentiles are the "also" included, not the "only" included. Relations between the two will be set right, thus upholding the Torah in which God promises that the descendants of Abraham will be a blessing to the Gentiles (Gen. 22:18).

Last Sunday after the Epiphany/Year A

Transfiguration Sunday

2 Peter 1:16–21

The congregation to which this letter is addressed is made up of Gentiles who turned away from idol worship to the God of Israel and have been annexed to the Jewish mission of witnessing to the living God (1 Pet. 4:3–4; 2:9–10). By the time of 2 Peter, the theme of suffering so prominent in 1 Peter is almost mute and the community faces challenges not from pagans outside (as in the case of 1 Peter) but from false teachers within the community (2:1–2; 3:1–4).

The false leaders downplay the coming of the apocalypse (2 Pet. 2:3–10; 3:1–17) and allow community members to engage in behaviors that drift in the direction of a return to their preconverted, destructive Gentile life (2:1–22). The writer adapts the literary genre of testament to call the congregation to realize that the apocalypse is coming and that they need to prepare for it by avoiding the self- and community-destroying behavior of unregenerate Gentiles and by living faithfully for God. In a testament, an ancient figure was pictured as assembling the wisdom a community would need in the figure's absence. Evidences of the testament character of the letter are clear in 1:3–15; 2:1–3; and 3:1–4.

As we note in connection with 1 Peter (Second Sunday after Easter/Year A), while 2 Peter purports to be written by the apostle Peter, it is more likely from the quill of someone writing pseudonymously. It was written in the name of a teacher to adapt the teacher's wisdom to a new time. Many testaments were pseudonymous—for example, the *Testaments of the Twelve Patriarchs* and the *Testament of Job*.

The language of 2 Peter 1:16–21 suggests that the false teachers had accused the writer of articulating a "cleverly devised myth" when the writer claimed that Jesus would return (a prominent theme in 1 Peter: for example, 1:3–12; 4:7–19; 5:6–11). Here the author uses "myth" (*mythos*) in the derogatory way characteristic of Jewish writers who used it to speak of untrustworthy stories, especially regarding deities other than the God of the Bible (as in Philo, *Creation* 1; Josephus, *Ant.* 1:22).

In response to this charge, the author claims in verse 16 to have been one of the three "eyewitnesses of [Jesus'] majesty" (*megaleiotes*), referring to the transfiguration of Jesus (Matt. 17:1–8 and par.). The latter event revealed Jesus in the resurrection body in which he will return at the apocalypse. The transfiguration was a prolepsis—an occasion when an event expected in the future occurs momentarily in the present. The writer not only saw the vision but also heard God speak (2 Pet. 1:17), making the report even more reliable, since the Jewish community often gives priority to the spoken word over sight.

The experience on the mountain "more fully confirms" (*bebaioteros*) the prophetic message (*propetes logos*), an expression in Judaism for the sacred Scriptures (note 1:20; cf. Philo, *Plant.* 117). The writer does not allude to a specific passage but presumes that the Scriptures point to an apocalypse ahead. The congregation needs to attend to this message in the same way that they would to a lamp shining in a dark place until "the day [the apocalypse, 3:10] dawns and the morning star rises in [their] hearts" (v. 19). Here the writer uses language familiar from Hellenistic Judaism not to reduce the apocalypse to psychological experience but to speak figuratively and evocatively of its effect on the self: the experience of the second advent will be as if the morning star arises within (Philo, *Drunkenness* 44; *Decal.* 49).

The writer reinforces the trustworthiness of the claim that Jesus will return by asserting that the message of the coming apocalypse found in prophecy in Scripture is not subject to interpretation, for this message (like others in Scripture) did not come from human speculation but from the Holy Spirit who spoke from God (1:20–21). The writer's interest is not in articulating a particular theory of inspiration but in calling to mind the Jewish contrast between true and false prophets: the former under the power of the Spirit and the latter creating messages to serve their limited and unfaithful ends (e.g., Jer. 23:16; Ezek. 13:3). While today's preacher likely recognizes that all statements, by nature, contain interpretive elements, the preacher could certainly help the congregation consider points at which they are in danger of heeding the words of false prophets and could encourage the congregation to return to faithful ideas, values, and practices.

Ash Wednesday/Years A, B, and C

2 Corinthians 5:20b–6:10

The broad context of today's text is Paul's attempt to restore his relationship with the congregation in the face of criticisms in Corinth that have come from super apostles (2 Cor. 11:5; 12:11) who preach that believers can experience near-fullness of glory through religious ecstasy. Paul's theology centers in the cross and resurrection as pointers to the coming apocalypse; the apostle suffers as present rulers entrench to resist the apocalypse. The immediate context begins at 5:16 and reveals that Paul's ambassadorial ministry invites people into the restored eschatological world (the new creation). We discuss 5:16–21 in connection with the Fourth Sunday of Lent/Year C.

When Paul initially visited Corinth, those in the congregation welcomed God's grace as interpreted by Paul. For the apostle, grace (*charis*) is not simply "unmerited favor" but God's covenantal faithfulness that reaches its climax when the new age comes and all people are together with one another and with God in love. However, by following the super apostles, the Corinthians are in danger of negating their initial embrace of the gospel (2 Cor. 6:1).

In 2 Corinthians 6:2a, Paul cites Isaiah 49:8, a salvation oracle that calls to mind the fact that when Israel was exiled in Babylonia (as a result of unfaithfulness), God remained faithful to the covenant with them and returned them to their homeland. The "acceptable time" in Isaiah is the day when God acts in deliverance. In verse 6b, the apostle draws a parallel from the time of Isaiah to the time of the Corinthians: the acceptable time is upon them. When the apostle says, "Now is the day of salvation," the point is that the apocalypse (ushering in the new world with its complete salvation from the vicissitudes of the present) is soon to come and the Corinthians need to act now to be ready for it.

While the Corinthians may have been unimpressed with Paul's modest personal appearance and his theology that interpreted present suffering as the journey toward future glory (in contrast to the super apostles whose ecstatic experiences yield immediate good feeling), the community needs to realize that Paul's circumstance and theology do not discredit Paul's person or message (6:3a). Indeed, from God's point of view, such matters are not a "fault" in Paul's ministry but are signs of its trustworthiness (6:3b–4a).

In 6:4b–5 Paul lists negative things that occurred in his ministry: afflictions, hardships, calamities, beatings, imprisonments, riots, labors, sleepless nights, and hunger. These conditions are typical of those that befall faithful witnesses in the tribulation suffering prior to the apocalypse and are evidence of his endurance (*hypomone*), which apocalyptic writers regard as a demonstration of faithfulness (Rev. 13:10). Further evidence of Paul's trustworthiness are the virtues that he continues to show: purity, knowledge, patience, kindness, holiness, love, truthful speech, and the power of God (6:6–7a). The Corinthians should respect Paul, for such virtues demonstrate the presence of the Spirit, who is a first installment of the coming world (2 Cor. 1:22; Gal. 5:22–23).

In 6:7b–10 Paul continues the same line of thought through a series of contrasts of ways and circumstances that demonstrate the apostle's reliability: he shows the armor of righteousness in both hands, in honor and disrepute as well as in good repute and ill repute (very important notions in the honor/shame culture of antiquity). Regarded as an imposter, he is yet a truthful messenger, unknown and yet known, dying and yet alive, punished but not killed, in circumstances that should generate sorrow but in which Paul rejoices. He is poor yet makes many rich; having nothing, he possesses everything. The perceptive reader recognizes, of course, that the positive qualities associated with Paul result from his being a part of the new creation that is already beginning to be revealed in the present. Paul hopes that the Corinthians will want to share in that life now and in the world to come.

First Sunday in Lent/Year A

Romans 5:12–19

Romans 5:12–19 carries further Paul's contrast between Adam and Christ and the impact that each of them has, particularly on the Gentiles whom Paul addresses in Romans (1:5, 13). Paul characterizes the importance of Christ by contrasting him with Adam, the parent of all human beings, Jews and Gentiles. It is Abraham who became the first member of the people Israel by turning his back on his idolatrous past (4:12). In today's passage, Paul reflects a traditional Jewish view of Adam as the one through whom death came into human history (*Sifra*, 27a; *Sifre Deuteronomy*, 141a). This tradition is ultimately rooted in Genesis 3:19:

> By the sweat of your face
>   you shall eat bread
> until you return to the ground,
>   for out of it you were taken;
> you are dust,
> and to dust you shall return.

Second-temple Jewish literature notes, as in *4 Ezra* 3:7, "You [God] laid upon him [Adam] one commandment of yours, but he transgressed it, and immediately you appointed death for him and for his descendants." Jewish literature, however, does not interpret Adam's transgression in the sense of original sin, which is a distinctively Christian teaching. Rather, God forgave Adam: "When he sinned, the Lord pronounced sentence upon him, but when the Sabbath came the Lord set him free. . . . So the Lord made the attribute of mercy take precedence over the attribute of judgment."[2]

It is a misreading to interpret this passage as throwing cold water on the torah of Judaism. Verses 13–14 comment, "Sin was in the world before the law. . . . Yet death exercised dominion from Adam to Moses." Gentiles apart from the law (and prior to Abraham all people were Gentiles) died, and after Moses they continued to die, as we do still. What the law brings to sin Paul earlier characterized as "recognition" or "awareness," *epignosis* (3:20). As Paul puts it in today's reading, "sin is not reckoned where there is no law" (5:13).

Paul treats sin, *hamartia*, and death, *thanatos*, as independent powers that are able to get control of human beings because of our weakness. We exist in a solidarity of sin and death—"Death spread to all because all have sinned" (5:12). All human beings are in Adam's "field of force," vulnerable to his powerful influence. Paul provides no account of how sin was able to do this (although the later Christian tradition offered various explanations: from the claim that we are all conceived in sin to the view that each generation corrupts the next by institutionalizing its prejudices in ways that shape upcoming generations).

The gift of God's active righteousness in Jesus Christ, however, effectively counters the rule of death over human beings. If one man's sin caused many to die, "much more surely have the grace of God and the free gift in the grace of the one man, Jesus Christ, abounded for the many" (5:15). Whereas Adam brought condemnation, Christ sets things right. The contrast between Adam and Christ comes to its full expression in verse 18: "Just as one man's trespass led to condemnation for all, so one man's act of righteousness leads to justification and life for all." All are ultimately redeemed from death by Christ; sin and death are subject to his dominion and will not, ultimately, be victorious. Christians are fond of quoting passages that stress that only some will be saved; here Paul claims, to the contrary, that the "gates of Hades will not prevail against" the gift given by God in Christ (Matt. 16:18).

Death for Paul is not merely physical death but the "sting of death" (1 Cor. 15:56), which is everlasting alienation from God. It is defeated by the "grace" available through justification "leading to eternal life through Jesus Christ our Lord" (Rom. 5:21).

Second Sunday in Lent/Year A

Romans 4:1–5, 13–17

Paul begins this reading with a question: "What then are we to say was gained by Abraham, our ancestor according to the flesh?" (4:1). Paul's major task in Romans is to explain his mission not only as "apostle to the Gentiles" but also as announcing that God has acted to set right the relationship between Gentiles and the people Israel. This is why Abraham is so terribly important to Paul.

Abraham was called by God to leave Ur of the Chaldees and to trust the promise that God would give him many descendants through whom "all the families of the earth will be blessed" (Gen. 12:1–3). Pamela Eisenbaum remarks of Paul and Abraham;

> Both are called by God to a purpose that benefits not only them
> and their families, but the rest of humanity. Both Paul and Abraham

become alienated from their communities of origin as a result of their experience. In Abraham's case, God literally calls him away from his family and kin; in Paul's case, God's call implicitly results in his alienation from the Jewish community of which he was once fully a part. Both Paul and Abraham become travelers among other peoples.[3]

Abraham is first and foremost "father" and "ancestor" for Paul, as Jews then and now widely understood Abraham.

Abraham functioned in postbiblical Jewish literature as the "first proselyte," a Gentile who turned his back on idolatry in favor of worship of the one God (*Jub.* 11: 16–17, Josephus, *Ant.* 1.154–57). Notice that in Romans 4:5 Paul alludes to Abraham's previous idolatry when he says that God "justifies the ungodly" (*asebes*). Paul's exegesis here is thoroughly Jewish. For him, Abraham is the "father [*pater*] of all who believe without being circumcised" (4:11) as well as the "father of the circumcised . . . who also follow the example of faith that our father Abraham had before he was circumcised" (4:12; we translate "father" rather than "ancestor" in order to stay close to Paul's point that Abraham is the current parent of both Jews and Gentiles, not a remote "ancestor").

Protestants typically luxuriate in this passage as extolling "justification by faith." In their more reflective moments, they realize that we should speak of being justified by God's grace, appropriated by faith. Paul is not asking us to put our trust in our faith. Our faith is too shaky a thing for us to put our ultimate trust in it. Rather, we trust God's faithfulness made clear in Jesus Christ.

In 4:13–17, Paul renews his discussion of Abraham as the "father of many nations" (4:17). Abraham trusted in God's promise, God's gift (4:13) before he was circumcised (4:6–12). Paul's long discussion of Abraham's being justified before he was circumcised suggests that circumcision was the major issue in his effort to affirm the election of Gentiles aside from the law (*torah*); Paul did not reject the torah or advocate that Gentiles were now free to commit murder and idolatry. Circumcision and/or the dietary laws are always the bone of contention in Paul's letters when he seems to be negative on the "law" (a poor translation of *torah*).

Paul's point in 4:13–17 is that everything "depends on faith, in order that the promise may rest on grace and be guaranteed to all his [Abraham's] descendants," both Jews and Gentiles. Hence, Abraham is indeed the "father of many nations" (4:17). Neither Abraham's age nor Sarah's barrenness caused Abraham to lose faith, and they had a son, Isaac (4:19–20).

In spite of all Paul's talk of grace and faith, Abraham still remains, as he was in the opening paragraph of the chapter, the "forefather according to the flesh," *kata sarka*, of the people Israel and of the Gentiles.

Annunciation/Years A, B, and C

Hebrews 10:4–10

This pericope is part of a longer discussion (10:1–10) in which Hebrews discusses the human sacrifice of Christ on the cross; the conversation turns from talking about Christ's offering in the heavenly sanctuary (9:23–28) to his offering of his body (*soma*, 10:10). Verse 4 sums up the point that Hebrews makes in 10:1–4. There he argued that "the law has only a shadow of the good things to come, and not the true form of these realities" (v. 1). Hence the sacrifices in the desert sanctuary could never "make perfect those who approach" (v. 1). The first half of the periscope ends with "For it is impossible for the blood of bulls and goats to take away sins" (v. 4).

Two points need to be made about this argument. First, the contrast between shadow and true form later became a way of contrasting Judaism unfavorably to Christianity, a belittlement that justified abuses committed against Jews by followers of Christ who thought that they had the "true form" of religion. "Shadow" exists in every faith tradition; it is not an adequate way to distinguish faith traditions from one another. Second, Hebrews's later exhortation to the community to quit persisting in sin (10:26–31) questions whether the new sacrifice has made "perfect those who approach."

Verses 5–10 are the second half of the pericope. Verses 5–7 quote Ps. 40:6–7:

> Sacrifice and offering you do not desire,
>   but you have given me an open ear.
> Burnt offering and sin offering
>   you have not required.
> Then I said, "Here I am;
>   in the scroll of the book it is written of me.
> I delight to do your will, O my God;
>   your law is within my heart.

Hebrews drops the last half-sentence, possibly because it disagrees with its earlier claim that only the new covenant was written on the heart

(8:8–13). Originally a psalm of thanksgiving for deliverance, Hebrews takes the psalm as spoken by Christ. Either Hebrews or its source changed Psalm 40 significantly. "You have given me an open ear" becomes "a body you have prepared for me"; "I delight to do your will" becomes "I have come to do your will." In Israelite faith an "open ear" was a way of talking that indicated readiness to "hear," *shema*, and carry out God's *mitzvot*.

Note that Hebrews emphasizes Christ's voluntary carrying out of God's will. Verse 8 begins an interpretation of the quotation from Psalm 40. The interpretation begins by listing the sacrifices of the desert tent—sacrifices, offerings, burnt offerings, and sin offerings—and adds that "these are offered according to the law" to reinforce the point made throughout that therefore they are inadequate and merely external. (How we can know that they were merely external is impossible; we cannot.)

Counter to this are the words taken as said by Jesus: "I have come to do your will, O God." From this Hebrews infers that Christ "abolishes [*anairei*] the first in order to establish the second" (v. 9). Here Christ himself becomes the agent who renders the old form of worship "obsolete" (8:13). We need to remember here that Hebrews claims only that one form of worship replaces another; it never even hints at the notion that a new people replaces the original people of God. Rather, the text reflects the prophetic preference for moral behavior over cultic ritual and the reframing of cultic language into moral language characteristic of Hellenistic Jewish writers. The writer also shares with every sectarian Jewish movement of the time a conviction that his own cult is the true temple and its members the true priests, although in Hebrews's case Christ is the true priest.

The text concludes that all this is by God's will: Christ's human body has been offered "once for all." This earthly offering makes access to God and eternity possible.

Third Sunday in Lent/Year A

Romans 5:1–11

In this section of his discussion of the hope of future salvation (Rom. 5:1–8:39), Paul makes two shifts in his articulation of the gospel. He has been talking about (1) the relation between God's faithfulness and our appropriation of God's faithfulness through our responding faith and (2) about the relation between Abraham and Christ. Now he shifts to talk about hope in future salvation in the midst of and in spite of present suffering

(5:3) and about the relation between Adam and Christ: "Sin came into the world through one man . . . [but] more surely have the grace of God and the free gift in the grace of the one man, Jesus Christ, abounded for the many" (5:12, 15).

The new era in human history has begun, but is far from fully present: "I consider that the sufferings of this present time are not worth comparing with the glory *about to be* revealed to us" (8:18; emphasis ours). Paul remains confident in the imminent return of Jesus in glory, bringing into history the rule of God. Because this new age has dawned, we can hope in spite of present suffering. Hope is contingent on God's love, which was freely given to us "while we were still weak" (5:6), situated in the old age of sin and oppression and beset by death, suffering, and weakness.

Verses 1–2 segue from the earlier discussion of justification by grace through faith to the discussion of hope. Because we Gentiles (the explicit addressees of Romans) have been justified (reconciled with the God of Israel and the Israel of God), "we have peace with God through our Lord Jesus Christ." No longer hostile to God, we are at peace and have "access to this grace in which we stand," access itself graciously given to us. We can now look forward "in our hope of sharing the glory of God."

Verses 3–4 make it clear that we can do this in spite of "our sufferings." In this in-between time, between the dawning of the new era in history and its final consummation when Christ will return in glory, we must still cope with death, suffering, and weakness (a major theme in Paul, often overlooked). But suffering itself produces endurance; endurance, character; and character, hope—important themes in Lent. However much the counterargument is true, that suffering is often merely destructive (one need only think of the thirty children per minute around the world who die of starvation), it is also the case that Christian communities should shape people who can persevere, develop a character described by Christian virtues, and hope even in apparently hopeless situations. One thing they should have the character to do is to put an end to needless suffering. Suffering does not reflect the will of God; it is caused by the powers of this old age.

Verse 5 gives voice to the most important motif of this section of Romans—our experience of God's Holy Spirit "poured into our hearts." Apocalypticists (see Ezek. 36–37) had long regarded the Spirit as the most important eschatological gift; the gift of the Spirit for Paul demonstrates that the community already lives in the age to come.

Verses 6–10 proclaim that God's love is the ground of hope: "While we were still weak, at the right time [*kairos*] Christ died for the ungodly . . . while we still were sinners." Paul's logic here is that if it is true that God in Christ did this for us while we were weak, how much more "now that we have been justified . . . , will we be saved through him from the wrath of God" (v. 9). We "*were* reconciled" by his death, we "*will be* saved by his life" (v. 10, emphasis ours). "His life" refers not to the lifetime of the historical Jesus but to the present life of the risen Christ who is actively present to the community.

Verse 11 articulates the theme that we may "boast in God through our Lord Jesus Christ, through whom we have now received reconciliation." The "we" who may boast, however, are the new eschatological people of God—Jews and Gentiles—who have been reconciled with each other.

Fourth Sunday in Lent/Year A

Ephesians 5:8–14

The three readings from Ephesians that lead into today's passage are discussed on Propers 12, 13, and 14 of year B; they contextualize today's reading.

Throughout, Ephesians addresses its readers as Gentiles: "You must no longer live as the Gentiles" you once were (4:17). Today's reading announces Ephesians's advice to dissociate from the nonbelieving Gentiles in the larger community (5:7). If the community is to witness to that to which it claims to witness, its behavior must be appropriate to its witness; if not, its behavior will be indistinguishable from that of the children of "darkness" (v. 8). Allusions to baptism abound in Ephesians—believers are to "clothe yourselves with the new self, created according to the likeness of God in true righteousness and holiness" (4:24).

The then/now contrast is strong throughout Ephesians: "Once you [Gentiles] were darkness, but now in the Lord you are light. Live as children of light" (v. 8; see 2:1–22). Through the faithfulness of God we no longer walk in darkness but are indeed "children of light." The imperative "walk" (*peripateo*) follows the indicative "you are light." Being precedes doing; new being precedes new doing. We are asked to do nothing that God's grace does not already empower us to do. We are to become who we are.

"The fruit of the light [*photos*] is found in all that is good and right and true" (v. 9). Good trees produce good fruit (Matt. 7:17; Luke 6:43). "Fruit" is an appropriate metaphor for the relation of moral behavior to God's enabling grace—good deeds are not difficult to do; they grow naturally from life in the "light," from the new person who has been recreated by God's grace and said "yes" to that grace in baptism.

What we ought to do requires thinking—"Try to find out what is pleasing to the Lord" (v. 10). To "find out" (*dokimazo*) is to test, not simply to follow whatever seems (*dokeo*) or is said to be pleasing to the Lord. Moral decisions are not automatic, and the situations in which they must be made are sometimes complex. Sometimes we have to jump the gap between moral imperatives and situations that the imperatives do not quite fit; sometimes inherited moral codes obstruct doing what is right in changed circumstances or in the light of new knowledge and understandings. Creative justice or imaginative love are required; then we need to "find out what is pleasing to the Lord."

Verses 11–14 deal with the "unfruitful works of darkness" in which believers in Jesus are to "take no part." The Greek says "do not have fellowship" (*synkoinoneite*) with them. Instead, we are to "expose them"—force them out into the light and show them for what they are. The church is to shine the strong light of day on racism, sexism, greed, and war—not fearfully to remove itself from a sinful society but, instead, to meet it head-on.

It is "shameful even to mention what such people do secretly" (v. 12). We cannot know what sins the writer had in mind (licentiousness is usually suggested). But, most people work hard to keep their sins from being exposed to the light. For example, perpetrators of corporate scandal go to great lengths to keep their machinations hidden from view. Neither is it clear what is meant by saying that "everything exposed by the light becomes visible" (v. 13). Perhaps the point is simply that if we would be ashamed for what we do to be in tomorrow's headlines, we should not do it.

Verse 14 says, "Sleeper, awake! Rise from the dead, and Christ will shine on you!" This suggestion of the transformation that has occurred in baptism stresses again that we are to "walk" as the people whom we "are" —new creatures in Jesus Christ.

Fifth Sunday in Lent/Year A

Romans 8:6–11

Please see Proper 10/Year A for commentary on this passage.

Palm/Passion Sunday/Years A, B, and C

Philippians 2:5–11

The same word for "mind" that occurs in Philippians 2:2 (see Proper 21/Year C) appears again in 2:5, thus suggesting that the phrase "in Christ Jesus" indicates that the self-emptying "mind" of Christ is to shape the common "mind" of the community. The members of the community are to embody the mind of Christ in their relationships with one another.

Several commentators point out that the phrase that Jesus was "in the form of God" (v. 6) is not fully developed Trinitarianism. Several Jewish theologians affirm the preexistence of agents of God who became manifest: wisdom, the logos, and torah (Prov. 8:22–31; Wis. 9:1–9; Sir. 24:1–12; Philo, *Spec. Laws*, 3:175). That Christ is such an agent is clear when we recognize that the term "form," *morphe*, is sometimes synonymous with *eikon*, "image" (Gen. 1:26–27; *Sib. Or.* 3:8). Paul describes Christ in this way in Romans 5:12–21; 1 Corinthians 15:22, 45; and 2 Corinthians 4:4.

Jesus did not count "equality with God" (v. 6) as something to be "exploited" (*harpagmos*) or "robbed." The preexistent Christ had the opportunity to try and grab equality with God but chose not to do so. Instead, Christ emptied himself, that is, descended from his preexistent state into the world and took the form of a *doulos* for the sake of others, an expression drawn from Isaiah 52:12–53:12. The Suffering Servant in Isaiah is the faithful remnant of Israel whose suffering provides the occasion whereby God can reveal the divine will to forgive and restore. In this vein, later Jewish thinkers refer to "servants of God" who suffered in behalf of the community (for example, the martyrdom of the seven sons in 4 Macc. 17:7–18:5).

The resurrection of Jesus both confirms God's faithfulness to Jesus (as to the Servant of Isaiah) and demonstrates how believers will be changed in the world to come (1 Cor. 15:20–28, 35–49). Even more importantly, God exalted Jesus to God's right hand (a place reserved for the most important representatives of God). This image assures the church that God authorizes the mission of the church in and to the Gentile world.

God gave Jesus "the name that is above every name" (v. 9). The immediate context suggests "Lord" is the name, a frequent term for God. Yet Paul does not say God made Jesus into God. Rather, in the ancient world a name revealed character and purposes. Those who speak and act in the name of another person do so with the authority of the other (1 Sam. 17:45; 1 Kgs. 21:8; Jer. 29:25). To be called by the name of another is to belong to that other (e.g., 1 Sam. 12:28; Isa. 4:1). The name of God can act through an agent, for example, angels (Exod. 23:20–21). The name of God functions similarly for Jesus.

Philippians 2:10 brings to mind a theme from Isaiah 45:22–25, a passage inviting Gentiles to bow before God. Paul's point is that through Christ, Gentiles now confess the God of Israel. When Philippians says that everyone will confess that Jesus Christ is Lord, it means not that everyone will become Christian but that the day is arriving when all inhabitants of the cosmos will recognize the validity of the mission of Jesus and the church as gathering Gentiles to the God of Israel. The confession of the name of Christ is not for its own sake but points to the work of the God of Israel as verse 11c makes clear: "to the glory of God the Father." The ministry of Christ and the church glorify the God of Israel by showing that God makes good on the promise to bless all the families of the earth through Israel (Gen. 12:1–3).

The event of Christ Jesus, then, does not introduce a new element into the story of Israel. On the contrary, the story of Israel gives the church a theological framework by which to interpret the significance of Christ's self-emptying and exaltation as a representation of love and faithfulness of the God of Israel to the Gentile world. This theme is accentuated in verses 9–11. Christians need to avoid triumphalism and supersessionism when handling these themes.

Monday of Holy Week/Years A, B, and C

Hebrews 9:11–15

Today's reading should end with verse 15, which we include here. The text deals with the eternal offering of Christ the High Priest in the heavenly Holy Place. It ends by hailing Christ as the "mediator of a new covenant" that redeems those whom he calls "from the transgressions under the first covenant" (v. 15). Hebrews 9 presumes Hebrews 8 with its interpretation of Jeremiah 31:31–34 and its new covenant in which the Lord promises to "put my laws in their minds, and write them on their hearts" (8:10). Hebrews interprets this as rendering the old covenant "obsolete" (8:13) and soon to disappear.

Hebrews does violence to the imagery of the First Testament that it uses. First, the Torah was always to be on the heart. Deuteronomy says of it: "The word is very near to you; it is in your mouth and in your heart for you to observe" (30:14). Jeremiah spoke of a renewed covenant, not a brand-new covenant. Second, Jeremiah does not breathe a word about the older covenant being rendered obsolete. Hebrews does note, however, that God made this renewed covenant "with the house of Israel and with the house of Judah" (8:8). We Gentiles are not mentioned here; that we are graciously included should prompt our gratitude and deter us from triumphalistic interpretations of the new offering and the new covenant.

Hebrews says that Christ came "through the . . . perfect tent (not made with hands, that is, not of this creation)" (v. 11). We are to remember 4:14 where Jesus "passed through the heavens." "Made with hands" (or "manufactured") is garden-variety disparagement of conventional forms of worship, frequent in Jewish sources. The temple not made with hands is usually the cosmos as such, that is, God's creation, not our creation. For Hebrews, it is the "heavenly" temple (8:5).

Verse 12 speaks of Christ entering "once for all into the Holy Place, not with the blood of goats and calves, but with his own blood, thus obtaining eternal redemption [*lutrosis*]." Hebrews assumes that sacrifice is necessary; what it claims is that Christ improves on the older priests by offering an "eternal redemption" instead of one that had to be repeated annually. By "his own blood" most likely refers to the sacrifice of Christ on the cross although it could refer to his ongoing life in heaven. *Lutrosis* here finds its one use in the Second Testament. It refers to "ransom," as in buying a slave or prisoner out of captivity.

Verses 13 and 14 make an argument from the lesser to the greater: "If the blood of goats and bulls, with the sprinkling of the ashes of a heifer, sanctifies those who have been defiled so that their flesh is purified, [the lesser] how much more will the blood of Christ, who through the eternal Spirit offered himself without blemish to God, purify our conscience from dead works to worship the living God [the greater]." Adding the "ashes of a heifer" to Hebrews's use of the Yom Kippur ritual is strained; the red heifer had nothing to do with priests on whom Hebrews has focused. The stronger argument claims that Christ's sacrifice purifies the conscience because it is an offering of his own blood and was made through the Spirit by one without blemish. A perfect work had to be done in order for God's grace to be effective. One might be cautious about this; that justification is by God's grace would indicate that Christ is God's gift to us rather than a work that is a necessary condition for God to be gracious.

The "dead works" should not be confused with the *mitzvoth* of torah. "Dead works" are not "deeds of loving kindness"; they are sins that pollute the conscience.

Tuesday of Holy Week/Years A, B, and C

1 Corinthians 1:18–31

Please see the Fourth Sunday after the Epiphany/Year A for commentary on this passage.

Wednesday of Holy Week/Years A, B, and C
Hebrews 12:1–3

Today's reading spans two sections of Hebrews: the end of the litany of praise for the faithful Israelite elders in chapter 11 and the section focusing on Jesus "the pioneer and perfecter of our faith" (12:1–3). As the elders were steadfast in faith in spite of persecution and suffering (11:32–38), so Jesus "endured the cross" (12:2) and so may we "not grow weary or lose heart" (12:3).

This reading first celebrates the faith of the exodus generation, beginning with Moses' parents and Moses (vv. 23–28) and then turns to the whole people Israel (v. 29): "By faith the people passed through the Red Sea as if it were dry land." It has been noted that just how their faith was evidenced by this is not made clear by Hebrews. But the little phrase "as if" (*hos*) may provide a clue; "as if it were dry" does not mean that the crossing was without peril. After all, "when the Egyptians attempted to do so, they were drowned." Faith is, in part, courage, and Hebrews wants to encourage its readers.

"By faith the walls of Jericho fell" (v. 30), says Hebrews, appealing to a story that still stirred the hearts of Jews in the first century (Josephus, *J.W.* 2.13.5). Then Hebrews strikingly lists "Rahab the prostitute" (v. 31) as one of the great exemplars of faith who "did not perish with those who were disobedient, because she had received the spies in peace," recalling the story of Joshua 2:1–20. A woman, a Gentile, and hardly reputable by conventional moral standards, then or now, Rahab the foreigner is included in the people of God because she practices the classic Israelite virtue of hospitality. The most frequently repeated commandment in the First Testament, "You shall love the stranger as yourself," is affirmed here.

Verses 32–39 shift the topic and celebrate the faith of Israelites who endured persecution, as the writer of Hebrews indicates his own community must do. Verses 33–34 attribute military and national success to faith; verses 35–36 deal with faith in times of loss and persecution, and verses 37–38 lift up themes of death, destitution, and torment. Of all these sufferers, "the world was not worthy" (v. 38).

Yet these staunch heroes, "though they were commended for their faith, did not receive what was promised" (v. 39). Note that this is not because of any failing on their part but because God's intention was they "would not, apart from us, be made perfect" (v. 40). Clearly, neither will we (Hebrews's readers) be made perfect apart from them. Hebrews here uses an inclusive logic: finally, by extension, none will be fully saved until all are saved because each and all of us are essentially related to the rest of us. We are not made perfect apart from each other.

Our endurance through difficulty is made possible not only by "so great a cloud of witnesses" (12:1), but ultimately by "Jesus the pioneer and perfecter of our faith" (12:2). At 12:1, Hebrews turns from the indicative to the imperative: "Let us run with perseverance the race that is set before us." Whereas earlier Hebrews had often said we have a high priest, now it says we have this "cloud of witnesses," and because we have them we should put away every encumbrance (excess weight) and sin—in other words, we should get in shape to "run . . . the race." Sin is a weight that hinders our living the life of faith. Hebrews uses the Greek term *agon*, "athletic contest," that is translated "race." The life of faith is not a one-hundred-yard dash; it is a long-distance race that requires "perseverance" (v. 1). Christ endured "so that you may not grow weary or lose heart" (v. 3). Perseverance through difficulty would help many a congregation.

Holy Thursday/Years A, B, and C

Maundy Thursday

1 Corinthians 11:23–26

The social world of antiquity was organized in strict pyramid-like fashion with the few wealthy and powerful at the top and the many more numerous persons of lower economic and social power below. A primary reason Paul wrote 1 Corinthians was to help the people replace division in the congregation with a sense of community that embodied the life of the world to come. The divisions in the congregation took place along the lines of social class with the upper class and the well-educated acting in ways that diminished persons of lower economic class and less education. Today's passage, like much of 1 Corinthians, is largely addressed to the upper-cut Gentiles.

The lection is part of a discussion that begins in 11:17 and continues through 11:34. Paul begins by indicating that the congregation's coming together to partake of the Lord's Supper (Paul's name for the sacred meal instituted by Jesus) actually does the congregation more harm than good. Indeed, when the people eat together, they do not really eat the *Lord's* supper but their own meals (11:17–20). The wealthy partake of their own food without sharing with those in the congregation who do not have enough to eat. Some members of the wealthy class became inebriated and were therefore unable to be fully responsible for living the covenantal life (11:21–22). In behaving this way, they violate a fundamental tenet of Jewish life: those who have food are to share with those who do not, so that no one will be hungry and all can experience blessing. Indeed, shortly after the time of the Second Testament, rabbis sometimes opened the door of the house and posted a flag in the street when a meal was being eaten so that the poor could enter and partake.

The apostle recalled the institution of the Lord's Supper in 11:23–26 to remind the wealthy of the quality that should permeate the eating of the Lord's Supper. The point is in verse 26: "For as often as you eat this bread and drink the cup, you proclaim the Lord's death until he comes." Most of the second-person pronouns ("you") in this part of the letter are plural and refer to the community. Paul frequently refers to Jesus' death as shorthand for his confidence that through the death and resurrection of Jesus, God was working to end the present evil age and replace it with the eschatological realm of God in which all circumstances and relationships would mediate peace, justice, and love. The life of the community is to "proclaim" this message, that is, to witness to it by living in community in ways that embody qualities of the new world. They are to do so "until [Jesus] comes," a reference to the expected return of Jesus very soon.

In 11:27, Paul calls attention to what is at stake. After the apocalypse (Jesus' return), when people face the final court of judgment expected with that event, members of the community will be judged on the basis of whether they enacted the Lord's Supper in ways that embody the world to come. Paul puts the matter with stark clarity: "For all who eat and drink without discerning the body, eat and drink judgment against themselves" (v. 29). The "body" (*soma*) here refers to the congregation as the body of Christ. "Discerning the body" means to relate with one another according to God's design of providing food for all. The behavior of the wealthy brings eschatological condemnation upon them.

According to 11:30–32, some in the community were sick (and even died) because of their attitudes. In a theological move that today's preacher cannot follow, Paul suggests that such sickness is "discipline" from God whose purpose is to alert the community to their error so they can correct it and be saved from condemnation.

The practical remedy, according to 11:33, is for the congregation to wait until everyone is present and then share the food equitably among all. If the wealthy are hungry, they can snack at home before they come (11:34).

Good Friday/Years A, B, and C

Hebrews 4:14–16; 5:7–9

Today's reading from Hebrews picks up after Hebrews's celebration of Christ's faithfulness (chap. 3) and summons the readers to be faithful as Christ was faithful (4:1–11). It concludes, "Let us therefore make every effort to enter that rest, so that no one may fall through such disobedience as theirs" (4:11). The "disobedience" referred to is that of the grumblers among the wilderness wanderers (3:16).

There is an equilibrium in today's passage; verses 12–13 stress the ability of God's word to "pierce" the human heart while verses 14–16 stress that Christ the high priest is able "to sympathize with our weaknesses." God's word here is the word of the living God, not the words of Scripture, although Hebrews's metaphors for God's word are drawn from Israel's Scriptures, which speak of it as creative, judging, and able to effect what it proclaims:

> So shall my word be that goes out from my mouth;
>   it shall not return to me empty,
> but it shall accomplish that which I purpose,
>   and succeed in the thing for which I sent it.
>   (Isa. 55:11)

> You desire truth in the inward being;
>   therefore teach me wisdom in my secret heart.
>   (Ps. 51:6)

Wisdom 18:14–18 depicts God's word as a warrior "carrying the sharp sword of [God's] authentic command." For Hebrews, God's word "divides soul from spirit"; it can "judge the thoughts and intentions of the heart" (v. 12). Hebrews reflects a Jewish tradition of uncompromising honesty with God in prayer: we might as well be honest, because God knows our thoughts and intentions anyway.

Verse 13 continues the theme of verse 12. That everything is "laid bare to the eyes of the one to whom we must make account" was a theme well known in Israel; Jeremiah speaks of God as one who judges righteously, who tries "the heart and the mind" (Jer. 11:20). Delighting in word play, Hebrews speaks of the "account," *logos*, we must render to God.

Verses 14–16 balance 12–13 with their talk of the "throne of grace." The warning of verses 12–13 is not negated. Grace is important because judgment is real. Hebrews articulates its Christology by emphasizing Christ's compassion. Verse 14 starts with its talk of Jesus as the "great high priest who has passed through the heavens." This becomes clear in 6:19–20 where Hebrews speaks of Christ as having entered the eternal temple.

Verse 15 is the linchpin of the passage: Hebrews urges its readers to hold onto their faith because they have a high priest who can "sympathize with our weaknesses . . . one who in every respect has been tested as we are, yet without sin." The Scriptures of Israel speak frequently of God's compassionate love for God's creatures using the word *rahamim* (from the word *rehem* for "womb") to speak of God's "womb-like love," God's "motherly" love, for God's children. Hebrews borrows such language to speak of Christ's compassion. It adds the idea that Christ was "tested as we are" as the reason why he is compassionate. With the word "tested," the author of Hebrews refers to the tough times through which his readers are living that, he fears, lead them to doubt God's promises.

Verse 16 rounds off today's reading by urging the reader to "approach the throne of grace with boldness, so that we may receive mercy and find grace to help in time of need." We may speak honestly to God in prayer and are to "approach," that is, enter the covenant with God courageously. Hebrews's words are ever pertinent, addressed as they were to a community being "tested," as we always are in some ways or other.

We discuss Hebrews 5:7–9 as part of our larger discussion of Hebrews 5:1–19 on Proper 24/Year B.

Good Friday/Years A, B, and C

Hebrews 10:16–25 (Alt)

Today's reading comprises two paragraphs; the first (vv. 11–18) restates Hebrews's view of the consequences of Christ's offering of himself, and the second (vv. 19–25) is an imperative (or paranetic) "therefore this is what you should do" section.

As elsewhere Hebrews contrasts the sacrifices of the priests with Christ's. They stood daily at the altar, repeating "sacrifices that can never take away sins" (v. 11). Priests did stand in the desert tabernacle (Deut. 10:8). By contrast, Christ "offered for all time a single sacrifice for sins" (v. 12); he does not need to repeat it. Then "he sat down at the right hand of God" (v. 12). Earlier Hebrews introduced the theme of "rest" (4:4, 10). Here Christ "rests" as God did (4:10) after completing God's labors. Hebrews then introduces an eschatological note (v. 13): having completed his offering Christ now waits "until his enemies would be made a footstool for his feet." Again the author quotes Psalm 110:1, a royal psalm about God's promise to the king of Israel that his enemies would be defeated, and takes it as addressed to Christ. Verse 14 claims that Christ's one offering "has perfected for all time those who are sanctified." Sanctification introduces the note of holiness, indicating the kinds of lives to be led by followers of Christ and preparing the reader for the injunctions to follow (vv. 19–30). Since Hebrews earlier declared that Christ had destroyed the devil (2:14), the aim of Christ's salvation is universal; the sanctified are not a small, cliquish group.

Verses 15–18 again invoke Jeremiah 31:31–34, quoted previously in 8:8–12. Whereas Jeremiah said that the new covenant would be made "with the house of Israel and the house of Judah," Hebrews says it will be made "with them." To whom Hebrews refers is a disputed question. Given that Hebrews never mentions any new people who replace the people Israel and because the scope of salvation in Hebrews is inclusive, we should take "them" as meaning everyone. In Israelite faith the Torah was supposed to be taken to heart and, indeed, even written on the heart (Deut. 30:11–14), and practical ways are prescribed for internalizing it. Hebrews adds (vv. 17–18) that because sins are now fully remitted, "there is no longer any offering for sin," that is, after Christ's singular offering.

Verses 19–25 shift from the indicative (what God has done for you in Christ) to exhorting the community to a way of life that should follow from such good news. The author addresses the community as "my brothers and sisters" (*adelphoi*), describing them as having confidence (boldness: *parresian*). This is a confidence "to enter the sanctuary by the blood of Jesus" (v. 19). In his first exhortation, Hebrews advises his community that because we have "a great priest over the house of God," we should "approach with a true heart in full assurance of faith" (v. 22). Hebrews's point is that Christ entered into the presence of God and in doing so enables us to do so as well. He accomplished this by his dutiful compliance with God's will in giving up his body (5:7–16).

The second exhortation (v. 23) is to "hold fast to the confession of our hope without wavering [*akline*], for he who has promised is faithful." Hope is not a formula. Hebrews is not urging adherence to a creed but to hope; we may hope because God is faithful (*hesed*, God's faithfulness, is a constant theme of Israelite Scripture). The last two exhortations are to "provoke one another to love and good deeds" (v. 24) and not to abandon one another (v. 25), but to meet together and encourage each other. As we have been loved, so we should love. Indeed, we should extend the exhortation to provoke each other to love and good deeds to all peoples and all faiths.

Holy Saturday/Years A, B, and C

1 Peter 4:1–8

The letter of 1 Peter was written to a community that was suffering. The author speaks of its suffering as "trials" that strengthen the community in the same way that smelting purifies ore (1 Pet. 1:7) and as similar to the suffering of Christ that he endured in order to receive the glory of resurrection (1:11). Slaves are to endure unjust suffering—suffering that is inflicted upon them because they do *right* (2:18–25)—as, indeed, is the community as a whole (3:13–20), for Christ himself suffered unjustly but in so doing witnessed to God's faithfulness and was raised from the dead.

The aim of today's text is stated in 4:1–2: to encourage the congregants to commit themselves to suffer faithfully in the same way that Christ suffered. The reading reminds the reader of the importance of doing so. The "human desire" (v. 2) is to end the time of suffering by departing from the life of discipleship.

The congregation was made up primarily of Gentiles. In 4:3–4, the ancient author characterizes the qualities of Gentile life that the readers have left behind: licentiousness, passions, drunkenness, reveling, carousing, and lawless idolatry. These work together as a catalogue of vices more to create a general impression of Gentile life than to recall specific behaviors of the Gentiles in the world of the congregation. Although each of these characteristics has its own nuance, they all share the trait of making it difficult if not impossible for Gentiles to live in covenantal community with one another and with God. Licentiousness likely refers to sexual immorality. The passions are not simply sexual urges but appetites of all kinds that consume the self. The drunk is not conscious and, therefore, cannot be responsive to God's desires. Reveling is an excessive meal that gets out of hand. Carousing is a drinking party. Idolatry, of course, is the regard of entities as ultimate when they are not. Typically, an idol is little more than a community's projection of its own self-interests. Consequently, such communities are lawless, that is, their life is a violent chaos that works against God's purposes for living together.

However, when converting from the idols to the living God of Israel, the members of the congregation left behind many associations with their idolatrous friends. In 4:4, the author says that their pagan neighbors "are surprised that you no longer join them in dissipation and so they blaspheme," meaning, "so they malign you." Some of their former friends, evidently, now harass them and cause them to suffer. In the socially stratified world of antiquity, to leave an established social group for one that was lower (or less defined) on the social pyramid could carry with it a powerful stigma. Moreover, in the ancient world, identity was communal: the suffering experienced by members of the church to whom this letter was written had likely caused them to question their new identity as members of the church.

The writer emphasizes why it is imperative for the addresses to remain faithful. The "end of all things is near," that is, the apocalypse that brings with it a day of judgment on which all people—the dead as well as the living—must account for the degree to which they have lived according to the purposes of the God for Israel for all people (4:5–7). The congregation needs to "be serious and discipline" themselves to be true to God in the face of suffering. The writer desperately wants the readers "to live in the spirit as God does," that is, to be a part of the age of imperishable, undefiled, and unfading life.

Although today's congregation may not share the belief that "the end of all things is near," members of the community may experience tension with the larger world when faithful witness requires that they go against values commonly assumed by the political, social, and economic systems that rule our world. The preacher would want to assure the congregation that such suffering is not the will of God (contra 1 Pet. 1:2b), but, indeed, that the knowledge of the presence of God can help sustain the community.

Easter Vigil/Years A, B, and C

Romans 6:3–11

In the preceding paragraph in Romans, Paul had commented, "But where sin increased, grace abounded all the more" (5:20). That comment occurred in the context of discussing human history from Adam to Christ. Now he is dealing with a question that his comment raises: "Should we continue in sin in order that grace may abound?" (6:1). This question is one that Paul could well have encountered as he carried out his mission to Gentiles; it could have been raised either by moral rigorists who regarded it as the natural implication of Paul's doctrine of grace or by moral libertines who rejoiced in Paul's apparent bashing of the law.

Neither group, however, understood Paul's thought, which in fact held that we are to keep all the law (*torah*): "Circumcision is nothing and uncircumcision is nothing; but obeying the commandments of God is everything" (1 Cor. 7:19). Paul never says that Gentiles are not to obey God's commandments; as we have just seen, he says quite the opposite. He simply says that Gentiles are not justified by doing so; they (as are Jews) are justified by God's grace. Grace frees and empowers us to do what God asks of us.

Paul's earlier discussion had been about the big picture—from Adam to Christ, sin and death exercised dominion; but now, lately, in Christ, grace has abounded to lead "to justification and life for all" (5:18). The question, "Are we to continue in sin in order that grace may abound?" is not about the big historical picture but about individuals now. It asks, Should we keep sinning in order to keep grace flowing? Paul answers, "By no means!" (6:2). The Greek, *me genoito*, is a strongly negative response, as if Paul had said, "That's ridiculous!" But the question for Paul is how he is going to get out of the logical trap that the question sets for him.

He does so by resorting to the practice of baptism (he also discusses it in 1 Cor. 1:13–17; 10:2; 12:13; and 15:29, and it is mentioned in Col. 2:12 and Eph. 4:5, which are post-Pauline). His answer reaches down to his root understanding of the Christian faith; it is a radical answer, one that goes to the root, *radix*. The import of the Greek word *baptismatos* is "drowning"; baptism is a word for shipwreck, dying, death. "How can we who died to sin go on living in it?" (6:2). Although sin is a power, we have been liberated from it by God in Christ. Further, all who are baptized into Christ are "baptized into his death" (6:3). The preposition "into" is important; members of the community live "in Christ"; Christ encompasses them. The pattern of Christ's ministry, which for Paul climaxed in his crucifixion, burial, and ongoing risen life, is to be the pattern of life of his followers—dying with him in baptism, rising to "walk in newness of life" (6:4). "Walking" is the Jewish way of understanding life with God; *torah* means "way" or "path," with the Scriptures as "light" for the way (Ps. 119:105).

Verses 5–6 seek to persuade Paul's Gentile readers of what he has just said. "If," says Paul, "we have been united with him in a death like his, we will certainly be united with him in a resurrection like his." A new prospect has been opened up for us, a new "prototype" for life—one found in Christ's dying to sin, self-giving love, and obedience. God's loving grace empowers us to live the righteousness that has been given us.

Verses 7–11 give voice to the hope that we who have died with Christ "will also live with him." We will live "to God" (6:11). Set free from the tyranny of sin and death, we can live for the neighbor and for God. Sin no longer has dominion over us (6:14).

Easter Day/Year A

Colossians 3:1–4

Today's reading looks backward and forward in Colossians. It looks back to the discussion of the counterfeit teachings and practices that have been repudiated (2:8–23) and forward to the discussion (3:5–17) of how the Colossians should live given what Christ has done for them. One theme running throughout Colossians is the strong communion between Christ and the community.

"So if you have been raised with Christ, seek the things that are above, where Christ is, seated at the right hand of God" (v. 1). Notice that believers "have been raised." Like Ephesians, with which it is fruitful to compare Colossians, the emphasis is that believers are already "in the heavenly places" with Christ. God, says Ephesians, "has blessed us in Christ with every spiritual blessing in the heavenly places" (1:3); God has "raised us up with him and seated us with him in the heavenly places in Christ Jesus" (2:6). Unlike the undisputed letters of Paul, where believers live in a time between Christ's resurrection and the hoped-for return of Christ, in Colossians and Ephesians believers are already "seated with Christ in the heavenly places." The Colossians are to understand themselves as already living in a resurrected reality.

That Christ is "at the right hand of God" does not imply that Christ is away and is, hence, absent from the community located in Colossae. The "right hand" is a metaphorical way of talking about God's rule of the world. But since there is nowhere that God does not rule, the right hand of God is everywhere (*dextra Dei ubique est*), and Christ is present with his followers wherever they are.[4]

Verse 2 says, "Set your minds on things that are above, not on things that are on earth." The Greek says, "Mind [*phoneo*] the things that are above," that is, concentrate on them. A constancy of commitment is required if we are to live as the new creatures that we are, having been raised with Christ. The distinction between "things that are above" and "things on earth" is not dualistic, nor does it call for indifference to such earthly matters as the needs of the neighbor. Verse 5 makes clear what is meant by "earthly": "fornication, impurity, passion, evil desire, and greed." And verses 12–13 equally clarify the "things that are above": "compassion, kindness, humility, meekness, and patience."

Verse 3 tells the Colossians, "For you have died, and your life is hidden with Christ in God." The believers' identification with Christ through baptism is stressed throughout this letter. It draws the strongest possible contrast between the "new" life of believers and their "old" life of hostility to God (1:21) by announcing, "You have died." "You have been raised" in verse 1 implies "you have died" in verse 3. The Greek makes it stronger: *apethanete gar*, "because you have died," therefore concentrate on the things that are above. As a result "your life is hidden with Christ in God." Believers have no need, looking backward to 2:8–23, of the false securities offered by the opponents in Colossae. You are with Christ and have no need of visible signs of acceptance; your life is "hidden" with him in God.

Verse 4 says, "When Christ who is your life is revealed, then you also will be revealed with him in glory." Today's text begins in the past—"you have been raised"—continues to the present—"your life is hidden with Christ in God"—and ends on the future—"when Christ . . . is revealed, you also will be revealed with him in glory." That we are encompassed behind, before, and above by Christ is the ground for the ethical life that God gives and calls us to lead (3:5–17).

Second Sunday of Easter/Year A

1 Peter 1:3–9

This document was written to congregations in Asia Minor (present-day Turkey) (1 Pet. 1:2) that were made up of Gentiles (1 Pet. 2:10; 4:3–4) who rejected idolatry and who were joined by Jesus Christ to the God of Israel in the church. The letter repeatedly mentions that the congregation (a minority in a larger culture) was suffering, apparently because nonconverted Gentiles harassed them, perhaps even excluding them from former social circles. The writer uses vivid theological images and ideas, largely from the First Testament, to interpret their identity as a minority (1:2, 3–9; 1:17–2:12), their suffering (1:6–12; 2:18–25; 3:13–4:19), and values in the larger culture which they should follow (2:13–3:7). Indeed, their minority status (exiles) is integral to their mission (1:2, 17–21) as they make their way to the second coming (1:3–5; 2:11–12; 4:5–11, 17–18; 5:1, 4). Although the historical Peter did not likely write the letter, the choice of the name of this Jewish apostle by the pseudonymous author (and drawing so heavily on the First Testament) indicates that the letter is to help Gentiles assimilate key elements of Jewish identity and purpose. However, the letter contains no suggestion that the church supersedes Israel. The mission of Israel is extended into the Gentile arena via the church.

The Jewish tone of the letter is immediately apparent as the writer replaces the thanksgiving of the Greek letter with a blessing (*eulogetos*) that has a Jewish character (1:3ff.). The importance of blessing in Judaism is clear not only in the use of that notion in the Jewish Scriptures but also in the facts that the first tractates of both the Mishnah and the Talmud are entitled *Berakah*, a key Hebrew word for "blessing." The blessing is directed to God for how God has helped the Gentiles through Jesus Christ (1:3).

God acted for the Gentiles out of mercy—a typically Jewish way of speaking of God's compassion for the world. The "new birth" (*anagennao* = be born again) is not a private psychological experience but is a fundamental change of social identity from the Gentile world to the community awaiting the return of Christ to end the present age and to reveal from heaven the imperishable and undefiled new world (1:3–5). The writer uses a term "inheritance" (*kleronomia*) with a long history in Judaism (for example, Exod. 34:9) that in the Hellenistic age came to describe the promise of God for a new age (Dan. 12:3; 2 Esd. 7:9; 8:45; *Pss. Sol.* 14:10; 15:15; Rom. 4:13). Typical of apocalyptic theologians, the author assumes that the inheritance (the new era) is already present in heaven and needs only be revealed as the last act of this age of history. God faithfully protects it for them.

Because of this hope, the congregation can rejoice even in the midst of its suffering. They do not rejoice that they suffer but because God has given them the insight that their suffering (*lupeo*) will be brief because the final apocalypse will occur (relatively) soon. Indeed, the writer uses a term, "trials" (*peirasmos*), that sometimes refers to the period of intense suffering just before the end of history (Zeph. 1:5; Hab. 3:16; *1 En.* 95:5; 96:2–3).

The suffering is testing "the genuineness of their faithfulness" by fire. The "testing" (*dokimazo*) by fire calls to mind taking ore and putting it into a fire in order to burn away the slag and leave the pure metal (as in Mal. 3:2b–4; Wis. 3:6; 11:10; Sir. 2:5; 31:10; 44:20). The tested or refined community will bring forth praise, glory, and honor at the second coming (1:7).

In verses 8–9, the writer seeks to fortify attitudes that are already present in the community. Although they have never seen Jesus Christ, they love him, trust him, and rejoice in the present with "indescribable and glorious joy" because they will receive, as "the outcome of their faithfulness, the salvation of [their] soul," that is, participation in the realm that is "imperishable, undefiled, and unfading" (v. 4).

Third Sunday of Easter/Year A

1 Peter 1:17–23

The congregations to whom this letter was written—made up of converted Gentiles—were suffering, probably because of harassment from their unconverted neighbors. The blessing in 1 Peter 1:3–12 affirms that this suffering will not last long because Jesus will soon return with "salvation ready to be revealed in the last time." In view of this situation, 1 Peter 1:13 begins a section of the letter that guides the congregation in understanding its identity and mission, which the author describes primarily in language taken from the First Testament adapted for the church.

The community needs to understand its identity and purpose so that it can live in a way that will prepare it for apocalypse (1 Pet. 1:13). Members are to be "obedient children" (*tekna hupakoe*), words that recall Israel ("children," Isa. 17:3, 9; Jer. 3:14; "obedient," Exod. 19:5; 24:7; Deut. 11:27). As children in the tradition of Israel, they are not to "be conformed to the desires [*epithumia*] that they formerly had in ignorance [*agnoia*]" when they lived by Gentile values and practices (Wis. 14:22).

Instead, in 1:16, the author cites Leviticus 19:2 to explain the identity and mission of the congregations. They are to be holy because God is holy. The terms for "holy" (*hagios, hagiazo*) mean, like their Hebrew counterparts, "set apart." God is holy in that God is not like any other deities and lives in integrity, by which God inevitably says and does what is right. The congregation is to be like Israel—holy in the sense of set apart from other peoples by living according to the precepts of God and not compromising with the false values and practices of the peoples around them, who worship idols and are unjust, exploitative, and violent.

The congregation needs to enact holiness during its "exile" because God "judges all people impartially" (Deut. 10:17; 2 Chr. 19:7; Sir. 35:12; *Pss. Sol.* 2:18). The term *exile* (*paroikias*) with its cognates bespeaks resident aliens or strangers—people who live in an area (sometimes temporarily but often permanently) but who are not fully integrated into the life of that area (Exod. 2:22; 18:3; 25:6; 23, 35, 45–47; 1 Chr. 29:15; Ps. 38:12; Wis. 19:10). It is unclear to what degree the writer uses the term figuratively to describe the situation of the church (a resident alien in Gentile culture) or more literally to indicate that the community was made up of persons who were aliens in social terms.

The community was "ransomed" (*lutroo*) from "futile [Gentile] ways" (1:18–19). The language of "ransom" is that of liberation. In the economic world it refers to money paid to free slaves, prisoners of war, or someone from a bond (Lev. 25:25, 30, 48–49); in the religious sphere it speaks figuratively of God's actions in freeing people from exile and other forms of debilitation (Isa. 35:9; 43:1). The means of liberation is the "precious blood of Jesus, like that of a lamb without defect or blemish" (v. 9). This language contains multiple allusions. It recalls the Passover lamb (Exod. 12:13) as well as more general Jewish sacrificial customs where the offering is an animal; it communicates release from sin (Lev. 2:9–12; 22:17–25). It also brings to mind Isaiah 53:7, in which the suffering of the Servant (community of Israel) witnesses to God's actions in making things right. In these spheres of thought, the importance is less on the mechanics of the ransom or the sacrifice (and their effects on God) and much more on the *function* of this language. Just as Jewish sacrifice assured Israel of God's continued providence, so the death of Jesus assured the congregation that it was free from the vicissitudes of Gentile existence and is now in the sphere of the God of Israel. Indeed, the references to "silver and gold" may be a subtle statement of the impotence of idols and other Gentile religious practices (Deut. 29:16; Wis. 13:10).

In 1:20, the writer uses a notion, common in apocalypticism, that God had planned many events to end the present perishable age and begin the imperishable one before the world was created. The theocentric character of this letter surfaces in 1:21: through the event of Jesus Christ, the community "has come to trust in *God*" (italics ours).

The change from Gentile futility to covenantal life in the church makes it possible for the Gentile converts to love one another "deeply from the heart." The congregation becomes, for them, a new (and unending) society, replacing the ones from which they were excluded because of conversion (1:22–23).

The writer brings this part of the discussion to a close by summarizing with Isaiah 40:6–8. The prophet compares Gentile existence to grass that withers and fades. The Word of God (in which the Gentile believers now live) "endures forever" (1:24–25). In such assurance, the community can endure suffering.

Fourth Sunday of Easter/Year A

1 Peter 2:19–25

In 1 Peter 2:4–10, the author states the mission of the Petrine community: to live as a chosen race witnessing to God's call out of darkness into light. In 2:11–17 the writer begins an extended explanation of ways to put this vocation into practice while living as resident aliens in the larger Gentile arena, which includes living in concord with the hierarchical social pyramid of the Hellenistic age.

The reading for today should begin at 2:18, which exhorts slaves to accept their place in that pyramid. The term "accept the authority" (*hupotasso*) means to place oneself under the authority of those ranked higher in the social order. We discuss slavery in the ancient world in connection with Philemon (Proper 23/Year C).

The author admonishes slaves to be submissive to harsh masters, not just kind ones. Obedience to a kind master is not a "credit," nor is suffering when one is beaten for wrongdoing. God approves when the slave does right but is beaten (or otherwise caused to suffer) without cause (2:19–20). Indeed, 2:21 echoes the notion of call in 1:9 by implying that God *calls* the community to such innocent suffering as part of its mission. They are to follow the example of Christ by walking in his steps.

While preachers often mine 2:22–25 for insights into the Christology of this document, the author uses this passage as a warrant for slaves to accept the authority of their masters. The author draws on Isaiah 53 with its picture of the Servant (the community of Israel), who suffered because Gentiles wanted to extinguish Israel's faithful witness to God's will for justice for all. The slaves are to follow the example of the Servant (and Jesus) and suffer quietly and submissively like a sheep led to the slaughter.

Since verses 22–25 focus on the suffering of Jesus, it seems likely that the author intends for Isaiah 53:9, quoted in 1 Peter 2:22, to mean not that Jesus was eternally sinless but that at the time he suffered, he did not sin. When abused, Jesus did not return abuse, nor threaten his abusers, but "entrusted himself to the one who judges justly" (2:23).

Jesus "bore [*anaphero*] our sins in his body on the cross" (Greek: "tree"). The image of "bearing our sins" derives from Isaiah 53:12. To be sure, Isaiah 52:12–53:12 uses the language of sacrifice to interpret the suffering of the Servant. However, commentators often miss an overriding point, revealed in 52:12–53:1: suffering gives God the opportunity to demonstrate the divine power and will for setting things right by *restoring Israel*. The death of Jesus, similarly, gives God an opportunity to demonstrate that Gentile converts are now "free from sins."

The community can now "live for righteousness," that is, live in right relationships with one another and with the wider world in anticipation of the coming world. Because Jesus faithfully died, he can now return and complete the healing of the wounded world. Though the Gentiles were once going astray like sheep, they are now gathered to the shepherd and guardian (2:25). With the death and resurrection of Jesus, God has begun to restore the fortunes of the community (as God promised in the case of Isa. 52:12–53:12) so that unconverted Gentiles can see the faithfulness, power, and covenantal life available through the God of Israel.

Although we might understand the text, as well as similar concerns in the larger context of 2:11–3:7, as part of a survival strategy for a struggling minority community, the preacher should rightly help the congregation understand that the arbitrary hierarchical social structure is theologically inappropriate to a God of unconditional love whose purpose is for all people to live together in egalitarian relationships of love. With respect to the motif of suffering, the preacher has a triple calling: to help the community understand (1) that God does not *want* people to suffer, (2) that God feels such suffering and supports people through it, and (3) that God is actively working to end conditions that lead to suffering. Indeed, in direct opposition to the point of this text, we believe the preacher should usually encourage the congregation to resist authorities who cause arbitrary and unjust suffering through abuse, exploitation, and other injustices.

Fifth Sunday of Easter/Year A

1 Peter 2:2–10

First Peter 2:1 admonishes the Gentiles to be sure that they are free of behaviors that are characteristic of Gentile existence—malice, guile, insincerity, envy, and slander. Such attitudes and actions destroy self and community. Suggesting that the congregation should be like newborns and take in "spiritual milk" (*logikos adolos*, 2:2), the author employs an antidote found in Jewish sources (Philo, *Agr.* 9; *Migr.* 29; cf. *Odes Sol* 8:14; 19:1–5; 35:5; 1 Thess. 2:7; 1 Cor. 3:2). In 2:3, the author offers Psalm 34:8 as a rationale: they should want God's milk because they taste that God is good. The church is in a situation similar to that of Israel in the psalm: calling to God in a time of distress.

The author continuously uses Jewish imagery to interpret the church in 2:4–10. As noted in connection with previous lections from 1 Peter, the writer implies not that the Petrine community replaces Israel but rather that the community provides a way for Gentiles to share in the life and vocation of Israel as they await the apocalypse.

The community is to come to Christ, who is a "living stone" (*lithos zontos*, 2:4). This image directly contrasts with the impotent idols of the Gentiles, many of which were made of lifeless stones (Deut. 4:28; Wis. 13:10; 14:21). Anticipating the appearance of Isaiah 28:16 in 1 Peter 2:6, the writer points out in 2:4 that the stone (Christ) though rejected by mortals, was chosen and precious, and therefore could enable the community to become "living stones," a spiritual house (*ho oikos pneumatikos*), that is, a community animated by the living Spirit. The author implies a dramatic contrast between the impotent temples of the Gentiles (built of lifeless stones) and the misguided communities that inhabit them. The church is a "holy priesthood" (on which we comment at 2:9, below) that offers "spiritual sacrifices [*pneumatikas thusias*] acceptable to God" through Jesus Christ. The church did not, of course, literally perform sacrifices, but apropos of our discussion on the Fifth Sunday of Easter/Year A, the language of sacrifice communicates to Gentiles that participation in the church has the same assurance of God's favor for them as participation in the sacrifices in Israel had for Jewish people.

In 2:6, the author cites Isaiah 28:16 as a rationale for the preceding assertions. The first-century reader would finish the quote from the Septuagint: "And the one who trusts on that stone will certainly not be ashamed" (author's translation). The point is that God has confirmed Christ as the cornerstone of the Gentile church, so the community can trust in God through Christ and live confidently in the community as prescribed in this letter.

Since the author has Gentiles in view, the citation of Psalm 118:22 and Isaiah 8:14 in 1 Peter 2:7–8 refers to them: They reject the God of Israel revealed through Christ (2:6) and stumble (2:7), which in the context of Isaiah 8:14 means to fall under condemnation.

In 2:9, the author draws from Exodus 19:6 and Isaiah 43:20–21 to give one of the most lyrical interpretations of the church in the Second Testament. The community is a "chosen race" (*genos eklektos*), chosen to be a light among the Gentiles in a manner similar to Israel. They are a "royal priesthood" (*basileion hierateuma*), that is, a community whose life functions in a priestly way among the Gentiles: to mediate the knowledge of God. They are a "holy nation" (*ethnos hagios*), that is, a community of Gentiles that, like Israel, is holy—living differently from the other communities of the world because they live in the manner prescribed by the God of Israel, who is holy (1 Pet. 1:16). They are "God's own people" in the sense of belonging to God (in contrast to the unconverted Gentiles, who belong to idols). The mission of the congregation as chosen race, royal priesthood, and so on, is to "proclaim the mighty acts of the one who called you out of darkness [a characteristic description of Gentile existence and condemnation] into . . . marvelous light [a stock designation for eschatological salvation and the community witnessing to it]" (Isa. 9:2; 42:6—called to give light to the Gentiles; 47:5; Wis. 17:2, 17, 21; 18:4; 2 Esd. 7:42, 97; Eph. 5:8; Col. 1:12; 1 Thess. 5:5).

The author summarizes these themes by citing Hosea 1:9 combined with 2:23. The Gentiles in Peter's community, like Israel, have received God's mercy and, consequently, are to live through suffering in the strength of that mercy, compassion, and faithfulness.

Sixth Sunday of Easter/Year A

1 Peter 3:13–22

The community to whom 1 Peter was written was composed of Gentile converts who were harassed by other, unconverted Gentiles. Today's lesson encourages the congregation to "do what is good" (witness faithfully) even when unconverted Gentiles cause them to suffer. While this theme is instructive for today's congregation, a preacher should not forget that it follows theologically problematic guidance in 1 Peter 2:11–3:12 (especially 2:15, 19–25, Fourth Sunday after Easter/Year A).

The question of 3:13 is ironic: the letter assumes the community is suffering for doing good. The question has a Jewish undertone: the expression "if you are eager" contains the word *zelotes* ("zealous"), which is often associated with fidelity to Jewish tradition (Sir. 25:43; 1 Macc. 2:26–27, 50).

The community is "blessed" (*makarios*) in suffering. The reference is to blessing from being in the coming eschatological world (4 Macc. 17:18; 18:19; Matt. 5:3–11; Rev. 19:19). Because of such confidence, the writer adapts Isaiah 8:12–13 to urge the community not to fear nor be intimidated by those who harass them, but to "sanctify Christ as Lord," that is, live holiness ("sanctify = *hagiazo* = "be holy") similar to Christ (3:14–15a).

The author wants the congregation to "be ready to make [their] defense [*apologia*] to anyone who demands an accounting for the hope that is in [them]." (3:15b). Here *apologia* refers to the congregation and explains why, while suffering unjustly, they continue to be faithful to the God of Israel. Josephus's work *Against Apion* reminds us that Jewish people frequently had to answer questions about why they lived differently from unconverted Gentiles. They are to do so in "gentleness and reverence" (*prautetos kai phobos*—with humility and reverence toward God) and by keeping a clear conscience, that is, responding to their questioners and persecutors by not repaying evil with evil (2:23). The congregation thus shames their accusers (3:16). Echoing 2:19–20, the writer says that if suffering is God's will, it is better to suffer for doing good than to suffer for doing evil. The former is meritorious while the latter is deserved.

As in 2:18–25, the writer draws on the example of the suffering of Christ to justify quietude in response to undeserved suffering. We considered this letter's theological interpretation of the suffering of Jesus, which surfaces again in 3:18–19a, on the Fourth Sunday of Easter/Year A. Here, however, the author expresses more clearly that the death of Jesus is not itself the ultimate point but, rather, that his death provides the occasion whereby the resurrection can demonstrate God's purpose and power to save. The intensity of the divine purpose in this regard is revealed in the resurrected Jesus visiting the spirits in the underworld, where they are awaiting the apocalypse, and announcing the good news to them (2:19–20a). Although some scholars think these "spirits" (*pneumasin*) are not human but rather heavenly beings from apocalyptic mythology, 3:20 suggests they are people, for they include folk who were disobedient in the days of Noah (cf. *1 En.* 22). Since the letter is addressed to Gentiles, and the author describes the dead with language frequently used of Gentiles ("did not obey") and refers to people in Noah's time (also Gentiles), we presume that these are Gentile dead. With the eschaton at hand, the God of Israel seeks to save even Gentiles who lived prior to the apocalyptic moment.

In 3:20b–22, the author makes a point directly applicable to the Petrine congregation. Just as God used water to save eight people from the great flood in the days of Noah, so God uses the water of baptism to assure the Gentiles in the congregation that their consciences are clean. They have not only turned from idols but are living in ways that are consistent with the example of Jesus (on conscience, 3:16–18; cf. 1:6–12; 2:9–10; 2:19–25), especially in responding to undeserved suffering, and they otherwise make what the author regards as a faithful witness (1:13–16; 22–23; 2:11–17; 3:8–12). They can trust this assertion on the great day of judgment because Christ is already at the right hand of God (Ps. 110:1), where angels and other beings are subject to him.

Ascension of the Lord/Years A, B, and C

Ephesians 1:15–23

Ephesians 1:3–15 is a *berakah* (blessing) for all the things God has done for Gentile believers (2:11–22 makes it clear that Ephesians is addressed to Gentiles). Today's reading is a thanksgiving prayer to God on behalf of "all the saints" (v. 15). It concludes (vv. 20–23) by "unpacking" the meaning of Christ's ascension: "God . . . raised him from the dead and seated him at his right hand in the heavenly places" (v. 20).

"I have heard of your faith in the Lord Jesus and your love toward all the saints" (v. 15). "Faith" here is not individualistic—the church is the "body" of Christ (v. 23); Ephesians speaks of the community's faith. "Love" is important in Ephesians and is mentioned twelve times. In verse 18, "hope" becomes the theme of the latter part of today's reading. With it, we have the well-known Pauline "faith, hope, and love." Ephesians then says, "I do not cease to give thanks for you as I remember you in my prayers" (v. 16). Significantly, the thanksgiving follows the blessing of 1:3–14; the two were closely associated in Jewish worship, on which Ephesians draws.

In verses 17–18 the writer prays, "[May God] give you a spirit of wisdom and revelation as you come to know him, so that with the eyes of your heart enlightened. . . ." Wisdom and revelation are one and the same thing here, with the emphasis that the readers are still coming to know God. God "has made known to us" God's will; Ephesians prays that we will comprehend what we have been given to know. We are on the way to fuller understanding; we have not arrived. God takes the initiative in our coming to wisdom. As the writer praised God in 1:3–14 for all that God has done for us, so here the stress remains on God's grace; "by grace you have been saved" (2:5).

The writer offers this prayer so that "you may know . . . the hope to which he has called you" (v. 18). Note two points about hope in Ephesians: (1) it plays a crucial role in forming the contemporary lives of believers (as does its absence!), and (2) its object is "the riches of his glorious inheritance [*kleronomias*] among the saints" (v. 18). The riches of glory and the inheritance refer to God's having called forth a people from among both Jews and Gentiles (2:11–22). "Inheritance" recalls the frequent use of "adoption" in Romans and in the election of the people Israel. We Gentiles who "once were far off have been brought near by the blood of Christ" (2:13). "Among the saints" echoes "all the saints" in verse 15 and points us toward the universal church, an emphasis in Ephesians.

Verses 19–23 deal with God's power and Christ's exaltation to "the right hand" of God "in the heavenly places, far above all rule and authority and power and dominion, and above every name that can be named" (vv. 20–21). Several important points are made here. First, at God's right hand, Christ is not "away" or "gone." The right hand of God, said Luther, is everywhere, because God rules the entire cosmos (*dextra Dei ubique est*).[5] God and Christ are always with us, wherever we are.

Second, Christ now is over, on top of, and ruling all other powers, rulers, and authorities. We are no longer in any ultimate sense under their control, whether they be understood as supernatural (for example, Satan) or utterly earthly (for example, despots such as Caesar). "All things," including all powers that would destroy the well-being of God's creatures, are under God's dominion. We are freed from them and freed for love of God and love of the neighbor. This is good news indeed.

Seventh Sunday of Easter/Year A

1 Peter 4:12–14; 5:6–11

These texts tie together three themes that weave in and out of 1 Peter—the final judgment, the return of Jesus in glory, and the suffering of the Petrine community in the last days. The particular focus on suffering in this part of the letter is more on suffering that results from faithful witness and less on unjust suffering, as in 2:18–25. This witness will not have to last long because "the end of all things is near" (4:7).

The term "beloved" (4:12) was often used in antiquity to indicate kinship, such as that between parent and child, and its use here indicates that the author (who is portrayed as the Jewish apostle Peter in 1:1) and the Gentiles in the community (4:3–4) are kin in the household of the church (Tob. 3:10; *Odes Sol.* 3:1–11).

The author speaks of the "fiery ordeal that is taking place to test you" (4:12) to interpret the meaning of the community's suffering (likely harassment from their unconverted Gentile neighbors). The experience of the community is similar to the "fiery ordeal" (*purosis*) by which ore is purified by putting it into a fire and burning off the slag to leave pure metal (Prov. 37:21), a notion that came to be used of "testing" the faithfulness of the community as suffering increases and as the enemies of God resist the coming of the apocalypse (1QS 1:17; 8:4; 1QM 17:1, 9). On *peirasmos*, "test," in this regard, see Second Sunday of Easter/Year A.

In this circumstance, the community is to "rejoice" not simply in the fact of suffering but because by sharing in the suffering of Christ it will be prepared to "shout for joy when his glory is revealed" at the apocalypse (4:13; Matt. 5:11–12, and *2 Bar.* 48:48–50; 52:5–7). The community is blessed when reviled because the Spirit is among them. The Spirit was associated with the last days, including among the Gentiles (Joel 2:28–29; Gentiles = "all flesh").

However, community members should live so they do not suffer punishment for community-destroying activities (4:15). The term "Christian" occurs in 4:16 one of the only three times in the Second Testament (also see Acts 11:26; 26:28). Since the author counsels that suffering as a "Christian" is not a disgrace, the term was likely used as a slur by those who abused the community. At such times, the community is to glorify *God*.

The sober verses 17–19 underscore the importance of faithful witness, for "the time has come for judgment to begin with the household of God" (4:17). The faithful are judged first. While the text does not directly say what "the end will be for those [Gentiles] who do not obey," the citation of Proverbs 11:31 implies that they will not be saved.

The Gentile congregation joins the Jewish people in "humbling themselves"(*tapeinoo*), that is, limiting themselves according to God's expectations (Lev. 16:29; Dan. 10:12) as they await the final deliverance "under God's mighty hand" (4:6). The latter phrase is often used in the First Testament in reference to God's delivering Israel (Exod. 3:19; Deut. 3:24). Drawing from Psalm 55:22, which laments treachery afflicted on an individual by a former friend (a situation similar to that of the Petrine community), the author urges the community to "cast their cares on" God (5:7). The psalm asserts that God will sustain the community. On God's care, see also Wisdom of Solomon 12:13.

The community needs to be "disciplined" and "alert" because the devil is like a roaring lion on the prowl—a dramatic depiction of the intensified activity of the devil in the last days (5:8; 4:12–13). The adversaries of Israel sometimes attack like roaring lions (Ps. 22:13; cf. 1QH 5:9). The author implies in 5:9 that the devil operates through the abuse perpetrated on the congregation by their idol-worshiping Gentile neighbors. The congregation resists the devil (5:9) by engaging in the practices described in this letter—such as suffering in silence without making retribution, maintaining their places in the social hierarchy, and avoiding Gentile patterns of destructive living (4:1–6).

The community will not need to engage in such resistance and endurance long. "After you have suffered for a little while," God will bring about the apocalypse, which, for the faithful, will be a time of restoration, support, strength, and security (5:9–10). The main body of the letter ends on a theocentric note (v. 11).

Day of Pentecost/Year A

1 Corinthians 12:3b–13

The congregation at Corinth was divided in ways that interfered with its ability to carry out its purpose of embodying the realm of God (1 Cor. 1:10). The major division was between people of higher and lower social status, and Paul encouraged the elites to set aside their status to help the congregation become a community embodying the gospel. Today's text was designed to help the community interpret spiritual gifts in ways that build up community (12:1–14:40).

The Corinthians wrote Paul for help in understanding and exercising spiritual gifts (*pneumatikoi*) (12:1). To set the stage for the ensuing discussion, Paul reminds the Corinthians that they once worshiped idols (v. 2). When Paul says the idols "could not speak," he uses a quintessentially Jewish characterization of idols as powerless (Ps. 114:4–5; 135:15; Hab. 2:18–19; Wis. 15:15–17). Fractiousness in community (such as that in Corinth) is one of many difficulties that result from idolatry (see further Rom. 1:18–32).

Although Paul mentions people who say, "Jesus be cursed" (12:3), it is less likely that people in Corinth actually said such a thing but more likely that Paul uses this dramatic expression to shock the Corinthians into agreeing with him about a matter that is foundational in the subsequent argument. The Corinthians know the Spirit operates among them (1:17; 2:4, 10–14; 3:16; 6:11, 19; 9:11), so they would think, "Of course, no one led by the Spirit would say 'Jesus is cursed.' When we say 'Jesus is Lord' [one of the earliest confessions of the church—Phil. 2:11; 2 Cor. 4:5; Rom. 10:9], it is by the Spirit." The apostle wins their assent in the hope that they will assent to the rest of his argument.

In 12:4–6 the apostle articulates a theology of difference within shared purpose to explain the relationship among the various spiritual gifts (12:8–11), acts of service (12:28), and activities. Through the Spirit, the same God animates each person with a gift in order to contribute to the *common* good, not to elevate the status of a few.

The destructive effects of status that permeate 1 Corinthians surface in today's reading. In antiquity, for example, speaking in tongues was associated with high social standing.[6] In Corinth, those who practice this gift are the same ones who speak "eloquent wisdom" (1:11–4:21) and whose behavior disrupts the community (5:1–11:33). Paul wants the Corinthians to recognize that while glossolalia is a gift of the Spirit, it is only one such gift. By embracing the value of all gifts, the congregation can become the *body* of Christ.

Differences among the lists of gifts in Romans 12:6–8 and 1 Corinthians 12:8–11, 28–30, as well as Ephesians 4:11 and 1 Peter 4:10–11, show that the list in today's passage is not exhaustive but representative of the kinds of gifts the Spirit gives. Paul's interest in 12:8–11 is less in the content of the list than in the relationship of the gifts to one another to serve the common good.

At the head of the list, Paul places uttering the "wisdom"and "knowledge" of God as described in 1:18–4:21 and 8:1–11:40. In the view of 13:2, "faith" is likely the capacity to remove mountains, a rabbinic expression for performing difficult acts of faithfulness. Some people have the gift of healing, and others, that of working miracles (signs other than healing). The early Christian prophets received messages from God or Jesus and relayed them to the congregation. Discerning the spirits is critical in order to determine which gifts and possibility are of the Spirit and which are of other spirits. Speaking in tongues is the experience of ecstasy overflowing into sound while interpretation of tongues gives the meaning of the ecstasy in conventional speech (see 14:1–40). By placing these gifts last, Paul dresses down the elites who regard their gift as most important. The point of 12:11 is polemical. The *Spirit* allots gifts not to maintain social hierarchy but to create a community of witness.

Trinity Sunday/Year A

2 Corinthians 13:11–13

Letter writing in antiquity followed conventions, particularly at the beginnings and ends of letters—for example, by concluding with remarks that evoke main themes in the letter, greetings, and a benediction. Just as Paul reshaped the content of the opening conventions for theological purposes (for example, see our comments on 1 Cor. 1:1–9 on the Second Sunday after Epiphany/Year A and the First Sunday of Advent/Year B), so Paul adapts the concluding conventions to reinforce the message of the letter and the practice and sense of covenantal community in the congregation.

Paul addresses the Corinthians as "brothers" (*adelphoi*), which the NRSV expands to "brothers and sisters" to indicate that the apostle included all in the community. The familial terms are further important because they indicate that the community is much like a family. In antiquity, kinship was much more important than today. The members of the church are bound to one another like kin in identity, tradition, and support. Paul addresses the Corinthians as *community*, people who are inseparably interrelated.

The NRSV translates *chairete* as "farewell" whereas other versions more satisfactorily render "rejoice." Even the latter, however, does not catch a subtlety deriving from the fact that *chairete* is related to *charis*, usually translated "grace," which evokes God's covenantal faithfulness. As the letter ends, the apostle wants the community to rejoice because their life is supported by divine faithfulness.

Given the tensions between himself and the community that Paul catalogued through 2 Corinthians, the apostle wants the Corinthians to "put things in order" (*katartizo*), that is, restore the life of the community to the purposes God has for it. The means to do so is to "listen to my appeal" (*parakaleo*) for the Corinthians to turn away from the glitzy message advocated by persons described as super apostles (2 Cor. 11:5; 12:11) and to return to Paul's interpretation of the gospel. When the apostle encourages them to "agree with one another" (*to auto phroneite*), he employs an expression typical of a partnership (*koinonia*), in which the partners make a commitment to work for a common purpose. The Corinthians can thus "live in peace," that is, embody the core Jewish vision of *shalom*—a community in which all members live together in mutual support.

The members of the community are to greet one another with a holy kiss (2 Cor. 13:12). While it was customary in many circles in Mediterranean antiquity to greet with a kiss on the neck or cheek, the adjective "holy" (*hagios*) indicates that the greeting (perhaps as a part of worship) expresses mutual commitment to the holy purposes of God for all people to know blessing and includes commitment to one another.

Virtually all scholars agree that the fully developed doctrine of the Trinity is not found in the Second Testament but was extrapolated by the later church from passages such as 13:13 and Matthew 28:19. The parallel structure of the elements of 2 Corinthians 13:13 remind the reader of the close relationship among God, Jesus, and the Spirit, but in the broader context of Paul's thought they are not proto-Trinitarianism. As a Jewish theologian, Paul was monotheistic and theocentric (for example, 2 Cor. 1:3, 20; 3:4; 4:15; 12:19; Phil. 2:11; Gal. 3:20). The apostle repeatedly describes the work of Christ and the Spirit as pointing to (or deriving from) God. Although Christ and the Spirit are agents of God, Paul never describes them as God. The love of the God of Israel may appear at the center of the tripartite benediction as a symbol of its centrality in theological reality. Whereas Israel came to know God through Jewish tradition, the Gentile Corinthians came to know God's grace (*charis*, as noted above, God's covenantal faithfulness) through Jesus Christ. The Spirit energizes the congregation as a "communion" a *koinonia*, a partnership (as noted above) whose purpose is to embody the life of the eschatological age and invite others into it. Paul reminds the Corinthians that these realities are ever "with all of you."

Proper 4 [9]/Year A

Romans 1:16–17; 3:22b–28, (29–31)

Please see the Ninth Sunday after the Epiphany/Year A for commentary on this passage.

Proper 5 [10]/Year A

Romans 4:13–25

Today's reading deals with the promise to Abraham "that he would inherit the world" (4:13), that is, become the one through whom both Gentiles and Jews would find inclusion in the one family of God. To put this promise in the larger context of Romans, let us attend to how Paul speaks of faith and the wrath of God.

First, Paul often uses the Greek expressions *pistis Christou* and *pistis theou*. They were long translated as "faith in Christ" and "faith in God," where Christ and God are objects of faith. But as today's reading makes clear, such a phrase as *ek pisteos Abraam* means "faith of [not in] Abraham." The expression *pistis theou* is an objective genitive that should be translated "God's faithfulness" rather than "faith in God" because it refers to God's faithfulness or *hesed*, steadfast love.[7] What is at stake for Paul is God's faithfulness to God's promises and Christ's faithfulness to God. Romans 4 is not about our faith in God or justification by our faith. It is about the inclusion of Gentiles because God is faithful to God's promises to Abraham.[8] For Paul "the righteousness of God is revealed through faith for faith" (1:17); that is, through God's faithfulness for faith.

Second, in today's reading Paul claims that "the law brings wrath; but where there is no law, neither is there violation" (4:15). Readers might conclude from this that Jewish law, torah, works only to expose us to the wrath of God. But Paul has already made clear that all human beings, not only those who know the torah, are in the same predicament: "All who have sinned apart from the law will also perish apart from the law, and all who have sinned under the law will be judged by the law" (2:12). Gentiles, whose catalogue of sins is rehearsed in 1:18–32, know what they need to know about God "because God has shown it to them . . . through the things he has made" (1:19–20).

Romans 4:13–25 has to do with the claim that Abraham's faith "'was reckoned [*elogiste*, repeated nine times throughout this section of Romans] to him'. . . not for his sake alone, but for ours also" (4:23–24). It will be reckoned to us "who believe in him who raised Jesus our Lord from the dead, who was handed over to death for our trespasses and was raised for our justification" (4:24–25), that is, our inclusion in the one family of God. Now we turn to how Paul gets from Abraham to the resurrection.

Paul argues for the utterly inclusive nature of God's promise to Abraham on the basis of God's unfathomable and undeserved grace; our inheritance is reckoned "according to grace," *kata charin* (4:4). "It depends on faith, in order that the promise may rest on grace" (4:16). God's promise to Abraham is guaranteed to all his descendants (4:17). Yet Abraham, being about a hundred years old, knew that his body was "as good as dead" (4:19); and Sarah's womb was also dead, *nekrosin*. Nonetheless, Abraham's faith was in a singular God—a God "who gives life to the dead and calls into existence the things that do not exist" (4:17). The God who created the world in Genesis by saying, "Let there be . . . ," is the God in whom Abraham and we are to persist in faith; Abraham's faith was not only occasional; he remained faithful without "weakening" (4:19) when there was every apparent reason to weaken. Believing in such a God is identical with believing in the One who "raised from the dead Jesus our Lord" (4:24–25). Believing in this God is the same as believing in the God who justifies the ungodly.

Proper 6 [11]/Year A

Romans 5:1–8

Please see the Third Sunday in Lent/Year A for our discussion of this lection.

Proper 7 [12]/Year A

Romans 6:1b–11

Please see Easter Vigil/Year A for commentary on this passage.

Proper 8 [13]/Year A

Romans 6:12–23

In today's reading, Paul continues his discussion begun in 6:1–11 on the new life that followers of Jesus Christ have been given and empowered to live. Verses 12–14 anticipate Romans 12:1: "Present your bodies as a living sacrifice, holy and acceptable to God, which is your spiritual worship." This radical statement claims that how we present our physical bodies (*somata*) is worship, and Paul clarifies the everyday meaning of worship: it is how we preach, teach, administer, and give. Verses 12–14 take as the first indication of newness of life that we "no longer" grant sin tyranny over how we use our bodies: now they should be "instruments of righteousness," not of wickedness. We are to act as "those who have been brought from death to life," out of gratitude.

We are no longer, says Paul, "under law." Interpreters of this passage will want to keep in mind Paul's comment in 7:22: "I delight in the law of God in my inmost self." What Paul is concerned with, as Markus Barth long ago showed, is that Gentiles not adopt selected Jewish practices, such as circumcision and the dietary laws, and then attempt to impose them on others as a means of self-justification.[9] That Paul did not consider Gentiles as suffering from an overabundance of doing "deeds of loving-kindness," to use a rabbinic phrase, is made eminently clear in Romans 1:18–32.

Verse 15 begins with a fallacious question: "Should we sin because we are not under law but under grace?" Paul answers his own question: "By no means!" (*me genoito*, a strong denial). In verses 16–18 the analogy of the transfer of a slave from one master to another contrasts the newness of life in Jesus Christ with life in the "old age" tyrannized by sin. Paul almost apologizes for speaking this way (v. 19), and it is certainly different from his claim in Galatians 5:1: "For freedom Christ has set us free." Yet Romans would have been all too familiar with slavery and doubtless a majority of the Roman community was composed of slaves and "freedmen," emancipated slaves. They would have understood Paul's analogy; what they thought of it, we have no way to know.

The premise of the discussion is that all slavery implies submission to the will of a master. But when a slave is "handed over" (*paredothete*, v. 17) to a different master, that slave becomes submissive to a different master's will. In Paul's analogy, "you are slaves of the one whom you obey, either of sin, which leads to death, or of obedience, which leads to righteousness" (v.16). "Righteousness," in Paul, is synonymous with "God's righteousness," God's gracious justification (right-setting) of the ungodly. In this new form of slavery, obedience is "from the heart" (v. 17), whereas obedience to sin had been because of our weakness in the face of its tyrannical power. This new obedience is owing to "the abundance of grace and the free gift of righteousness" (5:17).

Verses 19–23 delineate the contradictory outgrowths of the two slaveries; Paul now exfoliates the consequences of the slave's being handed over from the mastery of sin to the mastery of Jesus Christ: (1) our "members" (of the body) are no longer presented to impurity and iniquity but to righteousness (19b); (2) the outgrowth of being slaves to sin was death (alienation from God), whereas that of being slaves to righteousness is sanctification and eternal life (20–22); and (3) the "wages of sin is death, but the free gift of God is eternal life in Christ Jesus our Lord" (v. 23). There is a payoff for slavery to sin: death. But Paul says nothing of the "wages of righteousness"; instead he speaks of the "free gift."

Proper 9 [14]/Year A

Romans 7:15–25a

Because Paul devotes all of Romans 7 to a discussion of righteousness and the law, a few comments about verses 1–14 will set today's reading in context. First, Paul is "speaking to those who know the law" (v. 1), Gentile converts in Rome (1:5, 13) who became somewhat knowledgeable about the law while they were "Godfearers" in the synagogue. There were thirteen synagogues in Rome at Paul's time and ample opportunity for Gentiles to learn about the law.[10]

Second, in Romans 7 Paul makes frequent use of the pronoun "I": for example, "I was once alive apart from the law, but when the commandment came, sin revived and I died" (v. 9). Traditionally, commentators interpreted Romans 7 autobiographically, as Paul's confession of his inability to bear the weight of the law. More recently, Paul's claim in Philippians 3:6 that "as to righteousness under the law" he was "blameless" has been taken as a sign of Paul's guilt-free consciousness. In Romans 7, Paul is not talking autobiographically, but representatively, as did many Hellenistic writers. He is also interpreting (*midrash*) Genesis 3; in a sense, the "I" is Adam speaking—that is, all people (Rom. 5:12–21 is restated here).

In 7:15–25a Paul describes what for him is the catch-22 with which the law confronts us: although without the law we would not even recognize sin, our very awareness of it gives sin an "opportunity" to draw us within its power. Paul describes the dilemma in three ways. First, he is at a loss to understand his own behavior (v. 15). Second, he recognizes that there dwells within him what Jews call an "evil impulse": that "nothing good dwells within" him (v. 18) or that which is not good (*ouk agathon*) is what really controls his behavior, not his true self (v. 22). Third, Paul sets one law in opposition to another—the "law of God" is opposed to "another law at war with the law of my mind, making me captive to the law of sin that dwells in my members" (v. 23). These three descriptions are three ways of describing the same dilemma.

Notice that the law that gives Paul fits is "another law, the law of sin," not the torah of God or the law of his inmost self. Paul opposes the law of sin to the law of God. "I delight in the law of God in my inmost self" (v. 22). "With my mind I am a slave to the law of God, but with my flesh I am a slave to the law of sin" (v. 25).

The problem for Paul here is not the law of God—it is sin, *hamartia* (v. 20): "Now if I do what I do not want, it is no longer I that do it, but sin that dwells within me." Sin for Paul is not individual sins or the piling up of all of them into some big thing called "Sin" with a capital S. Sin, indeed with a capital S, is a power that governs the world in the old age in which we still live, in spite of the fact that in Jesus Christ we have a foretaste of God's righteousness, the "first [but not the last] fruit" of the Spirit (Rom. 8:23). Paul not only does not express guilt for sinning—"it is no longer I that do it"— he does not admit responsibility for it, at least not so far as to be made guilty for it. Sin is a power in which individuals, groups, and nations can become ensnared, like fish caught in a net. It is our weakness that sin exploits.

What we should not do then is wallow in guilt feelings. We should do what Paul did—sing praises to God through Jesus Christ for the magnificent gift of grace (v. 25).

Proper 10 [15]/Year A

Romans 8:1–11

Paul begins by repeating the distinction he has made before between two different "laws": "the law of the Spirit of life in Christ Jesus" and "the law of sin and of death" (v. 2). Because of the law of the Spirit of life in Christ Jesus, we have been "set free from the law of sin and of death." There is no reason to think that Paul differentiates the "law of the Spirit of life" from "the law of God" (7:22) or torah, except that for Paul it was God's or the Spirit's (the terms are virtually synonymous in Paul) gift of God's own righteousness in Jesus that effected what the law of God by itself— that law in which Paul delighted (7:22)—could not.

The good news to which Paul gives voice in today's reading is that there is "now no condemnation for those who are in Christ Jesus [who] has set you free from the law of sin and of death" (vv. 1–2). Liberation theologians have emphasized God's liberating activity; the most basic liberation, according to Paul, is from sin itself. As he will go on to point out in Romans and elsewhere, being liberated means being freed to liberate the neighbor from not only the oppression of sin but equally from specific forms of oppression characteristic of the "old age."[11]

Verses 1–2 are an announcement of this good news. All who are "in Christ" are in a new state of affairs. We had been slaves; now we are freed. What was unattainable because of the tyrannical power of sin is now attainable—righteousness. It is not we who attained it however—sin's power and our weakness prevented that. God has attained it for us by giving it to us, thus setting us free.

Verses 3–4 explain how our ability to live morally responsible lives is possible: "God has done what the law, weakened by the flesh, could not do." God sent God's own son "for sin," *peri . . . hamartias*, and "condemned sin in the flesh." Paul uses "flesh" in this reading in two senses—one in the ordinary sense of the body of Jesus and the other to refer to a human life "curved in upon itself" and unable to reach out in love to God or the neighbor. Note that it was sin that crucified Jesus and that in doing so it brought upon itself its own condemnation. Note also that God did this in order "that the just requirements of the law might be fulfilled in us." Now we are able to keep the commandments (see 1 Cor. 7:19). We are now freed to "walk not according to the flesh but according to the Spirit." "Walk" is a Jewish metaphor; Scripture is light unto our feet (Ps. 119:105). The structure of Paul's thought here is both biblical and rabbinic—first he describes in the indicative what God has done for us, and then he describes in the imperative what we are to do, as Exodus describes what God did for the people Israel in liberating them and then describes what they are to do.

Verses 5–11 describe two mutually contradictory "ways" that we can walk—the way of the fleshly, self-centered life or the way of the Spirit. We are free, and sin remains powerful. But we do not have to walk in its way. The indwelling Spirit (vv. 9, 11) empowers us to do what God commands. God is faithful; hence we may hope that God who raised Christ will also raise us (v. 11).

Proper 11 [16]/Year A

Romans 8:12–25

We commented on 8:12–17 on Trinity Sunday/Year B; today's discussion will focus on verses 18–25. Throughout Romans, Paul has been concerned to show that God has been faithful to God's covenant with Abraham, that God's *dikaiosyne*, God's setting things right, has been announced in the gospel, *euaggelion*, of Christ. God's promise to Abraham that in him and his descendants all the Gentiles would be blessed has been enacted and is taking place in Paul's mission as apostle to the Gentiles. God had also made a covenant with Noah (not mentioned by Paul) and "'every living creature that is with you, for all future generations; . . . [an] everlasting covenant between God and every living creature of all flesh that is on the earth'" (Gen. 9:12, 16).

Romans 8:18–25 may be the most overlooked passage in Pauline scholarship. It contends that in being faithful to the covenant with Abraham,

"God has thereby been true to the implicit covenant with the whole of creation."[12] God has set things right with the whole world. Note that in verse 22, "the whole creation has been groaning"; in verse 23, "we ourselves . . . groan inwardly"; and in verse 26 the "Spirit intercedes with sighs [*stenagmois* = groans)]too deep for words." Just as believers suffer (8:17), so the entire creation suffers, and, indeed, God groans with them. The destiny of the earth, *Adama*, and the human being, *Adam*, have been tied up with each other from the beginning. The earth's fate is affected by our conduct and its fate is, in turn, our fate.[13] Adam's sin brings curses upon the earth (Gen. 3:17–19).

In verses 18–25, Paul proclaims that the coming eschatological redemption will also redeem the entire creation, "that the creation itself will be set free from its bondage to decay and will obtain the freedom of the glory of the children of God" (v. 21):

> The wolf shall live with the lamb,
>   the leopard shall lie down with the kid,
> the calf and the lion and the fatling together, . . .
> They will not hurt or destroy on all my holy mountain;
> for the earth will be full of the knowledge of the LORD
>   as the waters cover the sea.
>
>   (Isa. 11:6–9)

All this is in service of Paul's "theology of hope," articulated since Romans 5. We still "wait for adoption" (8:23). Paul, some decades after the resurrection of Jesus, knows that the full messianic redemption lies in the future: "Now hope that is seen is not hope. For who hopes for what is seen? But if we hope for what we do not see, we wait for it with patience" (vv. 24–25). Later, Paul will deal with relations between believers in Jesus and Jews who do not believe in Jesus (Rom. 9–11)—those Jews do not "see" that Jesus has messianically redeemed the world. Neither does Paul, or, if he does see it, he sees it dialectically, as both an already and a not-yet redemption. What he does see is that God is faithful to all—to Jews, to Gentiles, to the whole earth.

Paul is not a contemporary ecologist worrying about environmental destruction. However, Romans 8:18–25 does call to mind the covenant of moral responsibility between human beings and all the living things on planet earth. Human beings were given responsibility for the world (Gen. 1:28), and the fortunes of people and their created environment are, willy-nilly, tied up with each other.

Proper 12 [17]/Year A

Romans 8:26–39

Today's reading falls into two parts. In verses 26–30 Paul discusses the groaning of the Spirit with us amid our groanings and claims that "all things work together for good for those who love God" (v. 28). In verses 31–39 he reassures his readers that God's love is sovereign over all that afflicts them.

In groaning with us, the Spirit "intercedes for the saints according to the will of God" (v. 27). In verse 34 Paul says that Christ "intercedes for us." The Spirit's groaning, therefore, is not our "speaking in tongues" but the Spirit's guiding our prayers. In "our weakness," says Paul, "we do not know how to pray as we ought" (v. 26). In Greek Paul says that we do not know for what (*gar ti*) to pray. His emphasis is not on *how* to pray but *for what*. Nonetheless, God, "who searches the heart, knows what is the mind of the Spirit" (v. 27). Paul has just said (v. 24) that we do not "see" that for which we hope and for which we should pray. But God and the Spirit know and help us in our praying. Even prayer is to be understood within the initiative of God's grace for us.

Verses 28–30 reassure the Romans that "all things work together for good for those who . . . are called according to his [God's] purpose." "All things" probably refers to "the whole creation" (v. 22) and to the Spirit that groans with us for redemption. That all things work together for good for those who love God is a traditional theme of Israelite faith: "The LORD watches over all who love him, but all the wicked he will destroy" (Ps. 145:20; see also Deut. 7:9 and *Sirach* 1:10). As did the ancient Israelites, Paul's Roman community faces persecution, peril, and the "sword" (8:35).

He provides further grounds for hope by saying that their inclusion among God's elect, their adoption (8:15), has all along been part of God's graciously loving intent. They have been foreknown, predestined, called, justified, and glorified (vv. 29–30). This is not Calvin's doctrine of the predestination of individuals to salvation or damnation; it is, instead, God's age-old plan to include Gentiles within the community of God's people and to redeem and glorify them in the eschaton. God's blessing to Abraham included Gentiles; Paul did not recently invent it. It was there from the beginning (Gen. 18:18).

In verses 31–39 Paul lists every instrumentality and cause that could impede God's purpose for the community. Often these "powers" are interpreted supernaturally as "angels," and Paul obviously thought that angels attempted to frustrate God's plans; he attributed his "thorn in the flesh" to a "messenger [*aggelos*] from Satan" (2 Cor. 12: 7). Sometimes this list of adversities and adversaries is taken as being a statement about Paul's own ministry (2 Cor. 11), its difficulties and hardships. Another possibility is that at least some of these references are to the hostility of the empire—the "sword" (v. 35) and "rulers" (v. 38). The First Epistle of Clement says that Paul came "to the extreme limit of the west and suffered martyrdom under the prefects" (chap. 5). The prefects would have been Tigellinus and Sabinus, and the time, the last year of Nero's reign.

We should remember that the emperor cult claimed that the emperor was "savior" (*soter*), proclaimed the "gospel" (*euaggelion*) of his reign, promised his "faithfulness" (*pistis*) to the people and demanded their faithfulness to him, and attributed to him and the empire "justice" (*dikaiosyne*) and "peace" (*eirene*). A community that attributed all these to a different lord, Jesus Christ, could well have experienced persecution, peril, and the sword from the rulers of this present age, not all of whom were mythological.

Even if we "are being killed all day long . . . accounted as sheep to be slaughtered" (v. 36), nonetheless "in all these things we are more than conquerors through him who loved us" (v. 37). Nothing, says Paul (vv. 38–39), "will be able to separate us from the love of God in Christ Jesus our Lord." Paul's confidence in the sovereign love and grace of God emboldens him to be defiant of all arrogant powers that would seek to frustrate God's purpose. Hope in what is not seen (v. 24) triumphs over them by God's grace.

Proper 13 [18]/Year A

Romans 9:1–5

Paul wrote to Rome to explain his mission to the Gentiles and in Romans 1–8 made a case for the inclusion of Gentiles in the people of God. Now in Romans 9–11 he reminds the Gentiles that the people Israel are and have long been included in the people of God. In other letters Paul dealt with relations between Jewish and Gentile Jesus–followers in the same congregation. Romans 9–11 deals instead with relations between Gentile Jesus-followers and Jews who do not believe in Jesus. Paul makes this case to Gentiles: "I am speaking to you Gentiles" (11:13). He warns them against boasting over Jews (11:18) and does not want them to "claim to be wiser than you are" (11:25). Paul resists a disparaging attitude toward Jews and encourages, instead, an appreciative one: "Remember that it is not you that support the root, but the root that supports you" (11:18).

Today's reading introduces this discussion. Paul's argument so far has sought to establish the claim that the privileges of Israel have been extended to Gentiles. Now he faces the question of whether Israel itself is excluded from his inclusive gospel. He asks if God has been faithful to God's promises to Israel: "Has God rejected his people? By no means!" (11:1). Because his argument has been based on God's faithfulness to God's promises, he cannot argue otherwise lest he discourage Gentiles from trusting God.

In 9:1–2 Paul makes a triple declaration: "I am speaking the truth . . . I am not lying; my conscience confirms it . . . I have great sorrow and unceasing anguish in my heart" over the fate of the people Israel. Then he utters an astonishing prayer: "I could wish that I myself were accursed and cut off from Christ for the sake of my own people" (1:3). Paul here paraphrases Moses who said to God after the sin of the golden calf: "But now, if you will only forgive their sin—but if not, blot me out of the book that you have written" (Exod. 32:32). Moses would rather be blotted out of the book of life than that God reject Israel.

To make clear that the issue is God's faithfulness, Paul lists the privileges of Israel (9:4–5). "They are Israelites" (v. 4); they simply are what they have been since the election at Sinai, *bene Yisrael*, the people of God. These non-Jesus-believing Jews simply are God's people, by God's grace, by God's naming them "Israel" (Gen. 32:28). To know Israel is to know that Israel is the Israel of God and that God is a God of steadfast love, *hesed*, faithfulness. Israel lives from its reception of God's gracious election. "To them belong the adoption," *huiothesia* (v. 4). "When Israel was a child, I loved him, and out of Egypt I have called my son" (Hos. 11:1). God's adoption of Israel is the basis of Israel's hope and the reason that "all Israel will be saved" (Rom. 11:26). "To them belongs the glory," the *doxa*, the manifest presence of God. God dwells among the people and is always with them, Immanuel. To them belong "the covenants" (v. 4), covenants with Noah, with Abraham, with Israel at Sinai, with David— the gracious gifts of the God of a singular promise and a singular command. The covenants represent both *gift* and *call*, and "the gifts and the calling of God are irrevocable" (Rom. 11:29).

To them belongs "the giving of the law [*torah*]" (v. 4), way, path, instruction, which Paul takes as one of Israel's greatest blessings. Torah is one of the blessings given to Israel in which Gentiles may now share as the law of the mind, of the Spirit. To them belongs "the worship" with its means of grace making possible atonement and forgiveness. To them belong "the promises," including the one to Abraham that his descendants would be a light to the Gentiles. "To them belong the patriarchs [and matriarchs]" (v. 5); Paul has contended that Abraham is the "father" of Gentiles but here reminds Gentiles that Abraham is not their exclusive possession. "And from them, according to the flesh, comes the Messiah" (v. 5). Jesus took form in the history and Scriptures of Israel; he is a gift to Gentiles from the God of Israel and the Israel of God.

Proper 14 [19]/Year A

Romans 10:5–15

Prior to today's reading, Paul attributed Israel's "stumbling" with regard to the gospel to the fact that the people Israel strove "for the righteousness that is based on the law" (9:31). "They did not strive for it on the basis of faith, but as if it were based on works" (9:32). He then prays to God "that they may be saved" (10:1) and explains how gracious is "the righteousness that comes from faith" (10:3).

Deuteronomy 30:11–14 reads,

> Surely, this commandment that I am commanding you today is not too hard for you, nor is it too far away. It is not in heaven, that you should say, "Who will go up to heaven for us, and get it for us so that we may hear it and observe it?" Neither is it beyond the sea, that you should say, "Who will cross to the other side of the sea for us, and get it for us, so that we may hear it and observe it?" No, the word is very near to you; it is in your mouth and in your heart for you to observe.

In 10:5–7 Paul paraphrases by replacing "cross the sea" with "descend into the abyss" and "Christ" for "commandment." His point is the lack of difficulty in what God asks of us, its "nearness" (*engys*). The difference between the two ways to righteousness is that what the law required, the gospel proclaimed as having already been done for us by God—we are to "believe . . . that God raised him [Jesus] from the dead" and we "will be saved" (10:9). We need not "ascend into heaven" because God has already sent Jesus to us; and we need not "descend into the abyss . . . to bring Christ up from the dead" because God has already raised him. We have only to believe and confess (10:10).

Two points are important to note. First, Paul made it clear in 6:1–8:13 that the "obedience" required by Christ is morally demanding; he will later (chaps. 12–15) spell out what is required of the community to live out the gospel. He earlier argued that we will be judged by our works: "[God] will repay according to each one's deeds" (2:6). Therefore, he is not arguing here for a morally lax gospel. Second, he contends that the way to righteousness requires admitting that we have no good works of our own to offer, that we are to receive gratefully the gift of God's righteousness in faith.

But there is a nagging doubt raised by this passage, occasioned by the fact that Deuteronomy 30:11–14 makes precisely the point about the torah that Paul makes about Christ. Scholars have long pointed to three major differences between rabbinic Judaism and what Paul here calls "righteousness based on works." They are (1) the torah is God's gracious gift to the people Israel; (2) the heart of Judaism is expressed in the phrase "the joy of the commandments" (*Simhat Torah*); and (3) repentance and forgiveness were readily available: "Let a person repent but a very little, and God will forgive very much." Says the *midrash* on Psalm 71:2: "'Through thy righteousness deliver me.' Israel says to God, 'If thou save us, save us not through our righteousness or good deeds, but, be it today or be it tomorrow, deliver us through thy righteousness.'"

The doubt is resolved when we recognize that when Paul speaks of some Jews as not having "submitted to God's righteousness" (v. 3) he means that they did not recognize God's "righteousing" of the Gentiles by bringing them into the eschatological people of God, which is how Paul speaks of the righteousness of God throughout Romans.[14] "Faith" fundamentally refers to God's faithfulness, *hesed*, to God's inclusive promise embracing both Jews and Gentiles. Our faith is graciously made possible by God's prior faithfulness.

Proper 15 [20]/Year A

Romans 11:1–2a, 29–32

Today's reading concludes Paul's discussion of the inclusion of Israel in the eschatological people of God (Rom. 9–11). Having finished his discussion (Rom. 10) of Israel's resistance to God's "righteousing" of the Gentiles, including them in the people of God (or of the terms on which Paul wanted to include them—without circumcision and the dietary laws), Paul now turns to affirm Israel's own inclusion.

As he has often done, Paul begins by posing a rhetorical question that draws an illicit conclusion from the prior argument: "I ask, then, has God rejected his people? By no means!" (v. 1). We remember Paul's earlier question, "What if some were unfaithful? Will their faithlessness nullify the faithfulness of God? By no means!" (3:3–4). So now, after chapter 10, the refusal of some of Israel to accept God's inclusion of Gentiles will not nullify God's faithfulness to "unbelieving" Israel. God is, after all, the same God, YHWH, who justified unbelieving Abraham (Rom. 4:9–12) and "keep[s] steadfast love for the thousandth generation, forgiving iniquity and transgression" (Exod. 34:7).

To enhance his credentials for claiming that God remains faithful to the promises to Israel Paul describes himself as a member of the people Israel: "I myself am an Israelite, a descendant of Abraham, a member of the tribe of Benjamin" (11:1). For God to have rejected Abraham's seed would have been for God to reject Paul as a descendant of Abraham, thereby making Paul's salvation conditional on Paul's commitment of some act deserving of salvation—such as believing in Jesus Christ. But for Paul, God's grace is the unconditional gift of God's love. We may not take such a gift and turn it into a condition apart from which God is not free to love.

Then Paul simply declares, "God has not rejected his people whom he foreknew" (v. 2). The lectionary skips over the bulk of chapter 11 to get to Paul's conclusion: "For the gifts and the calling of God are irrevocable" (11:29). In doing so it omits Paul's olive-tree parable or allegory (11:16–24). Preachers might want to include this allegory in today's reading, and its exposition, in the sermon. Here and in his discussion of God's "hardening" of Israel (vv. 25–28), Paul contends that Israel's unbelief is, finally, God's doing. In verse 25 Paul uses the "divine passive" to indicate that God hardened Israel just as in verses 19–20 he contends that some branches were broken off the root "so that" Gentiles might be grafted into it. All this is part of God's mysterious purpose—"how unsearchable are his judgments and how inscrutable his ways!" (v. 33). Meanwhile, we Gentiles should "not become proud, but stand in awe" (v. 20) and remember that it is "not you that support the root, but the root that supports you" (v. 18).

The people of Israel remain "beloved," *agapetoi* (v. 28). In verses 29–32 Paul's logic is that as Gentiles were once "disobedient" but have now received mercy because of Israel's disobedience, "so they have now been disobedient in order that, by the mercy shown to you, they too may now receive mercy" (vv. 30–31). So, "all Israel will be saved" (v. 26) or, as the Mishnah puts it, "All Israelites have a share in the world to come" (*Sanh.* 10. 1).

Paul wraps it all up in one grand conclusion: "For God has imprisoned all [*tous pantas*] in disobedience so that he may be merciful to all [*tous pantas*]" (v. 32). God's gracious love is all-inclusive. None of us merits salvation; it is available to each and all as a gracious gift, Jews and Gentiles alike.

Paul's double use of *tous pantas* heavily emphasizes the all-inclusive character of God's love for Gentiles and Jews together.

Proper 16 [21]/Year A

Romans 12:1–8

With today's reading, Paul begins the third and last part of Romans. Romans 1–8 dealt with God's gracious "setting right" of Gentiles by including them in the apocalyptic people of God, and Romans 9–11 with God's gracious inclusion of Israel in this same people. Romans 12–15 spell out how Gentile believers are to live in the light of this gracious good news. Romans 1–11 declare God's unsearchable goodness to us; Romans 12–15 make clear how we ought to live. The overall pattern is one of the indicative and the imperative, proclamation and paranesis, "gifts and calling" (11:29), the same pattern that is found in Paul's other letters, in the Torah, and in the Rabbis.[15]

Paul begins (v. 1) with an appeal to his "brothers and sisters, by the mercies [*oiktiremon* = compassion] of God," speaking in a traditional Jewish way of God's love. His appeal is that they present their "bodies as a living sacrifice," also a Jewish way of distinguishing worship of God from the kind of worship offered to the many gods of polytheism. He refers to this as our *logiken latreian*, our "reasonable service" or worship. To translate *logiken* as "spiritual" misses much of Paul's point. In 12–15 there is a profusion of words for "thinking," of which *logiken*, logical or reasonable, is only the first. Verse 2 asks us to be "transformed by the renewing of your minds" and verse 3 urges Paul's reader not to "think of yourself more highly than you ought to think, but to think with sober judgment." Paul urges us to develop an intelligent faith.

There is no dualism of "body" and "mind" or "spirit" in Paul; our reasonable service is how we "present our living bodies" to others both within and without the community. By means of the body we interact with other persons, things, and events; the body enables relationships and interactions; it is a communal body; and, indeed, the entire community is a body with many members (v. 4). We do everything with our bodies and nothing without them. Embodied faith, a living offering, comprises intelligent words acted out in deeds and deeds interpreted by words. The "spiritual" meaning of faith, properly understood, is bodied forth in concrete deeds.

We are not to be "conformed to this world" (v. 2) that is passing away but "transformed by the renewing of [our] minds, so that [we] may discern what is the will of God." Paul is sometimes interpreted as extraordinarily convinced of our ability to recognize God's will. It does not take much experience of those who claim such ability to make us suspicious of this capacity. However, Paul did not mean that we were without resources for determining God's will. He has appealed to God's gracious righteousing of human beings, to Abraham, to the crucifixion and resurrection of Jesus Christ, and to the commandments (13:8–10) as patterns that we are graciously empowered to emulate.

In verses 3–8 Paul calls his Gentile readers away from theological "boasting" over Israel (11:13–32) to the "sober judgment" (*sophrosune*) that shapes chapters 12–15. We are to assess the "measure of faith that God has assigned" (v. 3) each of us and understand how we have been differently gifted by God (v. 6). The ruling principle is that we are not to think of ourselves "more highly than [we] ought to think" (v. 3). In the one body of many members each has a different gift (*charismata*) depending on the "grace" (*charis*) that has been given us. We are to find that gift and exercise it; the particular *charisma* of each of us expresses God's grace that we convey to other people: such as, faith, ministry, teaching, generosity, cheerfulness. We are to live grace-embodying lives.

Proper 17 [22]/Year A

Romans 12:9–21

Today's reading falls into two parts; verses 9–16 deal with how members of the church are to relate to one another and verses 17–21 deal with relations to outsiders. In both cases, the ruling principle is love (*agape*). Paul draws on the wisdom teachings of Israel and of Jesus in this passage (cf. 1 Thess. 5:12–22), and the whole is full of practical wisdom—knowing how (*phronesis*), being thoughtful, and having good sense.

Verses 9–13 elaborate on the opening comment: "Let love be genuine" (*anypokritos*). In other words, "Don't fake it," let it be unhypocritical, the real thing. While we were alienated from God, God nonetheless freely and unconditionally offered us God's love in Jesus Christ. That same *agape* is now to be our response to God and to the neighbor; as we are loved, so we are to love. By calling it "genuine" Paul means that, like God's love, which was extended to us while we were "strangers" to God and to Israel, our love is also to extend to the stranger and to the enemy (vv. 14, 20). That this is a radical love is conveyed by the closing comment: "Do not be overcome by evil, but overcome evil with good" (v. 21). We are to make a fundamental decision to hang on to the good for dear life.

In verses 10–13 Paul talks of relations within the community in language associated with the proximity of family members to one another. Affection within the community is to be mutual (v. 10), not hierarchical as in the patron-client relationships by which Roman society was organized. Jesus' followers are not to "lord it over" one another, as do the rulers of the Gentiles (Mark 10:42; Matt. 20:25; Luke 22:25). We are not to vie with each other but to "outdo one another in showing honor," acting out our mutuality.

"Do not lag in zeal, be ardent in spirit" (v. 11). As the parable of the Good Samaritan redescribed the neighbor as the one who acted like a neighbor, here *agape* is a proactive attitude; it is impatient to meet the concrete needs of the neighbor. Paul's "be ardent in spirit" uses the Greek word *zeontes*, "burning": be "aglow" in spirit. Ancient manuscripts differ over whether verse 11c reads "*kairos*" or "*kyrios*," "time" or "lord." The NRSV opts for the latter, translating 11c as "serve the Lord." It could also be translated as "seize the time," make the most of your opportunities to serve the neighbor in this old, passing age. In verse 12 Paul gives voice to some of the strengths of faithful people: rejoice in hope, be patient in suffering, persevere in prayer. Pastors are keenly aware of the need for learning patience and perseverance, of keeping hope alive amid misfortune, loss, and disappointment. Faith is not just a moment-by-moment affair. Meeting the needs of the most vulnerable and extending hospitality to strangers are ancient requirements of the Torah, indeed its most insistent theme.

Genuine sympathy, empathy, and harmony are the themes of verses 14–15. Paul closes the first section of today's reading with "do not claim to be wiser than you are" (v. 16), again emphasizing our need for sober judgment about ourselves.

Verses 17–21 focus on the community's relation to outsiders: persecutors, enemies, strangers (the latter already present in the insistence on hospitality). The overriding idea here is that radical love, *agape anypokritos*, extends even to them. We are to show this love by refraining from all violence, including retaliatory violence, but instead extend help—food and drink—to enemies and strangers. Do not take vengeance into your own hands—God can be trusted to deal with it in God's own way (which is not our way). Instead we are to "overcome evil with good."

Proper 18 [23]/Year A

Romans 13:8–14

Paul continues his discussion of living the new life in Christ by taking up two themes: love of the neighbor (vv. 8–10) and knowing the time, the *kairos* (vv. 11–14).

In verses 8–10 Paul touches briefly on the relationship between love and law (*torah*, way, instruction). "Love does no wrong to a neighbor," he says, "therefore, love is the fulfilling of the law" (v. 10). Paul spilled a lot of ink in Romans arguing that Gentiles are not "righteoused," set right, by keeping the law. What he meant was that Gentiles are included in the people of God by God's active righteousness in Christ, God's faithfulness, which justifies Gentiles or gets them into the family of God. In that sense, Christ is the "end" of the law, its aim or telos. Today's reading makes it clear, however, that once in, Gentiles are to live by the commandments, all of which are kept by loving our neighbors. That is, if we truly love our neighbors we will not commit adultery, murder, or theft and will not even intend to do so (we will not covet).

One of the main functions of torah in Israel was to be the voice of the vulnerable—the poor, the elderly, widows and orphans, strangers—and to guard and protect their well-being. At the heart of the covenant between YHWH and Israel lies a twofold love, the unfathomable love of YHWH for Israel and Israel's responsive love for YHWH. "It is not," says Jon Levenson, "a question of law *or* love, but law conceived in love, love expressed in law."[16] We express our love for the neighbor by keeping the *mitzvoth*, commandments. That Jewish view cannot be distinguished from what Paul expresses in today's reading.

Two other points are noteworthy: First, Paul lists only a few commandments but adds "and any other commandment," just before saying that they are "summed up in this word, 'Love your neighbor as yourself'" (v. 9). All the law is kept by loving the neighbor, not just some of it. Paul does not mention the ritual commandments because he is discussing ethics. But we may presume that he would not approve of idolatry, avoiding which was a ritual commandment. Note also that much ritual consists of reminders of moral obligations. Ritual and ethics are not easily distinguished from one another. Second, in summing up all the law in one phrase, Paul was doing what many teachers in Israel before him did. Micah 6:8 asks, "What does the Lord require of you, but to do justice, and to love kindness, and to walk humbly with your God?" Habakkuk 2:4 said, "The righteous live by their faith," and Paul sometimes said the same. Closer to Paul's time, Hillel and Philo also summarized the law.

In verses 11–14 Paul urges his Gentile readers to "know [*eidotes*, distinguish] what time [*kairos*] it is." We live in a *kairos*, a highly momentous time; *kairos* is a time that is "ripe," a time ready for important things to happen. For Paul this was the soon-to-occur return of Christ with the kingdom or rule of God: "Salvation is nearer to us now than when we became believers" (v. 11). It is a time when night is passing, the darkness and night of the passing old age of sin and oppression, and "the day is near" as the light continues to dawn. Morally it is time for us to wake up, to "lay aside the works of darkness and put on the armor of light" (v. 12). We are to live in the new day, not the old one.

The light dawned in the resurrection of Jesus and the gift of the Spirit, but it is not yet high noon when we can bask in its full glare. We still live in the "in-between" time between the passing old age and the perceptible dawn of the new day. Nonetheless we should avoid the kinds of deeds that people prefer to engage in under the cover of darkness when they cannot be seen and, instead, "put on the Lord Jesus Christ," that is, the new humanity of the new age (Rom. 8:29).

Proper 19 [24]/Year A

Romans 14:1–12

Paul, in Romans 14:1–15:13, addresses the community about issues that threaten its unity. Difficulties in understanding today's reading stem from two facts: we cannot be clear exactly what the issues are, and we cannot know with confidence who was raising them. Paul says, for example, that "some believe in *eating anything*, while the weak *eat only vegetables*" (v. 2), and "some judge *one day* to be better than another" (v. 5; emphasis ours). Later he suggests to the "strong" (15:1) that "it is not good to *eat meat* or *drink wine* or do anything that makes your brother or sister stumble" (14:21, emphasis ours).

The problems are that (1) the Torah did not require Jews to eat only vegetables and did not ban eating meat or drinking wine, and (2) we do not know *which day* some judged to be better than another. Meat that had been offered to idols, as meat in Rome was, could have been objectionable to both Jewish and Gentile followers of Jesus. Also, an early form of Gnosticism (proto-Gnosticism) could well have avoided meat and wine.

Sunday took a while to take hold as the Christian day of worship: as late as 386 Chrysostom pleaded with his congregation to avoid the Sabbath and the synagogue.[17] The Sabbath as a day of rest was attractive to Gentiles who liked one toil-free day a week, and the day that some preferred in Rome could have been Sunday.

When teaching, preaching from, and commenting on this passage, therefore, one should stick with the only matter that is clear: issues of eating and judging one day better than another were apparently causing dissension in the Roman community. Paul deals with issues of lifestyle and behavior that could become sources of division. He regards these matters as unimportant: "the kingdom of God is not food and drink but righteousness and peace and joy in the Holy Spirit" (v. 17). His principle for dealing with differences is that we should never coerce others to act against their convictions (v. 22).

Paul addresses the "strong" (one wonders how the "weak" felt about their epithet): "Welcome those who are weak in faith" (v. 1). Paul calls on those who eat meat "not [to] despise those who abstain" and those who abstain not to pass "judgment on those who eat" (vv. 2–3). Not passing judgment on each other (vv. 3, 4, 10, 13) is terribly important for Paul, as witnessed in the number of times he declaims against it. Instead, we all "stand or fall" before the Lord (v. 4), as "we will all stand before the judgment seat of God" (v. 10). We have died to the Lord in baptism (Rom. 6:1–12) and therefore to all ultimate loyalties other than to the Lord (v. 7); we have died, that is, to our loyalties to food and drink. They are not matters of ultimate importance.

Whether we eat meat or do not, observe one day or another, we should do so "in honor of the Lord" (v. 6); meanwhile we should be "fully convinced in . . . [our] own minds" (v. 5); the strong should not make the weak "stumble" in this regard (v. 21).

Paul's counsel is a good antidote to letting unimportant, idolatrous matters divide the community. God is the God of a singular grace, a grace that affirms that what is ultimately important about us is that we are loved by God, whether we are vegetarians or meat eaters. We are freed, then, to love others who are loved by God, whether they are vegetarians or meat eaters. God affirms us in our weakness; we should affirm our neighbors in their weaknesses.

Proper 20 [25]/Year A

Philippians 1:21–30

Paul struggles today with the fact that he might choose a future for himself that is different from what he is called to do as an apostle. He is vividly aware that he serves in partnership with the Philippians and not alone (see the Second Sunday of Advent/Year C). The prayers of the Philippians are a support as are their financial contributions to the partnership (Phil. 4:3–8), not to mention the Spirit of Jesus Christ. When the apostle says, "This [my imprisonment] will turn out for my deliverance" (1:19), he speaks in the language of Job 13:16 and thus interprets his experience in Jewish terms. For many Jewish contemporaries of Paul, Job was an exemplar whose patience in suffering provided the chance for God to demonstrate God's faithfulness (*T. Job*; Sir. 49:9; Jas. 5:11). The English word "deliverance" renders *soteria*, "salvation." In apocalyptic texts, "salvation" usually means participation in the eschatological rule of God. Paul will be declared innocent and will be a full participant in the new age. In the same way that God vindicated Job, so God will vindicate Paul. Paul touches one of the deepest chords in the shame/honor culture of antiquity, declaring that he "will not be put to shame in any way " (1:20). More than shame in human culture, however, Paul knows that he will not be shamed by condemnation in the presence of God (Ps. 25:3, 20; 31:17; 119:6; Isa. 45:17; 49:23; 50:7; Zeph. 3:11; 2 Esd. 7:87; 16:65).

Paul is certain that Christ will be exalted regardless of whether the apostle dies or lives (1:24–26). If the apostle lives, he is aware of the effect of Christ, that is, the turning of the aeons, and is empowered by the Spirit. He becomes a part of the Gentiles coming to saving relationship with God. Continuing to live does mean that Paul will experience tribulation: the suffering of the old age ends and the new one comes (e.g., 2 Esd. 4:52–5:13; 6:11–29; 8:63–9:12; Mark 13:3–23; Matt. 24:3–28; Luke 21:5–21; 2 Thess. 2:1–12; Rev. 7:14).

By dying, the apostle would avoid imprisonment, and, from a broader perspective, he would bypass the pain of tribulation. Most important, however, is the apostle's "desire is to depart and to be with Christ" (1:23) because, after the apocalypse, the world will be renewed. That is the "gain."

While the apostle speculates about whether it is better to live or die, he seems certain that he will return to Philippi. For such a return is a "necessity," *anagkaioteron*, which in Jewish sources bespeaks God's direction of an individual or community so they have no choice except to carry out the divine purpose (*T. Jos.* 2:4; 4 Macc. 5:16; Josephus, *J.W.*, 5:571; *Ag. Ap.* 1:60).

The expression "live your life" translates *politeuo* meaning "to be a citizen." Citizens partook of special rights and had special roles in public life to act for the common good. The Philippians are citizens of God's new realm who have a special call now to testify to the world to come (cf. 3:20).

The Philippians should stand firm in one spirit, an expression taken from the military that portrays the congregation as a detachment of soldiers who maintain their post. They should strive side by side with one mind. The verb "strive" was often used of athletic contests. In this race, they are to have "one mind," which is interpreted in 2:5–11. The congregation need not be intimidated (or, more vividly "stampeded") by the visiting missionaries (the dogs).

Proper 21 [26]/Year A

Philippians 2:1–13

Because this passage is thick with matters of central concern to Paul and to broader Christian reflection, we discuss some aspects of it today and others on Palm/Passion Sunday/Years A, B, and C.

As this passage begins, the word "since" would better translate *ei* than "if." The English "if" implies a contingency that is not in Paul's mind. The apostle wants the Philippians to assume that they *are* encouraged in Christ, that they already *have* an incentive in love, that they share in the Spirit, and that they have compassion and sympathy (2:1). Paul bases his specific suggestions for unity (in vv. 2–4) on these qualities.

Paul uses the expression "consolation of love [*agape*]" to speak of the experience of love the Philippians have known in Christ. Whether the reference is to Paul's love for them or God's love for them (both options are grammatically possible), the Philippians' behavior should be similar: as they have been loved, they should now love one another. Because *koinonia* in Philippians indicates voluntary partnership (discussed on the Second Sunday of Advent/Year A), the "sharing [*koinonia*] in the Spirit" means that the Holy Spirit is a participant, a partner, in the work of Paul and the Philippians. The Philippians' responsibility in the partnership includes maintaining the common bond so that they can carry out their obligations to Paul and to the mission.

Furthermore, the community should remember and be motivated by the fact they have received "compassion" and "sympathy." (We discuss compassion in connection with 1:8 [Second Sunday of Advent/Year A]). The Greek word translated "sympathy" (*oiktirmoi*) is sometimes translated "mercies." God is the prototype of merciful attitudes and behavior (Rom. 12:1; 2 Cor. 1:3).

An unusual concentration of terms comes together in 2:1–4 to reinforce the idea that the community is shaped by God's grace and can make Paul's joy complete by living out that identity. Beginning with 2:2, the apostle becomes more specific about how to do this. Community members are to be "of the same mind," an expression that Paul uses frequently (1 Cor. 12:16; 15:2; 2 Cor. 13:11; Phil. 4:2). In antiquity, to be of the same mind meant to strive after a commonly shared goal. Given the respect for pluralism that permeates today's culture, we should note that the term does not indicate rigid uniformity but assumes differences of approach in working for a goal.

Paul indicates that the community must put aside selfish ambition and conceit to gain a common mind. The term "conceit," *kenodoxia*, is used in Jewish sources to describe people who think that their opinion is correct but who are wrong and refuse to admit their mistake (Wis. 14:4; 4 Macc. 2:15; 8:18). According to Paul, the Philippians should count others better than themselves (2:3) and look to the interests of others (2:4). For the apostle, humility moves beyond self-negation to the development of a healthy perspective on one's limitations. At Qumran the community regarded the practice of humility as central (e.g., 1QS 2:24). The Philippians should count others better than themselves because they should remember that the God of Israel—their God—provides for the humble (e.g., Ps. 17:28; 101:18; Isa. 57:15).

The themes of 2:1–4 derive from Jewish convictions on community. Jewish communities understand themselves to be established by God's grace. They are to care for one another so that all can experience blessing. Paul's teaching in verses 3–4 is consistent with the command to love one's neighbor as oneself (Lev. 19:18). Indeed, the notion that God's purposes are revealed through the humble and seemingly unimportant is at the heart of Jewish thinking about how God works in the world (e.g., 1 Kgs. 18:23; Ps. 118:67; Wis. 2:3).

Proper 22 [27]/Year A

Philippians 3:4b–14

Much traditional exegesis regards Paul as criticizing Judaism in this passage. However, a closer look reveals that Paul seeks not to critique Judaism as such but to correct a misunderstanding and misuse of elements of Jewish tradition by Gentiles whom Paul calls "dogs" and who teach Gentile Philippians that circumcision is a necessary part of coming into the church. People in antiquity disdained most dogs (e.g., 1 Kgs. 14:11; 2 Kgs. 9:30; Prov. 26:11) and sometimes speak of Gentiles as dogs (Deut. 23:18; 1 Sam. 17:43; Ps. 22: 12–13, 16, 29; *Midr. Rab.*; Exod. 9:2; 31:3; cf. Matt. 15:26–27; Mark 7:27–28; Rev. 22:15).

In 3:2–23, then, Paul protests not circumcision but its misuse. The dogs "have confidence in the flesh," that is, they teach that circumcision is a work incurring righteousness. Judaism regarded circumcision not as a work but as a gift from God representing God's grace (Gen. 17:9–17; Jude 14:10; Rom. 4:9–12). In 3:3 Paul does not depart from Jewish teaching but echoes other Jewish writers (Deut. 10:10–22; 30:6; Jer. 4:1–4; 9:25–26; Ezek. 44:4–8; 1QS 5:5; *T. Lev.* 6:6; cf. Rom. 2:25–29).

The apostle recalls his Jewish background (3:4b–6) to prompt the Philippians to recognize the poverty of the dogs' awareness. Paul was circumcised as an infant (Gen. 17:12; 21:4; Lev. 12:3). The tribe of Benjamin was honored (Gen. 35:16–18; 1 Sam. 9:1–2). The Benjaminites were resistant to pagans. Paul's family spoke Hebrew in their home ("a Hebrew of the Hebrews"). The Pharisees were a highly respected, lay-led reform group. When Paul calls himself a zealous persecutor of the church, he likely means that he was appointed by the synagogue to help discipline Jews who violated synagogue perspective.

"As to righteousness *under* the law," Paul is "blameless" (v. 6). The Greek does not contain the word "under" and the passage is better rendered "as to righteousness with respect to the law, blameless." Judaism did not believe that a person achieved righteousness through obedience to the law (*Midr. Ps.* 119:24; *Midr. Deut.* 2:1). A person followed the law to embody the righteousness that God bestowed through grace.

Nevertheless, Paul now regards his former gains as losses, even as rubbish, because of the "surpassing value of knowing Christ Jesus my Lord" (vv. 7–8). "Loss" and "gain" are terms from first-century commercial life and refer to making or losing money. "Rubbish" can indicate garbage and even human excrement. Paul comes to a similar conclusion about "all things" from his previous life.

In using such strong language, Paul is not criticizing Judaism as such. Rather, he is convinced that, through Christ, God is fulfilling God's promises by welcoming the Gentiles and by drawing the history of the world to its soon-to-come apocalyptic transformation. This discovery shifted Paul's energy field. What the apostle discovered in Christ does not diminish the positive qualities of Judaism, though Paul longs for his Jewish colleagues to share his interpretation of Jesus, the Gentiles, and the new world.

In 3:9 Paul states what he now takes to be fact—that Paul beholds the righteousness of God (God acting rightly) in accordance with God's promises to Abraham and Sarah to bless the Gentiles. This possibility is confirmed when we recognize that the phrase "faith in Christ" (*pisteos Christou*) is better rendered "*faithfulness of* Christ." Paul's righteousness is the gracious result of Christ's faithfulness. Indeed Christ's faithfulness reveals the "righteousness from God."

In 3:12–16, Paul turns to the language of athletics and apocalypticism to exhort the Philippians to continue their witness until the day of Jesus Christ (cf. 1:3–11; Second Sunday of Advent/Year A). The congregation has not reached the goal, a notion that also appears in apocalyptic texts to refer to God's completed work in the new creation (Dan. 12; *2 Bar.* 21:8; 30:3; 59:4; 2 Esd. 5:41; 6:15; 13:18; 14:15). Paul employs a wordplay to depict the relationship between divine activity and his own: he presses on to "make it my own," (*katalabo*), that is, persevering until the coming of the new world because Christ "has made me his own" (*katelamphthen*). Paul's activity testifies to God's activity in behalf of the world.

Paul forgets "what lies behind" and, in response to the heavenly call, "strains forward to what lies ahead," namely, the prize. The "prize" is "the heavenly call of God" to participate in the new world (*1 En.* 14:9).

Proper 23 [28]/Year A

Philippians 4:1–9

The apostle reinforces the encouragement that began in 2:1 for the congregation to have the same mind as Christ Jesus. In 4:2–3, Paul applies the theological vision of the same mind to Euodia and Syntyche, people in conflict in the congregation. The content of their disagreement is not clear. Nor do we know anything further about Clement. In any event, they need to recognize that their names are written "in the book of life," an idea prominent in apocalyptic literature that assumes God kept a list of all who are to be saved or condemned (Dan. 12:1; 2 Esd. 6:20; *2 Bar.* 24:1; 1QM 12:3; cf. Exod. 32:32–33; Ps. 69:28; Isa. 4:3; Rev. 3:5; 13:8; 17:8; 20:12, 15; 21:27).

When turning to Philippians 4:4–9, the minister needs to be alert not to discuss the motif of joy casually. The apostle's celebration of joy takes place against the backdrop of the tensions in Philippi and in the conviction that God would soon bring about the consummation of history (4:5a). The NRSV uses "gentleness" for *epieikes* (4:5), a word that often refers to characteristics of the rule of God and of earthly sovereigns who should mediate divine rule (e.g. Ps. 85:5; Wis. 2:19; 12:18; 2 Macc. 9:27). The apostle admonishes the Philippians not to be anxious (4:6a) because God is about to end the present evil age and because God's provident and trustworthy character is known in the resurrection of Christ (2:9–11). The anticipation of that great transformation is the reason the community can be both thankful and utterly honest with God (4:6b). The hope of the apocalyptic transformation is also why Paul can say so confidently that the peace of God will protect their hearts and minds. The mention of "peace" evokes the Hebrew *shalom*, which speaks of the community's material well-being and supportive relationships—qualities that are expected in the age to come (Isa. 2:2–4; Zech. 9:10–11; *1 En.* 1:7; *T. Dan.* 5:9, 11). The congregation knows the *shalom* of the God of Israel through Christ. This well-being that the community knows proleptically now, and in full in the future, "surpasses all understanding." Another way of understanding the same phrase is, "which does more than human plans can do." Both understandings are possible and make Pauline sense.

The Philippian situation is tense enough that *shalom* seems elusive. Yet the same power at work that raised Jesus from the dead empowers the community to the self-giving that can lead to peace.

"Finally" (4:8) applies the thought of 4:4–7 to the life of the community by suggesting characteristics that contribute to a community of peace. While commentators sometimes turn to Stoicism to understand these expressions, we can more easily understand them in the light of their Jewish context. To be "honorable" is to do what God wants (Prov. 8:6; 4 Macc. 5:36; 17:5). In Judaism, justice is a relational notion; the "just" are those who relate to each other as God wants. To be "pure" is be prepared for mission, as for religious ceremony (e.g., Num. 6:2, 21; 1 Macc. 14:36; cf. Phil. 1:17). That which is "pleasing" is that which draws a positive reaction (e.g., Eccl. 4:7; 20:13). To be "commendable" is to live so that others will have reason to speak positively about you, and, conversely, it includes speech that elicits the best from others. "Excellence" speaks of moral fidelity (Wis. 8:7; 2 Macc. 10:28; 4 Macc. 7:22; 9:8). "Worthy of praise" is from the language of citizenship and denotes actions that could be honored in public.

Paul urges the community to keep living in these ways (v. 9). When the apostle says he received (*parelabete*), he uses a technical term for tradition (1 Cor. 11:23; 15:3). Paul thus recommends to the congregation more than his own interpretation of the faithful life. The fact that he appeals to tradition reminded the community then as it reminds the community now that we need to be rooted in something bigger than we are. Paul's approach to community in this document should help the Philippians actualize the peace of God (4:9b) as it should today's community.

Proper 24 [29]/Year A

1 Thessalonians 1:1–10

Scholars agree that 1 Thessalonians was written in the late 40s or early 50s and is the first of Paul's letters. The Thessalonian congregation, made up of Gentiles (1:9), had grown dispirited because some of their Gentile neighbors had responded negatively to their turn away from idolatry and other Gentile behaviors and toward a life that better reflected a sense of Jewish ethics and covenantal community. Paul wrote 1 Thessalonians as pastoral encouragement to remain faithful in the face of discouragement so the Gentile Thessalonians can share in the eschatological world to come (1 Thess. 1:10; 4:16–5:11). From time to time he uses language that contrasts the unlimited sovereignty of the God of Israel with the limited and repressive rule of the Roman emperor.

Letters in the ancient world began with a simple formula: sender(s), addressee, greeting, and thanksgiving. This letter comes from the three coworkers who brought the gospel to Thessalonica—Paul, Silvanus, and Timothy—and who care for the congregation. The composition of the letter suggests that life in the God of Israel is one in which people are responsible for one another. As noted on the Second Sunday after Epiphany/Year A, the terms "church" and "grace and peace" are drawn from the Jewish world as is the designation of God as "Father" [*pater*] (e.g., Ps. 89:26; Isa. 63:15; Jer. 31:9; Mal. 2:10; Wis. 14:3; Sir. 23:1). In the Hellenistic world kinship was one's fundamental source of identity, and the head of the house was the symbol of the community. Paul's use of "Father" affirms that the Gentiles are now included in the divine household with the Jewish people. The Gentiles entered this family through Jesus Christ.

In the context of giving thanks to God for the Thessalonians, Paul previews the main concerns of the letter. The writers model a communication strategy that many ministers would find useful: they begin the letter by reminding the recipients of positive qualities in the congregation's life. This strategy establishes positive rapport between the apostles and the Thessalonians and invites the community to rediscover and reimplement the positive characteristics of their earlier life in the gospel.

Paul thanks God for the characteristics of the congregation's life (1:2–3). The phrase "works [*erga*] of faith [*pistos*]" has to do with "faithfulness" in the sense of being faithful to the God of Israel. The "labor of love" (*ho kopos tes agapes*) of these Gentile converts contrasts with the wicked works of other Gentiles (Wis. 3:10–11). "Steadfastness" (*hupomone*) is of necessity difficult in the days before the apocalypse (2 Esd. 10:2; Rev. 1:9).

When Paul says God "chose" the Thessalonians, he uses an expression (*ekloge*) used in the Septuagint (e.g., Deut. 14:2; Isa. 42:1–6; 43:10; 41:8–10) and elsewhere in Paul of the election of Israel (Rom. 9:11; 11:28) to witness to God's will and means to bless all. The church does not supplant Israel in this mission but joins the people Israel. The trustworthiness of the gospel is confirmed by both the experience of the Spirit in the congregation and by the conviction and integrity of the lives of the apostles with the message that they proclaimed (1:4–5).

Although it may seem self-congratulatory to us today for the apostle to congratulate the Thessalonians on becoming imitators (*mimetai*) of the apostles, imitation was a standard part of education in the Hellenistic age, and its absence could have been interpreted as a lack of integrity on the part of the apostles. The community, like the apostles, responded to the presence of the Holy Spirit in the midst of persecution by their Gentile neighbors. Indeed, from the point of view of antiquity, the Thessalonians demonstrated the success of their education in the Spirit (so to speak) by becoming examples imitated by believers in Macedonia and Achaia (1:6–8).

The Thessalonian practice of the key Jewish virtue (shared with many other people in antiquity) of hospitality—not only welcoming the three apostles but providing food and lodging—is legendary (1:9a). This welcome includes the key act of turning from (*epistrepho*) idols to the true and living God. Jewish theologians considered idolatry a fundamental Gentile problem leading not only to substituting a lifeless idol for the living God but to destructive qualities of Gentile life (4:1–10; Rom. 1:18–32). For a biting Jewish analysis of idolatry from the world of Paul, see Wisdom 13–15.

The ultimate consequence of idolatry is condemnation at the last judgment. By turning away from idols, the Gentiles in Thessalonians look forward to the day Jesus returns from heaven, for Jesus "rescues us from the wrath that is coming" (v. 10). That is a hope for which to endure.

Proper 25 [30]/Year A

1 Thessalonians 2:1–8

The members of the Thessalonian congregation had converted from worshiping idols to the true and living God but found themselves harassed by unconverted neighbors. Not surprisingly, they grew discouraged. The reading for today continues Paul's encouragement to remain faithful in the face of discouragement and the temptation to return to idolatry.

In 1 Thessalonians 2:1, Paul encourages the congregation by recalling the ministry of the apostles (1:1) who brought the gospel to Thessalonica. The idea of imitation is in the background: people learn to live rightly by imitating exemplars. Such imitation can prepare one for the coming age: "Be imitators of [the good person] . . . because of [that person's] compassion, in order that you may wear the crown of glory" (*T. Ben.* 4:1). By imitating the apostles, the Thessalonians can shed their discouragement and live with the boldness and verve they once had and that they see in the apostles.

Before arriving in Thessalonica, the apostles had suffered and been mistreated in Philippi. Although some preachers turn to Acts 16:11–40 to explain the difficulties in Philippi, many scholars today (we among them) think that Acts tells us more about Luke's theology than about the historical Paul. We really do not know for certain what happened in Philippi, though Beverly Roberts Gaventa notes that the presence in this passage of terms used in Hellenistic public discourse, in which speakers debated, often harshly (*parrhesiazomai* = "to declare to you;" *agon* = "opposition" in a public debate), may suggest that Paul had been publicly ridiculed.[18]

Although 2:3–8 sounds as though Paul is defending himself against charges of being deceitful and manipulative, recent studies lead to the conclusion that Paul is neither defending himself nor on an ego trip but is instead using a recognized manner of speaking in order to establish his reliability. The Thessalonians can count on what he says. Paul's remarks also imply a model by which the members of the Thessalonian congregation can conduct themselves during their season of difficulty.

Paul did not speak to the congregation out of "deceit or impure motives or trickery" (2:3). The Hellenistic age was filled with religious and philosophical charlatans who peddled misleading and manipulative religious visions and practices and appealed to people with "words of flattery or with a pretext for greed" (2:6). They were so common that Lucian of Samosata penned a satire depicting the deceitful, exploitative, self-serving practice of *Alexander the False Prophet*. If they relinquish the life of faithfulness, the Thessalonians will be in danger of joining such company.

By contrast Paul speaks as a messenger "approved [*dokimazo* = tested and found reliable] by God" in no small part because the apostolic messengers do not adjust the content of their message to please human beings but to "please God who tests [*dokimazo*] our hearts" (2:4). Paul and his companions could have made financial demands on the Thessalonians (much like self-serving charlatans), but they did not.

In 2:7b Paul uses the provocative image of being among the Thessalonians "like a nurse tenderly caring for her own children." Just as Moses was "nurse" to the people Israel in the wilderness (a situation of discouragement similar to that of the Thessalonians; Num. 11:12), so Paul is in the warm, devoted, tenderly yet fiercely caring relationship with the congregation as a mother with a nursing infant. Paul's nursing of the community should remind them of God's care for them (Isa. 66:11–12). Indeed, according to verse 8, the apostles share "not only the gospel" but their "own selves" in the same way that a mother shares her milk and fiercely cares for her children.

Proper 26 [31]/Year A

1 Thessalonians 2:9–13

The apostles who wrote this letter (1:1) want the Gentile congregation to persist faithfully and to engage in behaviors appropriate to a community whose call includes embodying the world to come. Today's text continues the thought of 1 Thessalonians 2:1–8. It demonstrates Paul's witness to the gospel in the face of persecution and his care for the Thessalonians as incentives for the community to persist in its witness and to care in the manner of Moses for Israel and Paul for them. The apostolic attitudes and actions are an implicit model for the congregation.

According to 2:9, the apostles labored day and night to support themselves so they would not financially burden the congregation while they preached the gospel. Self-support was a sign of religious or philosophical authenticity in the Hellenistic world, clogged as it was by charlatans who profited from the people to whom they peddled teachings and miracles. Although Acts 18:3 says Paul was a tentmaker (or, perhaps, a leather worker, or a maker of leather tents), Luke's statement is never verified directly by Paul. Even if Paul was not such a worker, however, the pattern of work of such folk is probably similar to that employed by Paul, which also explains some of Paul's missionary activity. Such workers typically had areas in a public space where they carried out their trade. Philosophical and religious discourse often took place in such workplaces. Paul could easily have had a booth in such a space and engaged people who came through the area seeking religious and philosophical conversation.

The Thessalonians are witnesses to the fact that the apostles are "pure, upright, and blameless" in their conduct toward the congregation, terms that, while in general use in ancient language, all invoke living in covenantal community in Jewish texts. In some texts, to be "pure" (*hosios*) is to be a faithful Jewish people who distance themselves from Gentile predilections (1 Macc. 7:13; 2 Macc. 14:6). The term rendered "upright" is *dikaios* that is related to the word for "righteousness" and bespeaks relating with others (and God) in the way that God wants. Abraham, who follows God's ways, is the paradigm of the "blameless" (*amemptos*; Gen. 17:5; cf. Wis. 10:5; 18:21).

In 2:11–12, Paul and his companions pick up the language of kinship first used in 1:1. The apostles speak of relating to the Thessalonians like a father with children. In antiquity, the household often included many more people than the typical nuclear family (in its various manifestations) found in most non-Hispanic European homes in North America today. The household also had a more intense function in that it was the source of identity and social standing. The father was responsible for the well-being of all in the household. Paul indicates here, then, that he is the Jewish parent in a household made up of Gentiles—a coming together of ethnicities that anticipates the eschatological age. Furthermore, when some of the Thessalonians turned to the true and living God, their families of origin may have excluded them, which, in antiquity, meant a profound crisis of identity and loss of social standing. For such folk the church is a household where one can belong while witnessing to a new social order.

Although the church is a renewed social world, as long as it is this side of the second coming it needs familial guidance. Indeed, Paul must urge, encourage, and plead that the congregants "lead a life worthy of God, who calls you into his own kingdom and glory." Paul yearns in the deepest way for the congregation to live through the tribulation and apocalypse and into the eschatological world.

Proper 27 [32]/Year A

1 Thessalonians 4:13–18

The extended passage 1 Thessalonians 4:13–5:11, with its dramatic vision of the apocalypse of Jesus Christ, is the climax of the letter. This vision functions in two related ways. First it describes the hope that the Thessalonians need to help them through their season of discouragement and of being harassed by their unconverted Gentile neighbors. Second, it presses upon the community a sense of urgency to "restore whatever [was] lacking in [their] faithfulness" (3:13), such as the danger of returning to Gentile ways, which can mean condemnation at the time of the return of Jesus (4:1–12).

Jewish apocalyptic writings, such as *1 Enoch*, 2 Esdras, and *2 Baruch*, present diverse understandings of the detailed events that would take place at the apocalypse. While we do not have space for extended comparisons and contrasts of different apocalyptic scenarios, we can note that apocalypticists shared the common ideas that God would end the present evil age with a massive historical interruption (apocalypse) and launch a new world in which all things occur in accord with God's purposes. The resurrection is not as important in its own right as it is a sign and part of the eschatological renewal of the world. The major difference between the apocalypses described in Jewish writings and in the Second Testament is that the latter think of Jesus Christ as the agent through whom God effects the cosmic transformation.

Some in the community may be uncertain about what will ultimately happen to those who died before the apocalypse (4:13). The Greek describes them as "sleeping," an expression that figuratively describes what some writers believed happened at death: the self lost consciousness and awaited the resurrection. Note that the writers of this document do acknowledge that grieving is appropriate at the time of death. Expecting the apocalypse, however, they do not "grieve as those who have no hope." Even appropriate grief, however, is a sign of the brokenness of the present age (2 Esd. 7:11–12).

The resurrection of Jesus is the ground of the Thessalonians' hope (4:14). Just as God raised Jesus from the dead, so God will raise those who have fallen asleep by bringing them back to consciousness and life in a resurrection body (see the Seventh Sunday after Epiphany/Year C). Those who are alive when Jesus returns will not precede those who have died into the world to come.

Verses 16–17 describe how the writers of this letter think that the events of the apocalypse will unfold. As noted above, some apocalyptic writers view these matters differently, but nearly all Jewish apocalypses contain versions of these elements: Jesus ("the Lord himself") will give a command for the apocalypse to begin. An archangel will transmit the command. A trumpet will sound making sure the event is publicly known. Christ will descend from heaven. At that time, the dead in Christ will rise first. Those who are alive will be caught up in the clouds together with them to meet the Lord in the air.

This event launches the new age. It explains what happens to the dead, and the desire to be part of it should give the Thessalonians reason to want to endure in faith.

Some scholars think that elements of Paul's language echo that of the Roman imperial cult. The emperor's coming, for example, was described with the same word that describes Jesus' coming: *parousia*. The arrival took place with great fanfare including the sounding of a trumpet. The title "lord" was used for the emperor, and local leaders would "meet" (an official greeting) the emperor upon arrival. For many first-century Jewish theologians, however, the Roman government was the epitome of Gentile existence: idolatrous, exploitative, and violent. No matter how grand the emperor's arrival, it cannot compare to the apocalyptic coming of

Jesus. Not only that, but the emperor himself will have to stand before Jesus, the awesome judge of history.

Proper 28 [33]/Year A

1 Thessalonians 5:1–11

The writers assume that the Thessalonian congregation agrees with what is about to be said (5:1). They assume the strategy of asking the congregation to build in a positive way on what the people already know or do. They want the congregation not to revert to Gentile ways but to be ready for the apocalypse.

By referring to the apocalypse as "day of the Lord" (5:2), the authors conceive of it as similar to the one(s) of which the prophets spoke—a day when God would decisively intervene, often with condemnation for some and salvation for others (Isa. 2:11–20; Joel 1:15; Mal. 4:5). The unfortunate analogy of the day of God coming with the same unexpectedness as a thief in the night was evidently a stock image in communities expecting Jesus' return (Matt. 24:43; Luke 21:34–36; 2 Pet. 1:10; Rev 3:3; 16:15).

Just when the Thessalonians think "peace and security" (*eirene kai asphaleia*) have come about, the apocalypse will occur (5:3). This phrase appeared on some Roman coins, but the authors warn readers not to settle for the Gentile life of the empire.

This document joins others in comparing the coming of the Day with a woman who is having labor pains and who cannot escape (Isa. 66:7; 2 Esd. 4:40–42). However, the delivery will come. Although the immediate experience of the Thessalonians is painful in a way analogous to that of a woman in labor, they need to endure until delivery (the return of Jesus).

In 5:4–5, the apostles employ the familiar contrast between light and darkness for spheres of power—the former is the realm being redeemed by God while the latter opposes God. Again, the writers assume that the Thessalonians are living in the light and need only to be reinforced. The Qumran scrolls speak of the apocalyptic change as a war between the children of light and those of darkness. In 5:8, Paul employs war imagery to interpret the Thessalonian situation as a struggle against darkness. While today's preacher needs to explain such imagery in context, the preacher should also help the congregation understand the negative social consequences of associating the night (darkness) with evil and the day (light) with God. Such language unintentionally casts aspersion on people of color and falsely elevates others.

Continuing the images of light and darkness, the congregation is warned not to fall asleep but to keep awake and sober and avoid the night because that is when people get drunk (5:6–7). Other first-century writers can speak of living faithfully in anticipation of the apocalypse as being "awake" (*gregreo*) or "watching" (Matt. 24:42–43; Mark 13:34ff.; Luke 12:37–39). A sober person is alert and can live in response to God's instruction. A drunk, however, is no longer able to discern God's purposes and, therefore, is likely to violate them. Being drunk at night, under the principalities and powers, makes it difficult to identify and respond to God's presence and aims.

Because the Thessalonians are in a conflict zone between the communities of light and darkness, they need to arm themselves by putting on the breastplate of faith and hope and the helmet of salvation (2:8), language used similarly by other writers (Isa. 59:17; Wis. 5:18). Given the fervor for supporting national wars that sometimes uncritically sweeps through Christian communities, it is worth noting that the breastplate and helmet are to protect the wearer and are not instruments for killing.

The Thessalonians need to know that God has destined them not for wrath but for salvation. Wrath (*orge*) is suffering that begins, particularly for Gentiles, now and continues in the postapocalyptic condemnation as a result of idolatry, injustice, and other forms of unfaithfulness (Rom. 1:18–32). Salvation is the gift of release from domination by the powers now and a place in the world to come. Jesus Christ is the means whereby God brings about the cosmic transformation (5:10). Therefore, to be a part of that world, the congregation needs to build up one another. Paul often uses the verb "build up" (*oidodomeo*) to refer to the church as community: members are to work with and be responsible for one another in the same way as workers on a building site.

Given the way that many people in North America today speak of this hope as "pie in the sky," it is important to remember that the apocalyptic theologians regarded the apocalyptic hope as the means whereby God would set things right for people who had been denied blessing in the present evil age—for example, the poor, the enslaved, those who suffered injustice and violence. Today's preacher may not believe that Jesus will return to gather the bereft into the air, but the preacher does need to help the congregation develop both a believable hope that God is at work to set things right and a realistic understanding of how to join God in that work.

Reign of Christ (Proper 29 [34])/Year A

Ephesians 1:15–23

Please see Ascension of the Lord/Year A for commentary on this passage.

All Saints/Year A

1 John 3:1–3

First John's dual purpose in today's reading is to reassure the community that it is beloved of God and to instruct it on how to live as God's beloved children. The implied context of these concerns is made clear in 2:18–25, where the author describes those who left the community and who still shake its confidence. Hence, 1 John needs to reassure the community that it is on the right path and to teach it about how life should be lived if we do, indeed, "love one another."

Verses 1–3 reassure the community of God's love and introduce the idea of sanctification—growth in the life of faithfulness: "See what love the Father has given us, that we should be called children of God; and that is what we are" (v. 1). "See" is in the imperative; it means "look!" It points to something astounding, such as this amazing love that we receive gratis, as a gift—it has been "given us."

That we are "*called* children of God" highlights the fact that we are elected by God as God's own (not only) children. Children (*tekna*) is a term of endearment. What is amazing is that 1 John is written to Gentiles who now share in the adoption that is Israel's. What Paul had said of Israelites, "to them belong[s] the adoption" (Rom. 9:4), the author of 1 John says to his Gentile community: You, too, are God's children, by God's grace because Jesus Christ is the "atoning sacrifice . . . for the sins of the whole world" (2:2).

John's community lived as a minority group in the midst of Gentiles who adhered to local religions and regarded John's community as social pariahs for its refusal to worship the gods and goddesses that protected the city; it has been abandoned by some former members who deny "that Jesus is the Christ" (2:22). So John explains to his community, "The reason the world does not know us is that it did not know him" (3:1). That some did not recognize Jesus Christ ("did not know him") accounts for why they do not recognize John's community now. One failure compounds the other.

The ongoing reality for the church, particularly when its witness is appropriate to the gospel and therefore questioning of its context, is that the "world" still does not recognize it. John reassures us as well as them: we are beloved of God as are they, if they would but recognize it.

John repeats his reassurance in verse 2: "We are God's children now." The "now" is eschatological: "What we will be has not yet been revealed." When Christ is "revealed" in his parousia, "we will be like him, for we will see him as he is." The vision of Christ is a transforming vision; it does not leave us as it found us. We will be like him—"pure." This is the note of sanctification, of growth in the life of faith. We have a long way to go.

Verses 4–7 expound on this theme by stressing the irreconcilable conflict between faithfulness and sin. Christ was the atonement for the sins of the whole world: "He was revealed [by God] to take away sins" (3:5). First John reverts to the claim of the Gospel of John that we and Christ mutually abide in one another: "no one who abides in him sins" (v. 6). Sin, says John, "is lawlessness" (v. 4). He would not need to make this comment to Jewish readers; for them it would be a tautology. First John places a high value on law, making fourteen references to commandments. The great commandment for John is "This is the message you have heard from the beginning, that we should love one another" (3:11). Those who do sin do not abide in Christ. The community should not be deceived; they should do what is righteous and love each other and, by implication, the whole world for which Christ atoned.

Thanksgiving Day/Year A

2 Corinthians 9:6–15

Paul is planning to visit Corinth to add a monetary offering from that church to one from Macedonia for the congregation in Jerusalem. In connection with Proper 8/Year B, we discuss three major theological themes that form the backdrop of Paul's appeal in 2 Corinthians 9:6–15 to the Corinthians to give generously: the covenantal value of giving to the poor, the *koinonia* or partnership involving the congregations and Paul, and the wealth of the Gentiles flowing to Jerusalem as an eschatological sign.

In 2 Corinthians 9:1–5, Paul offers a model that many preachers would find useful when appealing for money or time or when inviting the congregation to express thanks. The apostle approaches the Corinthians not by nagging but by reminding them of their eagerness (*prothumia* = joyfully ready), which inspires the Macedonians (9:1–2). In a pastoral move, Paul sent emissaries ahead to help the congregation prepare the offering so that neither Paul nor the Corinthians would be humiliated (9:3–5). Paul wants the offering to be a voluntary act (*eulogia*) and not extortion (*pleonexia*; 9:5).

In 9:6, Paul makes a statement whose spirit was widely shared: "The one who sows sparingly will also reap sparingly, and the one who sows bountifully will also reap bountifully" (see Prov. 11:24; 22:8). The word translated "bountifully" is *eulogia*, which was rendered "voluntary act" in

9:5: participating in the voluntary act of offering creates bountifulness in one's life. (On the deeper resonance of sowing and harvesting, see below.)

When Paul advises the congregation not to give "reluctantly or under compulsion, for God loves a cheerful giver," he evokes Deuteronomy 15:7–11, which calls for a generous spirit toward the needy, with no hard hearts or tight fists. God uses liberality as means to blessing. The people do not give to earn God's love but to express the knowledge that they are loved. The analogy is apt: Deuteronomy gives this advice in anticipation of the seventh-year remission of debt just as the Corinthians await the apocalypse.

Recognizing the tendency toward insecurity when giving up material resources, the apostle reminds the congregation that only God provides, but God does so "with every blessing in abundance" (2 Cor. 9:8). These themes are reinforced in 9:10 with the citation of Psalm 112:9, a passage invoking the larger psalm that depicts the life of the righteous as blessed with land, descendants, and wealth. In gratitude to God and in commitment to the covenantal community, they deal generously with others and distribute their own goods to the poor (Ps. 112:1–9). Similarly God provides for the Corinthians so they can fulfill their covenantal responsibility by "sharing abundantly in every good work," that is, be a means through whom God provides for the needy of their day.

Paul touches a deeper chord in the memory of Israel in 2 Corinthians 9:10 by using language reminiscent of that used in Genesis 8:22 regarding God's covenant with the whole human family through Noah to provide seedtime and harvest as long as the earth endures. The church at Corinth was composed mainly of Gentiles, and this covenant reminds them that God provided faithfully for them before they knew God as God. They can continue to count on that sustenance as they give to the Macedonians. Moreover, because sowing and harvesting are fundamental life processes, the reader feels an intuitive resonance: as God works reliably through nature, so God provides through their life processes.

The Corinthians will find that their generosity not only provides for the needs of the saints in Jerusalem but enriches the Corinthians themselves and also adds to the quality of God's life by increasing the thanksgiving to God (2 Cor. 9:11–12). The latter is especially true as Gentile participation in the offering for Jerusalem signals that final manifestation of the divine realm is almost here, and with it the reunion of God's scattered peoples—Jews and Gentiles (Isa. 60:4–16; 61:5–6).

The points at which Paul's discussion draw from the taproot of Israel remind the community that being "obedient to the confession of the gospel of Christ" is a way God provided for the Gentile Corinthians to share in the blessing of the God of Israel at the edge of the apocalyptic denouement of the present age of history (2 Cor. 9:13). Given the magnitude of this development, the rendering "thanks" in 9:15 does not do justice to the Greek *charis*, which is typically translated "grace" and which evokes God's covenantal faithfulness to Israel which is now experienced by Gentiles through Jesus Christ. This is, indeed, an "indescribable gift."

Year B

First Sunday of Advent/Year B

1 Corinthians 1:3–9

A letter in antiquity often included a "thanksgiving paragraph," such as is in today's lesson in which the author thanked the gods for the recipients and their blessings. Always the theologian, the apostle not only offers thanks to the God of Israel but also presages some of the main themes in the letter. Even more, Paul uses the thanksgiving paragraph to orient the hearers to receive the letter in ways suggested in that paragraph.

In Judaism, giving thanks to God not only expresses gratitude but also implicitly acknowledges that God (and not other gods, idols, or one's own cleverness) is the source of life. Because we owe our life to God, thanksgiving also reminds us that we are accountable to God, a theme that is prominent in this and other letters from the apostle.

When Paul speaks of the "grace of God that was given you in Jesus Christ" (1 Cor. 1:4), he does not mean that God's grace (God's favor and faithfulness) appeared for the first time in Jesus. Most of the recipients of 1 Corinthians were Gentiles (12:2), so Paul reminds them that whereas Israel learned of God's grace through the call to Abraham and Sarah, the exodus, and the divine trustworthiness in Jewish history, these Gentiles have come to know the grace of the God of Israel by means of Jesus Christ.

In 1:5–7 the apostle anticipates themes that develop later in the letter: God has given the Corinthians speech, knowledge, and spiritual gifts. However, we soon discover that some people in the community have misused their speech, knowledge, and gifts, and that Paul needs to correct these misuses (for expanded discussion, see passages such as 8:1–13; 10:23–11:1;

and 12:1–14:40). By beginning with the affirmation of 1:5–7, Paul orients the readers positively to the changes the apostle will recommend, thus minimizing the resistance that sometimes arises in the face of correction.

Though Paul did not use the category of "prevenient grace," a similar idea surfaces when Paul says, "You are not lacking in any spiritual gift" (1:7). God has already given in the community the resources needed to await "the revealing of our Lord."

The phrases "the revealing of our Lord Jesus Christ" and "the day of our Lord Jesus Christ" refer to the second coming. Along with many other Jewish theologians in the first century, Paul was basically apocalyptic. He believed that God is about to bring the current evil era of history to a close through a dramatic historical interruption (the return of Jesus Christ from heaven; cf. 1 Thess. 4:16–5:5) and will then fully manifest the divine realm in a new world. This event would be accompanied by a great judgment in which God either condemned people or raised them with Christ. To be raised, one must be "blameless," a term sometimes used in the courts to bespeak innocence but one that can have deeper undertones, as in 3 Maccabees 5:31, where it is part of the reason a monarch (under divine guidance) would spare Jewish people from death: they have been without reproach in manifesting steadfastness and loyalty.

Human beings can be steadfast as they await the second coming because God is faithful (1:9a). Confidence in the trustworthiness of God is fundamental to Jewish tradition. Because God has promised them, the community at Corinth can count on the coming of the apocalypse and the new world. However, Paul will soon use this confidence in God to call the Corinthians to change the behaviors that would deny them a place in the new world. The community is advised, then, to live in the full awareness that they are in fellowship (or partnership—*koinonia*) with Jesus Christ.

Second Sunday of Advent/Year B

2 Peter 3:8–15a

The congregation that received this letter was made up of Gentiles who had converted from idol worship and destructive living to the God of Israel and covenantal life. False teachers had persuaded many in the community to abandon their confidence in the second coming of Jesus (which would be accompanied by the final judgment) and to engage in behaviors inappropriate to covenantal qualities of life in a community of the God of Israel. The lection appointed for today is designed to rekindle the congregation's confidence in the promise of Jesus' coming and to live in ways that are consistent with those of faithful Jewish people.

In 2 Peter 3:1–2, the author straightforwardly states the purpose of this part of the letter: "to arouse your sincere intention" to remember "the words spoken in the past by the holy prophets, and the commandment" of Jesus "spoken through your apostles" (the ones who brought the gospel to the Petrine community). As we learn from 1:16–22; 2:4–10; and 3:2–7, the words of the prophets, Jesus, and the apostles refer to the coming apocalypse (cf. Last Sunday after the Epiphany/Transfiguration Sunday/Year A). In 3:3, the writer alludes to a common expectation in apocalyptic literature that certain things would have to occur in the last days before the apocalypse itself could take place. The author of 2 Peter interprets the false teachers as "scoffers" (*empaigmone*), a term that denotes people who mock others, sometimes derisively (Wis. 12:25; Sir. 27:28; 2 Macc. 7:7), behavior obvious in their question "Where is the promise of his coming?" The world has continued much as it is ever since the beginning of creation (3:4).

The writer replies that the scoffers "ignore" the facts that the word of God with its promise of the apocalypse "existed long ago" (people in antiquity prized old things). God formed the earth through water (the primeval sea of Gen. 1:1–2) and later destroyed it through water (Gen. 6–8, esp. 7:11). The author (along with many other apocalypticists) believed that "the same word" of God contained (since the foundation of the world) the anticipation that God would judge and destroy the post-flood world ("the present world") by fire (*1 En.* 1:6–9; 52:2; 2 Esd. 13:10–12 *Sib. Or.* 2:187–213). The destruction by water is proof that the community can count on the same by fire.

The congregation turns to Psalm 90:4 to help them realize that "with the Lord, one day is like a thousand years, and a thousand years are like one day" (2 Pet. 3:8). God's perspective on the passing of time differs from that of human beings who are more limited and caught in the vicissitudes of history (3:9). Yet more is involved than simply a difference of perspective: the delay is a demonstration of patience on God's part to give all a chance to repent (3:10).

Different Jewish writers envisioned the events in the apocalypse itself in different ways. In 3:10, the writer offers one interpretation: the day will come suddenly ("like a thief"); the "heavens will pass away with a loud noise"; the "elements" (*stoicheia*, probably the elements of the world) will be destroyed by fire and the earth "will be disclosed" (that is, to the final judgment).

To prepare for the cataclysm, the community should lead lives of "holiness and godliness," by living out God's purposes articulated earlier and in 1 Peter. Although such lives may have the effect of "hastening" the final cataclysm, the community needs faithfully to wait for the coming of the "new heaven and earth" (the apocalyptic regeneration removes the barrier between the present heaven and earth; 3:12–13). Living as the writer has taught is the means whereby to be "at peace and without spot or blemish." From the author's point of view, the community should "regard the patience of our Lord as salvation" (v. 15), for the delay of the apocalypse increases the opportunity for repentance.

Before reaching the pulpit, the preacher might think about a couple of matters. First, it sounds suspiciously like the author of this letter is engaging in name calling by designating the false teachers as "scoffers." Name calling is theologically inappropriate and often short-circuits the possibility of meaningful conversation. For another, when these teachers say of the world "all things continue as they were," they seem to many contemporary people to be to the point. Evil still stalks the streets. The world is still unredeemed. Rather than stoke the fires of an apocalyptic expectation that is two thousand years delayed, the preacher might better help the congregation name a believable hope and how to live in witness to it.

Third Sunday of Advent/Year B

1 Thessalonians 5:16–24

The congregation at Thessalonica was made up of Gentiles who had turned away from idols to serving the true and living God (1 Thess. 1:9). Such faithfulness meant not only worshiping the God of Israel but also adopting values consistent with Jewish identity. Eventually, however, they became disheartened (1:6) and were in danger of returning to Gentile behavior (4:1–11). The apostles write 1 Thessalonians to encourage them to remain steadfast to avoid the chaos of Gentile existence now and be a part of the eschatological world to come (4:13–5:10). The writers urge the members of the congregation to encourage one another, that is, to build up one another (5:11). Today's lesson provides three kinds of practical guidance.[19]

First, in 5:12–13, the authors focus on the congregation's relationships with its leaders. The community should respect (*oida*) those who "labor" (*kopiao*) among them (as in 1 Thess. 1:3; 2:9; 3:5), those who "have charge" (*proistemi* = in 1 Macc. 5:19, those in charge of battle against Gentiles and often of leaders in combat), and those who "admonish" (*noutheteo*), emphasizing helping Jewish people avoid Gentile ways (Wis. 11:10; 12:2, 26). The verb translated "esteem" (*egeomai*) often means something like "to prefer in comparison to others" (Wis. 1:16). In sum, the congregation should lovingly prefer the guidance of their leaders who can instruct them in the ways that make for "peace" so the Gentiles experience the shalom of the Jewish community.

The focus then shifts in 5:14–15 to encouraging the community to attend to those in need of encouragement. Although the NRSV first mentions "idlers," a better rendering of *atakos* here is "disorderly" in the sense of disrupting community (3 Macc. 1:19; *T. Naph.* 2:9). The faint-hearted (*oligopsuchos*) are those with a "fearful heart" from Isaiah 35:4 (Septuagint) who, like some in the Thessalonian community, were disquieted by the exile. The "weak" (*asthenes*) could be those susceptible to drifting from the faithful life (as in 1 Cor. 8:7–13) or those who are repressed by physical or social circumstances (Prov. 21:13). In either case, the call is consistent with the Jewish value of caring for the poor. In such matters (and others) the congregation is not to repay "evil for evil but always seek to do good to one another *and to all*" (v. 15, emphasis added). Again, the Gentiles are to take up core Jewish values by not repaying evil with evil (Prov. 20:22; Rom. 12:17; Matt. 5:38–39) and by actively overcoming evil with good (*T. Jos.* 18:2).

In 5:16–22, the letter focuses (according to recent scholarship) on qualities that are to characterize the life of the congregation as community, especially in worship. The congregation is to "rejoice [*chairo*] always," which means not simply "Be happy" but rejoice liturgically (and live joyously even in the broken world) because God is graciously (*charis*, grace, is etymologically related to *chairo*) replacing the present evil age with a renewed world (5:16). Prayer is the opening of the community to God, so to "pray [*proseuchomai*] without ceasing" is to be ever conscious of being receptive to the movement of God, particularly toward the new world (5:17). Giving thanks to God for the divine presence and leading is essential to Jewish life (Ps. 107:1; Sir. 51:12). Through Jesus Christ, Gentiles join the Jewish community in giving thanks to God (1 Thess. 5:17b). To "give thanks [*eucharisteo*] in all circumstances" (as rejoicing always at 5:16) is to give thanks not *for* the circumstances (especially evil ones) but because God is leading the creation into a new world whose circumstances do prompt unending thanks.

The congregation is not to "quench [*shennumi* = as one would extinguish a fire] the Spirit" (5:19) which, in this context, is likely connected to prophecy in 5:20. Many early communities believed that prophets in the church spoke messages from the heavenly world through the agency of the Spirit, sometimes in a moment of ecstasy (1 Cor. 14:6). The community is to encourage such expressions but also to test them to determine what is good (and hold fast to that) and avoid "every form of evil." The criterion on which to gauge whether a prophetic utterance is truly inspired by the Spirit is the degree to which it is "good" (*kalos*) or a form of evil (*poneros*). Good is represented in thoughts and actions that are consistent with Jewish covenantal life (Deut. 6:18; 12:28; Amos 5:14; Mic. 6:8) and that point toward the new world. Evil is not only indicated by attitudes and behaviors that undercut God's desires for community and that reinforce complicity in the present evil age but sometimes also, in Hellenistic usage, by Gentile behavior (Wis. 3:12; 12:10; 1 Macc. 7:25; 11:8; *T. Reu.* 4:9; *T. Jos.* 3:10).

Fourth Sunday in Advent/Year B

Romans 16:25–27

Today's reading is the doxology with which Romans ends. Whether Paul wrote this doxology or it was added later is debatable; it is absent from some ancient manuscripts and others put it at different places in the letter. Although unique in Paul's letters, the doxology contains important themes to which we now turn.

Verse 25 begins as a prayer "to God who is able to strengthen [*sterixai*] you according to my gospel." Apocalyptic thinkers such as Paul tended to say that "strengthening" was necessary in light of the impending crises that would arrive as the eschaton came near, and verse 25 is usually interpreted as having meant just this. Earlier in Romans (8:18–39), however, Paul referred to what seem to be actual sufferings or trials of the community. Whatever their views of eschatology, pastors understand the need for strengthening among their congregants and God, as the One whose strength is sufficient for all our weaknesses.

The phrase "according to my gospel" (*to euangelion mou*) refers not to some gospel that is known only to Paul or to his idiosyncratic gospel but to the (by now) widely known gospel that Paul proclaims. This gospel is the "proclamation of Jesus Christ" or the proclamation that Jesus is the Christ (*to kerygma Iesou Christou*). Jesus Christ is not an adjunct to the gospel or a bearer of the gospel but *is* the gospel, the good news.

What this gospel is, however, Paul immediately says is a "mystery [*mysterion*] that was kept secret for long ages but is now disclosed" (vv. 25–26). This long-hidden but now-disclosed secret was revealed (v. 25) in Jesus Christ. Inasmuch as Paul worked hard throughout Romans to show that his gospel was in fact disclosed throughout the Scriptures beginning with God's promise to Abraham and Sarah to make their descendants a blessing to the Gentiles, readers might wonder just what is now meant by saying that this very gospel was for long kept "secret." For Paul, it was the "timing" of the eschaton that was once secret but has now been disclosed to have begun in Jesus Christ. The language is like that of deutero-Pauline writings: "In former generations this mystery was not made known to humankind, as it has now been revealed to his holy apostles and prophets by the Spirit; that is, the Gentiles have become fellow heirs." (Eph. 3:5–6; see Col. 1:26–27).

Romans 16:26 says that this gospel is now "made known to all the Gentiles" (*ethne*). The great good news that Paul has circumnavigated the Mediterranean to proclaim to Gentiles is that they, too, are included in God's promises to Israel and to remind them that if they can be included, so can Israel.

This gospel is made known not only through Jesus Christ but also through the "prophetic writings" (v. 26). "Prophetic writings" is a term that appears nowhere else in Paul or in the Second Testament. Obviously it could refer to the writings of the Prophets, particularly those such as Second Isaiah who spoke of the inclusion of Gentiles (Isa. 49:6). Equally well, however, it could apply to Paul's own letters, including Romans, which make known this same gospel. A clear purpose of Romans is to effect what it proclaims—including Gentiles in the praise and service of God.

The reason for this gospel's being made known to the Gentiles, "according to the command of the eternal God," is "to bring about the obedience of faith" (v. 26). "This is why I have let you live," God said to Moses, "to make my name resound through all the earth" (Exod. 9:16). The doxology concludes glorifying the God of all-inclusive grace.

Christmas Day/Years A, B, and C

Titus 2:11–14

Titus 3:4–7

Hebrews 1:1–4, (5–12)

Please see Christmas Day/Year A for commentary on these passages.

First Sunday after Christmas Day/Year B

Galatians 4:4–7

The congregation in Galatia is composed mainly of Gentiles. The passage for today continues Paul's appeal to them to abandon a version of the gospel offered by other missionaries who themselves, as Gentile adults, took up some Jewish practices (such as circumcision), believing that they need to earn God's favor. Paul's appeal is predicated on two meanings of the term *law*: (a) torah as positive covenantal instruction for Jewish people, and (b) torah as the standard by which Gentiles (who worship idols and ignore God's instructions) are condemned. The Galatian situation and the different uses of "law" are discussed in detail at Propers 4, 5, 6, and 7 of Year C.

In Galatians 3:23–29, Paul uses this second notion of *law* to assure the Gentile Galatians that through the faithfulness of God revealed to them through Jesus Christ they have been saved from condemnation at the last judgment. Indeed, through Jesus Christ they have been adopted as heirs of God's promise with Israel. In the apocalyptic context, this promise means not only immediate justification but also welcome into the salvation of the eschatological world.

Paul uses the pronoun "we" in order to identify with the Gentiles' situation in 4:1ff. With respect to salvation, he draws an analogy between a minor who is an heir to an inheritance and the Gentiles (4:1–3). In the hierarchical and abusive social pyramid of the times, a minor had much the same social standing as a slave until the date the head of the household decreed the minor could receive the inheritance. While waiting, the minor was under the abusive supervision of guardians and trustees.

Prior to the event of Jesus Christ, the Gentiles were in a circumstance similar to that of the minor. They were "enslaved to the elemental spirits of the world" (4:3). These "elemental spirits" (*stoicheia tou cosmou*) were powers, demonic in character and in league with the brokenness of the old age, who enslaved Gentiles and made it impossible for Gentiles to live as God wanted. The term "enslaved" (*douloo*) indicates that the Gentiles did not freely choose to serve these spirits nor could they simply will themselves to be free of the spirits' influence.

However, "in the fullness of time" God sent the Son to be "born of a woman, under the law" so that the Gentiles could receive "adoption as children" (4:4). The phrase "fullness of time" invokes the apocalyptic notion that God had predetermined a time to end the present corrupt world and replace it with the eschatological world to come. The phrase "born of a woman" emphasizes that Jesus was an authentic human being. The phrase "under the law" appears in Paul not in the sense of "under torah" but in the second sense of "law" above: the Gentiles under condemnation.[20] Paul means not that Jesus became a Gentile but that Jesus was born into a world under apocalyptic judgment and in which Gentile members faced condemnation.

God sent Jesus "to redeem those who were under the law" so that they might "receive adoption as children" (v. 5). Jesus Christ is the means whereby God "redeems" the Gentiles by communicating that God loves them and by preparing a community for them to prepare for the coming divine realm (the church).

One proof of the truth of Paul's claim is that God sent the Spirit into the Gentiles so that, like the Jewish community, they affirm that the God of Israel is "Abba! Father!" In the ancient world identity was communal and centered in one's family. The ecstatic presence of the Spirit (4:6) along with the earlier note that the Gentiles have been "*adopted* as children" (4:5, emphasis added), indicates that the identity of the Gentiles is now conjoined with Israel in the eschatological community (4:6). The Gentile believers are no longer slaves to the elemental spirits but heirs whose time for inheritance has come (4:7).

Second Sunday after Christmas Day/Year B

Ephesians 1:3–14

Please see the Epiphany of the Lord/Year A for commentary on this passage.

Epiphany of the Lord/Years A, B, and C

Ephesians 3:1–12

Please see the Epiphany of the Lord/Year A for commentary on this passage.

First Sunday after the Epiphany/Year B

Baptism of the Lord

Acts 19:1–7

In today's reading, Paul has come to Ephesus, a port on the Aegean Sea where he encounters a group whom the text initially describes simply as "disciples" but soon designates as "believers." In Acts, "believers" are those who believe that God, through the agency of Jesus Christ, is about to end the present, broken world by means of a cosmic apocalypse and replace it with a new one. To believe "in" Jesus, for Luke, is less to believe certain things about the nature of the person of Jesus than to believe that God is acting through Jesus for the transformation of the world.

Paul asks the disciples if they have received the Holy Spirit (Acts 19:2a). For Luke, the Spirit is an ecstatic presence that manifests qualities of the divine realm. In Acts 2:17–19, the Spirit both signals that the last days have come and begins to reshape the believers into a community in which roles and relationships demonstrate those of the world to come—sons and daughters, old and young, even slaves. Indeed, in Acts 2:1–22 and 10:34–48, a definitive work of the Spirit is to join people of different ethnicities and languages into a community of the new age. This latter trait suggests a norm by which a preacher can judge the degree to which an experience or movement is a work of the Spirit: the degree to which it brings together people who are otherwise separated.

The disciples in Ephesus reply to Paul in a way that many congregations today might as well: "We have not even heard that there is a Holy Spirit" (Acts. 19:2b). Although they have the essential insight concerning Jesus and the turning of the ages, they are not adequately instructed. Paul asks, "Into what then were you baptized?" (19:3a). The question reveals that, for Luke, baptism and the Holy Spirit are conjoined. Luke assumes that the disciples should have received the Spirit in conjunction with baptism, whether at the time of baptism or through the separate act of the laying on of hands. In Luke-Acts, baptism has an eschatological quality. By going into the water (very likely for immersion) a person repents of sin (participation with the corrupt powers and behaviors of the old age) and becomes part of a community empowered by the Spirit as they await the coming of the new age.

The disciples have received John's baptism (19:3b). John the Baptist also had disciples who debated Jesus' disciples as to which leader was greater. Luke wants the reader to interpret Jesus as the superior leader. Although John's baptism was important, indicating repentance in preparation for the apocalypse (19:4; Luke 3:1–17), according to Luke, John himself pointed his followers to Jesus (Acts 19:4b; Luke 3:16–17). While John baptized for repentance, Jesus baptizes with the Holy Spirit and with fire (Luke 3:16–17). By "fire" Luke means that Jesus is the eschatological judge.

To be fully initiated into the community of the new world, the disciples are baptized "in the name of the Lord Jesus." In the book of Acts, baptism is never performed in the name of the Father, Son, and Spirit but only "in the name of the Lord Jesus." Evidently the early church was diverse in its practices of baptism. To be baptized "in the name of the Lord Jesus" meant to be initiated into the community of believers (as defined above) and to live as part of a community witnessing to God's coming world while continuing in the present.

Following the act of baptism, Paul laid hands on them and the Holy Spirit came upon them. They spoke in tongues (presumably in the same way as in Acts 2:1–13) and prophesied. In the early church "prophecy" typically referred to receiving messages from the risen Jesus that helped the community faithfully interpret and live through their situations in the world.

Second Sunday after the Epiphany/Year B

1 Corinthians 6:12–20

As noted more fully in connection with the Second Sunday after the Epiphany/Year A, the Corinthian congregation has divided into fractious groups that impede the congregation's ability to (1) alert Gentiles to the impending final manifestation of the divine realm and (2) embody qualities of the realm in the life of the congregation. A major division of groups is by class—those who are impressed by signs of high social status such as "eloquent wisdom" (1 Cor. 1:10) lord it over those from lower classes. Paul calls the congregation to become a community whose common life witnesses to the gospel. In particular, he encourages the largely Gentile congregation towards faithful unity by adopting approaches to personal and corporate life that are Jewish in spirit.

The particular division in the congregation in today's lesson is revealed in the attitude voiced in 6:12. Scholars agree that the phrase "All things are lawful" is a slogan voiced by a group in the congregation. (The word "lawful" does not here refer to torah and could better be translated "permissible.") Paul reports a similar slogan in verse 13a: although food is meant for the stomach and the stomach for food, those facts are inconsequential since God will destroy both. Deprecating the body was common in philosophical circles in antiquity, and it led to the idea that what one did through the body was unimportant. A wise person need not be restricted in the use of the body. This idea likely came from the upper class because the wealthy could afford exposure to the philosophical schools.[21]

Some upper-class Corinthians, interpreting the slogans of verses 12–13a into their personal lives, were having intercourse with prostitutes. In response, Paul says (v. 13b) that the body is not for fornication [*porneia*] but "for the Lord." Paul presumes the Jewish view that a human being *is* a body (not *has* a body) and that embodied persons are to live "for the Lord," that is, in covenant. The body is so important that God raised Jesus with a resurrection body for the eschatological world, and God will raise the Corinthians similarly (v. 14).

In verse 15, Paul draws on the idea that a social group was also a body. People baptized into Christ become the body of Christ. Christ is present through the bodies of the Corinthians and the church as community is present through the individual Corinthians. In 6:16, Paul quotes Genesis 2:24 to show that two people become one body in the act of sexual intercourse. The body that is created by fornication, however, is a body contrary to God's purposes. In the Jewish view, sexuality is reserved for marriage, a covenantal relationship designed to mirror the covenant of God with the community; the intimacy of intercourse is to create an experience of covenantal oneness that embodies the intimacy of God with the people. Fornication with a prostitute exploits another person for sensual pleasure without covenantal commitment. Hence "Shun fornication!"

The body, indeed, is the temple of the Holy Spirit (6:19). In a way similar to the temple in the community of Israel, the body is a place wherein one can experience through the Spirit the assurance of God's presence and be empowered to live covenantally through the power of the Spirit. Indeed, "You are not your own but you were bought with a price" (v. 20). This expression from the slave market echoes the Hellenistic notion that each person serves a higher power. The Corinthians had been enslaved to the false wisdom of the present age (expressed by slogans such as 6:12–13a), but through Jesus Christ they now belong to God. In this new state, they are to glorify God in their bodies, that is, to use their bodies for God's covenantal purposes.

Third Sunday after the Epiphany/Year B

1 Corinthians 7:29–31

At 1 Corinthians 7:1 Paul responds to matters about which the Corinthians have written. The Corinthians are divided in how to respond to these issues. Indeed, many congregations continue to be perplexed regarding how to make theological sense not only of certain circumstances but of Paul's recommendations. Paul recommends that, to avoid fornication, a husband and wife should resolve their sexual desires by maintaining an active sexual relationship with one another in a spirit of mutuality (7:1–7). The unmarried and widows should remain single unless they cannot practice self-control (7:8–9). The apostle frowns on divorce, although if divorce is inevitable, divorcees should remain single or reconcile (7:10–11). The believer who is married to an unbeliever is advised to remain married except when the unbeliever wants to end it, for the believer might help the unbeliever be saved (7:12–16). Paul recommends not changing one's current social status—whether circumcised or uncircumcised, slave or free (7:17–24). Although it is preferable for virgins to remain unmarried, marriage is not sin (7:25–28). The call to hold fast in one's current circumstance is amplified in 7:32–40.

The lection for today articulates the underlying reason for Paul's suggestion that members of the congregation should remain as they are: "The appointed time has grown short" (7:29). Indeed, "the present form of this world is passing away" (v. 31). An apocalyptic theologian, Paul believed that people were living in the last days of the present evil age, that God would soon end that eon with Jesus' return from heaven, after which God would fully realize the divine realm when all circumstances and relationships would be in accord with God's desires.

Paul believes that the time is so short that people can live in the present with attitudes and behavior shaped not in response to corrosive powers and passions but by the coming realm of God. Those with wives can live with the undivided faithfulness of the single person. Those who mourn (perhaps, as in 4 Esd. 10:5–17, grieving the sin and brokenness of the present) can live as if there is no reason to mourn. Those who rejoice (presumably in having high social status in the present) can live as though not rejoicing. Those who attempt to make life secure by accumulating possessions can live as though they had none, and those compromised by economic (and other) entanglements with the old age can live as though they had no dealings with it. Paul does not seem to suggest a physical detachment from the present world (such as the withdrawal of a group of apocalyptic hopefuls to the desert community at Qumran).

For Paul, the first priority for the Corinthians is to remain faithful for the relatively short duration of history that remains before the apocalypse. Paul envisions the advice in 1 Corinthians 7 as survival strategies and not as systematic theological reflection for the long term on sexuality, marriage, the single life, circumcision, and slavery.

Relatively few Christians in the long-established churches today believe history will end soon. We cannot simply cut Paul's recommendations out of this first-century document and paste them into our current thinking about sexuality, marriage, the single life, and social movement. However, one aspect of Paul's theological reflection should still be at the heart of our considerations: the concern that we envision all dimensions of relationships and social movements from the perspective of their faithfulness to what we most deeply believe about God's purposes on these and analogous issues. Indeed, in the spirit of 7:29b–31a, we can seek to live "as if" the realm of God is already fully present.

Fourth Sunday after the Epiphany/Year B

1 Corinthians 8:1–13

The Corinthians had written Paul concerning whether members of the congregation could eat meat sacrificed to idols, and, like other controversies in Corinth, this one is related to class conflict. Only the upper classes regularly ate meat, virtually all of which had been sacrificed to idols. Worshipers would offer a tiny piece of flesh in a charcoal brazier in front of an idol, believing the sacrifice would bring the deity's blessing. The wealthy, who ate the meat in a small dining room at the temple, would then be in the sphere of the idol's authority (1 Cor. 8:10).

Paul quotes a slogan of this upper-echelon group who think it is permissible to eat such meat: "'All of us possess knowledge'" (8:1). By "knowledge" they mean the awareness expressed in the slogans that "'no idol in the world really exists'" (that is, an idol has no power), "'there is no God but one'" (8:4–5), and "'food will not bring us close to God'" (v. 8a). Whether the affluent eat meat offered to idols matters not with respect to relationship with God (v. 8b). In 8:4–6, the apostle agrees in principle with the wealthy, even bringing forth (v. 6) an early creed stressing the sovereignty of God.

Paul says that such knowledge "puffs up" (*phusioi*), that is, it destroys community by allowing one to become self-important and arrogant, whereas "love [*agape*] builds up" (*oikodomeo*) community. Those who subscribe to the slogans of the upper class do not yet have the "necessary knowledge" that will bring about the unity that will strengthen the church to carry out its purpose.

Those in the congregation from the lower strata of society do not recognize that idols have no power: "Their conscience, being weak, is defiled" (8:7). In antiquity "conscience" (*suneidesis*) referenced not the inner instinct or moral guide that comes to mind today but the capacity to reflect on one's present or past and to suffer pain at the awareness of having violated the moral precepts of the community. The behavior of the wealthy not only causes these weaker believers to suffer unnecessary pain but causes the community to disintegrate.

At 8:9, Paul implicitly draws on the Jewish notion that members in a covenantal community are responsible for one another. In and of themselves, the upper-cut Corinthians have the freedom to eat food offered to idols. However, they need to consider the possibility that others who do not share their knowledge could be encouraged to eat food sacrificed to idols and would be "destroyed" [*appolumi*], the same word rendered "perishing" in 1:18 that refers to those who are wiped out at the apocalyptic cataclysm.

Because Christ died for these latter folk, oligarchs causing the poor to be destroyed not only violate a fundamental more of antiquity—"sin against the members of your family"—but also sin against Christ (8:12).

The apostle uses his own behavior as an example (8:13): "I will never eat meat so that I will not cause one of them to fall." The wealthy should limit their freedom so as to not to destroy those who would be troubled by the eating of food sacrificed to idols.

This perspective challenges North American culture that venerates individual choice and expression. Can the preacher help the congregation identify points at which we could limit our freedoms to keep together a community that witnesses to God's purposes of love and justice for all? However, this text poses a difficult question. Are there points at which self-limitation inhibits witness? To witness adequately, do times come when a community must violate the consciences of some of its members?

Fifth Sunday after the Epiphany/Year B

1 Corinthians 9:16–23

In chapter 9, the apostle illustrates from his own life the principle articulated in 8:1–13 of limiting one's freedom for the sake of others. He is "free" in the same sense as the status-conscious members of the congregation. Furthermore, he is an apostle, and the fact that the Corinthian congregation exists is itself proof that he is an effective worker (1 Cor. 9:1–2). As an apostle, Paul is entitled to certain rights mentioned in 9:3–14, such as food, drink, being accompanied by a wife, and wages.

Paul "would rather die than" make use of such rights, for he does not want anyone to deprive him of his "ground for boasting." Paul "boasts" in the positive way that Israel "boasts" (exults, rejoices) over God's care (Deut. 33:29; Ps. 5:11; cf. Jer. 17:14, 1 Cor. 9:15). Paul's vocation as preacher is not because of his own achievement but because "an obligation" is laid on him. The Greek term translated "obligation" (*anagke*) refers to something over which one has little choice because God has ordained it. When Paul says, "Woe is me," he uses the apocalyptic "woe" meaning condemnation at the last judgment.

If Paul preaches the gospel because it is his choice, he would receive a conventional reward or wage. However, the apostle has a "commission," an *oikonomian*, a word related to "steward" in 4:1–2 that means he is responsible for preaching in the same way that a steward is responsible for a household. Paul's reward as a faithful steward of the gospel is seeing the gospel go forward free of charge (9:17–18).

In 9:19–23, the apostle illustrates how he turned away from apostolic rights and accommodated others. Paul reminds the elites that he is also elite with respect to being free in all things. However, his freedom in the gospel leads him to become a slave to others to win them (v. 19). The word "win" (*kerdaino*) is an economic term meaning to make a profit: that people accept the gospel is Paul's profit. Paul wins people by meeting them where they are, by not hitting them in the face with possibilities and demands that seem far-fetched, even impossible.

As a Jewish person, Paul identifies with the Jewish people in order to win them (v. 20a). By win them, Paul does not mean that they leave Judaism but that they recognize the death and resurrection of Jesus as a sign that the apocalyptic consummation of history is at hand and that God is now gathering Gentiles for the divine realm through the church.

The phrase "under the law" (v. 20b) is never used in Jewish literature to refer to Jews. As we explain further in connection with Proper 7/Year C, it refers to Gentiles who stand under condemnation because they have not fulfilled God's purposes.[22] In this sense, Paul cannot, as he says, be "under the law" (v. 20c), because he is Jewish.

Those "outside the law" (*anomos*) are not simply Gentiles but persons (Jews and Gentiles) who are especially wicked (v. 21).[23] The NRSV renders verse 21b poorly when it says, "though I am not free from God's law," for this reading could be taken to mean that "God's law" has a negative quality. The expression is *anomos theou* and would better be rendered "outside God's law," as if to say, "I am not wicked by identifying with the wicked for I am inside the law of Christ."

When Paul mentions the "weak" in 9:22a the reader remembers 8:1–13. The apostle thus implies that the elite Corinthians should relate similarly to the underclass.

Paul sums up: "I have become all things to all people" (v. 22b). Paul adapts his behavior and message so that people will initially feel that the gospel life is truly possible for them. Consequently Paul's reward is to "share in [the] blessings" of the gospel, that is, in the realm of God that will become fully manifest after the return of Jesus.

This passage raises an important question for today. Do members of the congregation relate with one another (and does the congregation relate with the larger world) in ways that are more like the Corinthian elites or more like Paul? What does the congregation need to do to act analogously to Paul, who became all things to all people?

Sixth Sunday after the Epiphany/Year B

1 Corinthians 9:24–27

In the interest of unifying the church, Paul encouraged the high bred in Corinth to adapt their attitudes and behavior to those who do not have their status and insight (1 Cor. 8:1–9:23). Today's lesson reinforces this call through a sporting metaphor that may be a double entendre: (1) Like an athlete in a race, the elite Corinthians should discipline themselves by limiting their freedom, and (2) since the church is the *body* of Christ, the congregation needs to discipline itself as a community.

In the background of today's text is the notion, widespread in the Hellenistic age, that the self is a conflagration of passions that, when undisciplined, make the self a chaos that has a hard time participating constructively in community. The conflicted condition of the self reflected the social conditions of the time: unsettled, tense, and chaotic. A common goal in Hellenistic culture was to master the passions and thereby to calm the self and create a peaceful social world.[24] The athletic metaphor that Paul uses (and was used by other writers in antiquity) draws from this worldview. Because the self *is* a body, many ancients believed that disciplining the body would discipline the passions.

The running imagery that Paul uses would have been familiar to the Corinthians from the Isthmian games (named for the isthmus on which Corinth is located), sited about eight miles outside the city and held every two years. Although many runners would race, only one would win. Paul exhorts the Corinthians to "run in such a way that they may win it" (v. 24).

Verses 25–27 point the way for the runner to be in a position to win the race. "Athletes exercise self-control in all things" (v. 25a). Self-control (*egkrateuomai*) refers to refraining from excess (e.g., Sir. 18:30; 4 Macc. 5:34). It is striking that the athlete practices such restraint in "all things" (*pantes*), not just in matters related to the race.

In verse 25b, Paul employs a multivalent symbol. The athlete receives a perishable (*hitherto*) wreath (perhaps made of pine or celery); the Corinthians who follow Paul's regimen will receive an imperishable (*aphtharton*) one. This language evokes the final judgment, as these terms reappear in 1 Corinthians 15:42, where the body placed in the tomb is perishable while disciplined believers are raised with imperishable bodies.

Consequently, in 9:26, Paul does not "run aimlessly" (*adelos*) nor "beat the air" (an image from boxing). Rather, he "punishes" and enslaves the body (v. 27a). The severity of the training is indicated by the fact that the verb "punishes" (*hupopiadzo*) means literally to get a black eye. These radical measures are necessary because the apostle does not want to get to the finish line and learn that he is "disqualified" (*adokimos*—a term used in the Greek athletic games). By extension the upper-class members of the congregation should not want to spend their limited time thinking they are faithful only to find at the apocalypse that their failure to respond adequately to the lower social class disqualifies them from the eschatological world.

Although the analogy between running a race and disciplining one's life in the body of Christ hardly needs explanation today, the preacher needs to handle the analogy with care. In antiquity athletics had a much deeper meaning than today, and athletics in North America can be shallow and riddled with false values as well as a way of avoiding deep encounters with life. Also, the preacher should remember that some parishioners are impatient with or uninterested or have attitudes toward sports that are similar to that of the person who said, "If I hear another golf story, I am out of here."

Seventh Sunday after the Epiphany/Year B

2 Corinthians 1:18–22

In 1 Corinthians, Paul dealt with divisions within the congregation. In 2 Corinthians he deals with tensions in his own relationship with the congregation. Apparently, the apostle had been attacked in some way by a member of the Corinthian congregation (2:1–2), and such bitter feelings resulted that he cancelled a visit. The Corinthians took his failure to visit as a sign of his unreliability. Now, however, the relationship between Paul and the Corinthians is improved, and he seeks in today's text to explain the cancellation and reconciliation (2 Cor. 1:13–14; 5:11–21) so that he can help them live faithfully in preparation for the last judgment (2 Cor. 4:13–16–5:5; 7:5–16).

In 2 Corinthians 1:15–16, Paul explains that he had planned to visit Corinth twice on his way to and from Macedonia, where he picked up a collection for the church in Jerusalem to which the Corinthians were to contribute (2 Cor. 8–9, esp. 9:1–5). The word "send" (*propempo*) indicates the congregation was going to support him financially (1 Macc. 12:4) as a part of their "partnership" (*koinonia*) with Paul (1:7; 8:4, 23; 9:13). The "double favor" (*deuteran charin*) of verse 15b is a double entendre that refers both to Paul's visiting twice and to the twofold favor or act of grace of (1) Paul's visit and (2) Corinthian participation in the offering (the word *charin* is related to *charis*, "grace"). Paul understands their offering from the perspective of Isaiah 60:4–7 as the Gentiles making offering to and thereby acknowledging the sovereignty of the God of Israel as a part of the eschatological world.

Paul asks the questions in 1:17 in a way that, in Greek, presupposes a negative answer. No, he says; he was not vacillating or otherwise acting according to "ordinary human standards" whereby one gives two contradictory answers simultaneously—"Yes" and "No." Such a lack of integrity is characteristic of the broken old age. In Paul's day, people may have used double expressions ("Yes, yes") to reinforce the reliability of one's statement.

In 1:18, Paul invokes the most powerful guarantor of authenticity in the Jewish tradition: the faithfulness of God (Deut. 7:9). By definition God is faithful because God is one (Deut. 6:4); that is, God by nature has integrity that allows only God to be faithful. The same kind of faithfulness and integrity flows through the apostle who, therefore, cannot say both "Yes and no" (v. 18b).

The Corinthians can understand this phenomenon because, although they are largely Gentiles, they now serve the God of Israel through Jesus Christ who is "not 'Yes and No'" (2 Cor. 1:19). Paul's theocentrism comes into focus as he asserts that for Gentiles every one of the promises of the God of Israel is in Jesus Christ a "Yes" (1:20), including a place in the eschatological reign of God. God has confirmed the divine promise to the Gentiles without implying that God's promises to Israel have been abrogated. God confirmed these promises to the Corinthians by putting the "divine seal" on them through baptism and giving them the Spirit as a "first installment" of the fullness of the divine realm (1:21–22).

Paul explains that he cancelled his visit as an act of pastoral integrity and faithfulness in order not to intensify the community's pain and disruption by appearing before them (1:23–2:2). Inflaming their emotions would be contrary to the apostolic purpose, which is to build up the church so that the congregation can embody the eschatological community. Instead, "out of much distress and anguish of heart and tears" Paul wrote a letter regarding the painful situation to let the congregation know of his love for them and to initiate reconciliation so that his next actual visit could be an occasion of joy for all (2:3–4). The wisdom of Paul's approach is now confirmed by experience: he and the congregation are ready for a joyous reunion.

Eighth Sunday after the Epiphany/Year B

2 Corinthians 3:1–6

Some Christian interpreters have used this text as the basis for the pernicious portrait of Judaism as a dead religion of works, legalism, and empty ceremony that has been superseded by Christianity. However, we join other scholars in suggesting that this interpretation of the text is mistaken and that Paul actually positively evaluated Judaism and sees a positive continuity between Judaism and the Corinthian community.[25]

Since Paul's writing of 1 Corinthians, other missionaries, "super apostles" (*huperlioi apostoloi*) (11:5; 12:11), visited the community and brought a dramatic theology and a style of ministry that emphasized immediate experiences of glory. Paul seemed unimpressive, in contrast, and his theology, centered in crucifixion and resurrection, presented that the transition from the present evil age to the realm of God would involve suffering, as rulers of the present resist the coming glory (10:1–12:21). Many in the congregation had turned away from Paul's message and embraced the glitz of the other missionaries, and Paul had been in conflict with some in the community (2 Cor. 1:23–2:11).

Paul writes 2 Corinthians to help restore his relationship with the congregation. His strategy is to compare his ministry with that of the super apostles, who themselves differ over how to interpret various aspects of Judaism. His comparison is thus not between two religions (Judaism and Christianity) but between two groups, both of whom believe that the event of Jesus Christ is the turning point from the old age to the new but whose interpretations differ.

In 2:14–16a, Paul compares the movement of the church towards the second coming with the triumphal procession of a Roman victor, which would include both the conquering heroes and the prisoners captured during war. In verse 16b, the apostle raises the key question that he answers in the next part of the letter: "Who is sufficient for these things?" That is, "Who is really competent to lead the movement toward the impending realm?" In Greek, questions are typically phrased to expect either a negative or positive answer, such as "No one is really competent." However, Paul and his workers are not "peddlers" like others (presumably the super apostles) but speak sincerely and on the authority of God (v. 17).

Much as today, in antiquity representatives of leaders and movements often carried letters of recommendation that identified them and indicated what they were commissioned to do. In 3:1–3, Paul reminds the Corinthians that they do not need such a letter. The Corinthians themselves are indisputable testimony to Paul's ministry, for they are written "not with ink but with the Spirit of the living God, not on tablets of stone but on tablets of human hearts" (v. 3). In Judaism, the heart is a symbol of the deepest center of the self, and many Jewish theologians want faithful identity and behavior to issue from the heart (for example, Jer. 31:33; Ezek. 11:19; 36:26).

Although commentators habitually assume that the "tablets of stone" are the Ten Commandments, nothing in the immediate context suggests this. The connection is rather with "letters of recommendation," which leads to the conclusion that Paul's reference is to the tablets as symbols of revelation received through mystical experiences that the super apostles used to demonstrate (like letters of recommendation) their superiority. Other people in antiquity used similar figures to describe ascending to a mountain or to heaven to receive visions from deities (for example, 2 Esd. 14:24, 42).[26]

In 2 Corinthians 3:4–6, Paul asserts that the only reason he and his companions have any competence or reliability is because God has given it to them as "ministers of a new covenant, not of letter, but of spirit; for the letter kills, but the Spirit gives life." The phrase "new covenant" (*kaine diatheke*) comes from Jeremiah 31:31–34 and indicates not that one covenant has been replaced by another but that the community *feels* the values of the covenant and embodies them as expressions of *heart* (on heart, see above). Paul, of course, is called as apostle to the Gentiles and the Corinthian congregation is largely comprised of Gentiles. The priestly theologians understand that the Gentiles share in a covenantal quality of life (Gen. 8:22) and that the life of Israel is to help Gentiles discover the fuller measure of covenantal living (Gen. 12:1–3). Deutero-Isaiah thinks of Israel as a signal of God's covenant with the Gentiles (42:6; 49:8) and notes that God plans to incorporate strangers and others fully into covenantal community (55:3–4; 56:3–8; 60:1–16). Many Jewish theologians in the first century looked forward to the time when Gentiles would share in the divine realm (for example *1 En.* 10:18–22; 50:1–5; *Sib. Or.* 3:768–95; *Pss. Sol.* 17:30–34). The "new covenant" is thus not a replacement for the old but the recognition that the moment has come when God is gathering Gentiles into covenantal relationship with God-self and Israel for the eschatological world.

Lloyd Gaston recognizes that the word "letter" (*gramma*) here refers not to the law but to the fact that the mystical revelations associated with tablets (see above) were often given in letters that the recipients needed to know in order to understand the revelation. Paul's point, then, is that the heavenly revelations—the teaching—of the super apostles will lead the Corinthians to condemnation on the great day of judgment.

In 3:7ff., Paul explains further why the Corinthians should regard his apostolic ministry as authoritative and, conversely, why they should disregard the ministry of the super apostles. This topic is discussed on the Last Sunday after the Epiphany/Year C.

Ninth Sunday after the Epiphany/Year B

2 Corinthians 4:5–12

This passage continues Paul's attempt to persuade the Corinthians to turn away from the gospel put forward by "super apostles" (2 Cor. 11:5; 12:11) and to return to Paul's gospel. (This background is further developed in connection with the Seventh, Eighth, and Last Sundays after the Epiphany/ Year B, where we discuss 2 Cor. 4:5–6, and the Last Sunday after the Epiphany/Year C.) Paul shows that although his ministry is less impressive than that of the false apostles, its understatement is a sign of authenticity.

Like the super apostles, Paul has a "treasure" (*thesauros*). Paul's treasure is his version of the gospel—the death and resurrection of Jesus as the turning point from the present sinful world to the coming world of peace and love (2 Cor. 4:7). Jewish writers conceived of the eschatological era as a "treasure" (2 Esd. 6:5–6; 7:77; 8:54). The treasure is in "clay jars"—useful but also plain, inexpensive, and easily broken. Unlike the impressive super apostles, Paul is a "clay jar" holding "treasure," that is, the news of the coming world.

Paul is a clay jar and not the treasure itself (2 Cor. 4:7b). The unimpressiveness of the jar demonstrates that the "extraordinary power" (*he huperbole tes dunmeos*) animating the treasure is God. First-century readers would remember that the God of Israel works through unimpressive people and circumstances to demonstrate that divine power transcends all others. For example, God worked through the aged Sarah and Abraham, the slaves in Egypt, and the small nation of Israel and is now at work through the death and resurrection of Jesus and the struggles of Paul.

In verses 8–9, Paul describes the apostolic life as afflicted, perplexed, persecuted, and struck down. These designations sometimes appear in apocalyptic literature to describe the quality of life in the tribulation—the time shortly before the apocalypse when the cosmic powers fight against the coming of the new world. People suffer as a result. Paul specifies these sufferings elsewhere (2 Cor. 1:1–11; 11:16–30).

As 4:10 shows, the apostle regards the death of Jesus as an act whereby the powers defied the coming of the new world. When Paul says that he bears in his body (*soma*) the death of Jesus, the apostle means that he shares in the suffering of the tribulation with Jesus. By "body" Paul means both his physical body and his experience: the apostle's body and life are a conflict zone between the powers of the two ages.

However, while the apostolic life embodies the tribulation, it is also an arena in which the power of God to bring the new world is manifest. Despite intense suffering, the apostle is not crushed, driven to despair, forsaken, or destroyed (4:8–9). Why not? Because the life of Jesus is made visible through the bodies of Paul and those who follow him. The "life of Jesus" (*he zoe tou Iesou*) is the life of the resurrected Jesus, the firstfruit of the age to come. The readers would expect Paul to be ground down by the wretched circumstances of his life. Paul's hope, however, results from recognizing that the present circumstances are temporary and will be replaced by life in the divine world. The apostle does not deny the painful realities of his life but interprets them as resulting from the conflicts that accompany the change of the ages.

According to 4:11a, as long as Paul and the Corinthians live prior to the second coming, they will be in conflict with the powers of the present age. They experience tribulation pain "for Jesus' sake," that is, to witness to what God is doing through Jesus to transform the ages. According to 4:11b, they experience the life of Jesus, that is, the assurance that they can endure their suffering until the apocalypse. Indeed, according to verse 12, the apostle faces the cosmic powers who intend death for him so the Corinthians can live through the difficult present with confidence in the world to come.

Last Sunday after the Epiphany/Year B

Transfiguration Sunday

2 Corinthians 4:3–6

The reading for today continues a line of thought Paul has been developing since 2 Corinthians 2:14 to respond to challenges to his understanding of the gospel and his approach to ministry that have arisen in the congregation because of a visit to the community by "super apostles" (2 Cor. 1:15; 12:11). For the context of today's lection, please see our remarks on the Eighth Sunday after the Epiphany/Year B and the Last Sunday after the Epiphany/Year B (2 Cor. 3:7–4:2).

Paul's gospel (2 Cor. 4:3) is the news that the death and resurrection of Jesus Christ is the sign that God is bringing the current evil world to an end and is about to bring into being the future realm of God, in which all things take place according to God's purposes. The church is to alert others to the apocalyptic moment and especially to prepare Gentiles for it. In the meantime, the cosmic rulers of the present age resist the coming of the new.

The super apostles and their disciples in Corinth accused Paul of "veiling" his gospel (2 Cor. 1:12, 17; 6:11–12; 7:4), a charge that Paul refutes (1:12–14; 3:1–3, 12–18; 4:1–2). The "veil" in 4:3 recalls the vivid and ironic interpretation of the "veil" in 3:12–18 where Paul claims that while the other missionaries accuse him of "veiling" his gospel, their message is really the one that is veiled because it misconstrues God's purposes.

In 4:3b Paul points out the consequence of their misinterpretation: failing to understand and embrace his interpretation of the gospel is "perishing." In the apocalyptic world of thought, to "perish" often meant to face condemnation at the last day (2 Esd. 7:31; 9:36).

The "god of this world has blinded the minds of unbelievers, to keep them from seeing the light of the gospel of the glory of Christ" (4:4). This instance is the only use in the Second Testament of the designation "god of this world" (*ho theos tou aiovos toutou* = the god of the current age) for Satan. Scholars debate whether the "unbelievers" (*apistoi*) are pagans or whether the term here designates the false apostles and their followers. The latter is more likely since they are under discussion in this context. By adhering to their false gospel, they are in the same situation before God as those who do not believe at all.

When Paul speaks of the "light of the gospel of the glory of Christ," he has the apocalypse in mind. As noted in 2 Corinthians 3:7–4:2, the super apostles reduced the notion of "glory" to immediate, effervescent spiritual experience and downplayed the importance of preparing for the coming apocalyptic glory. Paul underlines the distance between the super apostles and himself by pointing out that his gospel comes not from "the god of this world" but from Christ "the image [*eikon*] of God." Per Genesis 1:26–27, to bear the image of God is to act as God's representative in the world.

The apostle is polemical in 4:5 in saying, "We do not proclaim ourselves," for the super apostles proclaim their own spiritual experience (the esoteric visions they received). By contrast, the content of Paul's gospel is

God's actions through Christ to end the suffering of the present and to initiate the unending eon of love and justice. This gospel is so important that Paul has made himself a slave (*doulos*) of the Corinthians. In the rigid social pyramid of antiquity, slaves or servants were near the bottom.

While commentators typically understand 4:6, "'Let light shine out of darkness,'" as a reference to Genesis 1:3, Lloyd Gaston points out that the sentence is much closer in wording to the Septuagint version of Isaiah 9:1, where the prophet speaks of the Gentiles as having walked in the darkness in the past but on whom God's light will shine.[27] Paul's gospel is a concrete application of Isaiah 9:1, for it is God's message of deliverance to the Gentiles who make up a majority of the Corinthian congregation. This gospel is not veiled but graciously *shines* through the face of Christ as communicated by Paul so that Gentiles may live in the light of the God of Israel in the present and be prepared for the unabated light of the age to come.

Ash Wednesday/Years A, B, and C

2 Corinthians 5:20b–6:10

Please see Ash Wednesday/Year A for commentary on this passage.

First Sunday in Lent/Year B

1 Peter 3:18–22

Please see the Sixth Sunday of Easter/Year A for commentary on this passage.

Second Sunday in Lent/Year B

Romans 4:13–25

Please see Proper 5/Year A for commentary on this passage.

Third Sunday in Lent/Year B

1 Corinthians 1:18–25

This passage also appears in the lectionary on the Fourth Sunday in Epiphany/Year A. A brief discussion of the setting of 1 Corinthians 1:18–25 is found on that date.

Power is a fundamental issue in 1 Corinthians. To those with an upper-class mentality, the idea of a cosmic transformation signaled by a crucifixion is foolishness (*moria*). To them, death is the epitome of weakness. They, however, are perishing; that is, they are on the way to condemnation at the last judgment and suffering the consequences of a fractious world in the meantime. Others are being saved. That is, they are on the journey into the eschatological community as they recognize the "message of the cross" (which for Paul includes both death and resurrection) as a demonstration of the power of God. The rulers of the old age asserted their maximum power by putting Jesus to death only to face the fact that their worst was too weak to counter the power of the God of Israel who raised Jesus.

By turning to Isaiah 29:14 (in 1 Cor. 1:19), Paul reminds readers that the idea of God confounding the rulers of the present age is as old as Israel itself. Indeed, the story of Israel is one of less being more—a tiny nation whose people have been enslaved, conquered, and exiled demonstrates the purposes of the universally sovereign God.

Through the word of the cross, *God* makes foolish (*moria*) the so-called "wisdom [*Sophia*] of the world": that is, that power derives from social importance (1:20b). No amount of power gained by "eloquent wisdom" (1 Cor. 1:17) can raise the dead. If God revealed divine power through venues associated with "eloquent wisdom," who could distinguish the wisdom of God and that of the world that results in perishing? Instead, God reveals true wisdom but through the foolishness of preaching (1:21).

Preachers sometimes think that verse 22 criticizes Jewish and Greek peoples, but another interpretation is more likely. The translation "Jews *demand* [*aiteo*, emphasis ours] signs" casts the Jewish quest in an unnecessarily negative light. The verb *aiteo* more naturally means "ask," and a sign is simply a confirmation of God's presence (as at the exodus in Exod. 7:3, Deut. 4:34, and other settings, such as Isa. 8:18 or Jer. 32:20). "Greeks [Gentiles]" also seek authentic wisdom. To some but not all Jewish people the idea of the apocalyptic transformation beginning with a crucifixion is a stumbling block. To many Gentiles, the idea of wisdom emanating from the same source is foolishness. Nonetheless, when Paul says people recognize Christ as the power and wisdom of God (1 Cor. 1:25), the emphasis is less on the person of Christ and more on the death and resurrection of Christ as revealing God's end-time activity.

In this spirit, it is worth asking what it meant, at the time of Paul, for a Jewish person to recognize the power and wisdom of God in Jesus Christ. At this early stage, the church did not focus on the *person* of Jesus as much as on God's actions taking place through him. Jewish people at that time likely would not have believed "in" Jesus in today's sense of affirming his simultaneous divinity and humanity. Nor, in Paul's time, did it mean renouncing the synagogue and Jewish practice; to the contrary, we should think of the church as a sect within Judaism or as an outreach of Judaism to Gentiles. In keeping with what we have already said, a Jewish Jesus-follower in the first century simply recognized the death and resurrection of Jesus as a signal of the denouement of the present world and the final manifestation of the divine realm, with the church as a community in which Jewish and Gentile people awaited the consummation.

Fourth Sunday in Lent/Year B

Ephesians 2:1–10

Appropriately for Lent, today's reading articulates Ephesians's understanding of the import of life with Christ, that God "made us alive together with Christ" (v. 5). The passage falls into three sections: verses 1–3 describe what Gentiles were like before being saved by Christ; verses 4–7 describe God's gracious salvation of us in Christ; and verses 8–10 describe the new life in Christ as "walking" in good works. Walking the way of life and blessing are figures of speech taken over from Judaism's talk of torah as way or path.

Verses 1–2 say, "You were dead through the trespasses and sins in which you once lived" (the Greek has "walked," *periepatesate*). Verses 1–10 contrasts two different ways of walking the path of life. "Dead" is used metaphorically, as in the parable of the Prodigal Son: "this son of mine was dead and is alive again" (Luke 15:24). Note that it is "you" who were dead; in verse 5 Ephesians will speak of "we" as having been "dead through our trespasses," and the writer, being a good pastor, includes himself among the sinners.

Formerly we followed "the course of this world [*kosmos*] . . . the ruler of the power of the air, the spirit that is now at work among those who are disobedient" (v. 2). Here Ephesians speaks of "walking" obediently to the powers that rule the old, passing age. "Spirit" refers to evil powers. First John 4:1 reminds us to "test the spirits," a reminder to which we should pay heed in these days of rampant "spirituality." "Those who are disobedient" (literally the "sons [*huiois*] of disobedience") are all those who have not responded to Christ. Ephesians regards the "world" as dominated by sin: "All of us once lived among them in the passions of our flesh . . . and we were by nature children of wrath" (v. 3). Of all that Ephesians mentions of "flesh," this is the only verse that associates it with sin. Ephesians 2:1–3 is parallel to Romans 1:18–32 as a description of the sins of the Gentile world. It is a standard Jewish depiction of Gentile life at the time.

Verses 4–7 mark an abrupt shift in tone and content. God, rich in mercy and out of great love "loved us even when we were dead through our trespasses" and "made us alive together with Christ—by grace [we] have been saved." Grace is who God is; love is freely (graciously) given; freedom, lovingly given. God frees us to love and loves us into freedom, that is, freedom from sin and for doing deeds of loving-kindness. Since verses 1:20–23 Ephesians has talked about freedom in Christ—being exalted "above all rule and authority and power and dominion"—no longer under the control of such powers. God's saving us when we were "dead" recalls God's saving Israel from bondage. God's grace here is mercy; *eleos* translates *hesed*, God's faithfulness in Judaism. We have been "raised" with Christ and "seated with him in the heavenly places" (v. 6). We are already in heaven! This is "realized eschatology"; we seem to have been saved out of this sinful world. But verse 7 immediately counters this emphasis with a reference to the "ages to come" in which God will show his mercy to us with the return of Christ and the rule of God. Without verse 7, the passage could encourage withdrawal from efforts to transform this sinful world.

Verses 8–10 deal with the "faith/works" polarity, but the "works" are not, as in Paul's undisputed letters, those of circumcision and the dietary laws but "good works" in general. Ephesians reformulates Paul's teaching for a later generation that is no longer dealing with Paul's immediate issues. We have been saved "by grace, through faith," and this is the "gift of God—not the result of works"; faith itself is a gift. Therefore, do not feel self-important. Instead, be who you are: "created in Christ Jesus for good works" (*en autois perpatesomen*). God empowers us to do what God asks of us.

Fifth Sunday in Lent/Year B

Hebrews 5:5–10

In today's reading Hebrews elaborates the high priesthood of Christ, which was introduced in 4:14 where the writer announced the theme that Christ is able "to sympathize with our weaknesses" (4:15). Verses 1–4 describe "every high priest" in Israel; the description is entirely positive.

Like Christ the high priests were human beings, "chosen from among mortals" (v. 1). Jesus, too, was human ("in the days of his flesh," v. 7). Like Christ, they were "put in charge of things pertaining to God" on behalf of other human beings (v. 1).

Verse 2 points up the "weakness" of the high priests that enabled them "to deal gently with the ignorant and the wayward," as Christ sympathizes with us because he, too, has been tested (4:15; see also 5:7–8). Numbers 12:3 says that Moses, Israel's first priest, was "humble, more so than anyone else on the face of the earth." When God was incensed, Moses and Aaron "fell on their faces, and said, 'O God . . . shall one person sin and you become angry with the whole congregation?'" (Num. 16:22).

Because of his weakness, the high priest offered "sacrifice for his own sins as well as for those of the people" (v. 3). There were two daily sin offerings, morning and evening, in the desert tabernacle (Exod. 29:40–41). Hebrews interprets one as for the high priest and the other as for the people; this is not clear in the Torah. Later, Hebrews will contrast this with Christ, who in his sinlessness does not need to make an offering for himself (7:27; 9:7). Hebrews's last comment on the high priests is that they were "called by God, just as Aaron was" (v. 4); they did not grasp at the office.

Verses 5–6 are the second part of today's reading: "Christ did not glorify himself in becoming a high priest" (v. 5). In this he is like the high priests. He, too, was "appointed" by God who addressed him, "'You are my Son, today I have begotten you'" (v. 5). This citation is from Psalm 2:7, earlier quoted in 1:5. Originally Psalm 2 was about the enthronement of the king of Israel and the king's relationship to God, a relationship entailing priestly functions on the part of the king. Hebrews goes on to quote Psalm 110:4: "'You are a priest forever, according to the order of Melchizedek'" (v. 6). No other text in the Second Testament quotes this passage or mentions Melchizedek. Psalm 110, like Psalm 2, had to do with the kings of Israel. Note that Jesus was appointed "by the one who said [*lalesas*] to him" (v. 5). This comment recalls Hebrews 1:1: "Long ago God spoke [*lalesas*] to our ancestors." Jesus is who he is by virtue of God's initiative.

Verses 7–10 turn to the claim that Jesus was perfected through suffering for the role of high priest. Hebrews emphasizes that Jesus "learned" (*ema-then*) obedience (v. 8) and "became" (*egeneto*) the savior (v. 9). His human suffering was a process through which he became who he is and became able to do what he does. His humanity makes a definite contribution to who he is; he was not a Gnostic redeemer who merely "appeared" to be human nor an impassible deity (in the manner of Aristotle's God) unable to suffer.

Instead he prayed "with loud cries and tears" and was heard "because of his reverent submissions" (v. 7). Again, he is comparable to the high priests of Israel in that he fully participates in human weakness, "yet without sin," as Hebrews insists (4:15). This comment invites readers to remember Jesus' prayer in Gethsemane or his prayers from the cross. Through this suffering, the "Son . . . learned obedience," was "made perfect," and "became the source of eternal salvation for all who obey him" (vv. 8–9). Hebrews does not explain how suffering enabled Christ to become the source of salvation, but 7:1–22 explains the reference to Melchizedek; it is not in the lectionary.

Palm/Passion Sunday/Years A, B, and C

Philippians 2:5–11

Please see Palm/Passion Sunday/Year A for commentary on this passage.

Monday of Holy Week/Year B

Hebrews 9:11–15

Please see Monday in Holy Week/Year A for commentary on this passage.

Tuesday of Holy Week/Year B

1 Corinthians 1:18–31

Please see the Fourth Sunday after the Epiphany/Year A, for commentary on this passage.

Wednesday of Holy Week/Year B

Hebrews 12:1–3

Please see Wednesday of Holy Week/Year A for commentary on this passage.

Holy Thursday/Year B

Maundy Thursday

1 Corinthians 11:23–26

Please see Holy Thursday/Year A, for commentary on this passage.

Good Friday/Year B

Hebrews 10–16, 25

Please see Good Friday/Year A (alt) for commentary on this passage.

or

Hebrews 4:14–16; 5:7–9

Please see Good Friday/Year A for commentary on this passage.

Holy Saturday/Year B

1 Peter 4:1–8

Please see Holy Saturday/Year A for commentary on this passage.

Easter Day/Year B

1 Corinthians 15:1–11

Throughout this letter, Paul calls Corinthians of high social standing to live in covenantal ways. Chapter 15 is the pièce de résistance as Paul dramatically images the resurrection body in order to persuade the elite (and others) to use their bodies appropriately *in the present* in order to have *a resurrection body* in the realm of God. In Jewish thinking the body *is* the person—a person does not simply *have* a body. People will perish (1:18) if they use their bodies noncovenantally for such things as foolish concern with status.

Some in the community probably shared the view of the socially advantaged who looked down on the body and may have doubted whether the future life would include an embodied self.[28] In 1 Corinthians 15, Paul justifies belief in the resurrection body and explains the nature of that body. This turn to the resurrection is not theoretical speculation but is intended to motivate ethical reflection and behavior.

In 15:1, the apostle connects the teaching about the resurrection with issues discussed previously in the letter. Where the NRSV has "Now I would remind you," the verb is *gnorizo*, which is related to the authentic *gnosis* or "knowledge" from Paul (1:5; 8:7; 14:6) in distinction from the mistaken knowledge of the elites (8:1; 8:10, 11). The "message" (15:2) is the true *logos* Paul preached (1:5, 18; 2:13; 4:19–20; 14:19, 36) and the Corinthians received, in contrast to the false *logos* of the elites (1:17; 2:1, 4; 14:9).

Paul now establishes that Christ was, in fact, raised. Scholars have long agreed that 15:3–4 is a pre-Pauline summary of the core message of the Jesus movement. Although this early confession says, "Christ died for our sins," the death of Jesus has no saving effect by itself but only as a part of the complex of death and resurrection. The phrase "in accordance with the scriptures" means that the sacred traditions of Israel provide the theological categories by which to interpret the Jesus event.

The notion of resurrection in apocalyptic literature assumes a body. However, resurrection is not simply resuscitation of a corpse; it is the transformation of the present decaying body into a material body different in nature and existing forever (Dan. 12:3; *1 En.* 39:7; 51:4; *2 Esd.* 7:97; *2 Bar.* 51:3; 1 Cor. 15:35–57).

In Judaism truth is established when two witnesses agree. In 15:5–7 Paul recounts appearances of the risen Christ to many witnesses. The Greek *ophthe*, "appeared," is a divine passive meaning that *God* caused Jesus to appear. To Paul "the twelve" are not a "new Israel," an expression that Paul never uses. The number indicates continuity between Israel and the Pauline mission to the Gentiles that is authorized by the Jewish leaders of the Jesus movement (Gal. 2:1–10). Peter and James affirmed Paul's work with others in Jerusalem (15:5, 7; Gal. 2:1–10). We have no information about the appearance to the five hundred other than 15:6. The point is that many reliable witnesses agree.

In verse 8 Paul echoes his earlier interpretation of the apostle as a person of low status in comparison to the way the powers of the present age reckon status by noting that Christ appeared *last* to him. Even then it was "as to one untimely born," that is, a premature birth (or perhaps even a miscarriage)—to one who is unfit to be an apostle because of having persecuted the church (15:8–9). However, just as the grace of God made lowly Israel a witness of the universal God to the more prominent nations of the world, so this grace made the low-status persecutor Paul into the apostle whose commission to preach to the Gentiles brought him to Corinth. There the Gentiles turned away from perishing because of their worship of idols and complicity with the false values of the present age and toward the gospel that leads to salvation (15:10–11). It would be tragic for the educated in Corinth to have made such a dramatic change and then to perish because they have inadequate wisdom and knowledge. To receive the eternal status (so to speak) of a resurrection body, the Corinthians need to pay attention to this apostle.

Second Sunday of Easter/Year B

1 John 1:1–2:2

Today's reading falls into three parts: the prologue (vv. 1–5), three "If we say" statements that John rejects (vv. 6–10), and a christological statement (2:1–2).

The prologue focuses on "the message we have heard from him and proclaim to you" (v. 5). Three times the text says, "We declare [this message]" (vv. 1, 2, 3). This message has been "heard" and "seen" (v. 1); it is words that have been heard and a "life [that] was revealed" (v. 2). Jesus Christ and his message are one, as Jesus and God the Father are one. Hence the message is "that God is light and in him there is no darkness at all" (v. 5). In Johannine theology Jesus makes God known: "fellowship . . . with the Father" is through "his Son Jesus Christ" (v. 3). And fellowship with Jesus Christ is through fellowship with one another: "so that you also may have fellowship with us" (v. 3).

Notice that "what was from the beginning" (v. 1) alludes to the eternal Logos of John 1:1: "In the beginning was the Word." Yet "what we have . . . touched with our hands" calls to mind the Logos incarnate in the Galilean Jesus and as the risen Christ present with the community in the Eucharist.

The message is "that God is light" (v. 5). In the Gospel of John, Jesus Christ is "the true light" (1:9), but in 1 John the message is that "God is light." There is no disjunction here. God created by saying, "Let there be light" (Gen. 1:3), and Psalm 27:1 claims, "The Lord is my light and my salvation." God gives the people Israel as a "light to the Gentiles" (Isa. 49:6). Light is a highly appropriate metaphor for God. Light reveals. To say that God "is" light is to say that revealing is what God does and that God gives God's self in self-disclosure. Hence, "God is love" (1 John 4:8).

Verses 6–10 deny three positions apparently held by those who "went out from us," who "did not belong to us; for if they had belonged to us, they would have remained with us" (1 John 2:19). The first rejected position claims to have "fellowship with him while" those making the claim walk "in darkness" (v. 6). "Walk" (*peripatein*) is a metaphor for how we live our lives. The claim to have fellowship with Christ is not in itself false. It becomes false, however, when those who make it walk out on the fellowship of the community; then they walk in darkness. To have fellowship (*koinonia*) with him is to keep his commandment to love one another (4:11) and vice versa.

First John also rejects the claim (v. 8) "that we have no sin." Unlike the first claim, this one is just plain false, and if we say it, we simply "deceive ourselves, and the truth is not in us." We are to "confess our sins" (v. 9), not deny them. God's grace enables us to be honest with ourselves; it frees us from self-deception. Denying our sin is tantamount to denying God's gracious word (v. 10). The third claim, "that we have not sinned" (v. 10), restates the second claim and is also rejected.

In 2:1 John addresses his community with a term of endearment, "my little children" (*teknia mou*), saying that he writes to them so that they "may not sin." He does not want them to take a casual attitude toward sin because it will, after all, be forgiven (1:9). So he gives them a negative commandment: Do not sin (the sense of the Greek *me hamartete*). He wants them to persist in avoiding it. Yet he reassures them that if they do sin, they have an "advocate with the Father, Jesus Christ the righteous" whose atonement is sufficient "for the sins of the whole world" (2:2). The reading ends on an all-inclusive note of universal grace.

Third Sunday of Easter/Year B

1 John 3:1–7

Please see All Saints/Year A for commentary on this passage.

Fourth Sunday of Easter/Year B

1 John 3:16–24

Verses 16–18 provide the first part of today's reading. In them 1 John begins by describing the grounds of our knowledge of love, that is, our knowledge that we are loved and that we ought to love. The passage begins, "We know love by this, that he laid down his life for us" (v. 16). The revelation of God in Christ is how we have come to know the love of God. John's stress is on God's gracious initiative. The moral consequent of grace follows immediately: "and we ought to lay down our lives for one another." That we love one another is, for John, a test of our knowledge of God's love for us; it is not a condition placed on God's freedom to love or the source and origin of God's love.

However, John is not implying that we rush out and get ourselves sacrificed. He turns instead and appropriately to a more mundane example and asks, "How does God's love abide in anyone who has the world's goods and sees a brother or sister in need and yet refuses help?" (v. 17; the Greek uses the expression "closes off his compassion from him.") Refusing help signals an absence of compassion or love, and a person who so refuses has not passed from death to life (3:14). "God's love" is an objective genitive that speaks of God's love for us. First John 4:11 says, "Beloved, since God loved us so much, we also ought to love one another." Failure to love the neighbor discloses a prior failure to recognize that God loves us (and the neighbor).

Verse 18 addresses the community as "little children," saying to it, "Let us love, not in words or speech, but in truth and action." The opposition between words and action is relative, not absolute. John is clear about how the language should be used and would not allow such a dichotomy. The point is one of emphasis; words count, but actions count more. Faith is words acted out in deeds, deeds interpreted by words.

In verses 19–22, 1 John reassures its readers of God's love for them: "By this we will know that we are from the truth and will reassure our hearts before him" (v. 19). This time, "by this" refers to our love for one another, which has just been discussed. Although our love for one another originates from God's gracious gift, it is a test as to whether we have received the gift by loving one another. Our hearts sometimes "condemn us," says John, reflecting the view that the sense of right and wrong is located in the heart. Our anxious hearts are put at ease by the reassurance as to who God is: "greater than our hearts, and he knows everything" (v. 20), which we assuredly do not. Verses 21–22 continue to reassure the distraught heart: God's grace calms our self-accusations and grants us boldly to come before God in prayer knowing that what we do "pleases him." We do not appease God by obeying his commandments; God graciously enables us to love one another and, so, to please God. (Words have some importance.)

Verses 23–24 make clear what is "[God's] commandment: that we should believe in the name of his Son Jesus Christ and love one another." The one commandment is actually two, like the great commandment, considered as two aspects of one comprehensive commandment. The "name" of the Son is actually the name of God, as Jesus' mission in John is to make God's name known: "I have made your name known to those whom you gave me from the world" (John 17:6). The passage ends on the Johannine theme of mutual abiding: by loving one another we abide in Christ and he in us "by the Spirit that he has given us" (v. 24). That Christ abides in us enables us to keep his commandments and abide in him and each other.

Fifth Sunday of Easter/Year B

1 John 4:7–21

First John presents a string of "tests" of faith, because those who had left the community had made contrary claims, denying, for example, that

Jesus is the Christ (2:22) and "that Jesus Christ has come in the flesh" (4:2). In one of his most important lines, John writes, "Do not believe every spirit, but test the spirits to see whether they are from God" (4:1). In 4:1–6 he develops a christological test: "Every spirit that confesses that Jesus Christ has come in the flesh is from God" (4:2). Today's reading presents three more.

Whether we love one another tests our claim to love God—the theme of verses 7–12. We are able to love one another because "love is from God" (v. 7); it is in us but not from us. God's grace enables our love for God and each other, and that we love shows that we know God. Verse 8 draws the negative corollary: "Whoever does not love does not know God, for God is love." John had earlier said that "God is light" (1:5); here he says that "God *is* love" (emphasis ours) meaning that it is God's very nature to love. It follows that to know God is to love. One thing this means is that we do not abandon the community as did those who "went out from us" (2:19). The same attitude is found in rabbinic Judaism: "Rabban Gamaliel would say: 'Do not walk out on the community.'"[29]

God sent God's "only Son into the world so that we might live through him" (v. 9). Love is the opposite of the death-dealing ways of "the world." Revelation must be appropriately received if it is actually to reveal; it becomes revelatory for us when we understand why God sent Jesus—that we love the neighbor and the stranger. Revelation is for the whole world, but the test of whether we have received it (not of whether it has been given) is that we love one another. John defines love in terms of who God is (v. 10): "In this is love, not that we loved God but that he loved us and sent his Son to be the atoning sacrifice for our sins." Love is both gift and claim—God's gift to us and God's claim on us. God frees us to love and loves us into being free. We who have been so amazingly loved, should love in response.

Verses 13–16a constitute a second test of whether our claims to know God are true: "By this we know that we abide in him and he in us, because he has given us of his Spirit" (v. 13). The gift of the Spirit is that of love or mutual abiding. We are empowered by the Spirit to confess Jesus Christ and "abide in God . . . and believe the love that God has for us" (vv. 15–16). God sent Jesus "as the Savior of the world" (v. 14). John's language of love often seems limited to the community members' love for each other and to neglect love of the neighbor and stranger. That is probably due to the pastoral crisis he faces; his deeper logic puts no limits on God's love. We should note as well that John's claim about Jesus being the Savior of the world at least implicitly denies the claim of numerous Roman emperors to be Savior of the world.

Verses 16b–21 present the last faith test: "Those who say 'I love God,' and hate their brothers or sisters are liars" (v. 20). "We cannot love God whom we cannot see unless we love those whom we can see" (v. 20) people's claims that need to be tested, as do all theological claims. God is love; those who love God love their neighbors. Confidence in God's love "casts out fear" (v. 18). John may have in mind fear of the apocalypse, but the point is broader—fear often prevents us from loving because loving makes us vulnerable. We refrain from love because we do not want to be hurt. Confidence in God's love removes all such fear and enables us to love.

Sixth Sunday of Easter/Year B

1 John 5:1–6

First John is concerned with three matters: believing, belonging, and behaving, that is, confessing that Jesus Christ has come in the flesh (4:2), loving one another (3:11), and keeping God's commandments (3:22). Today's reading focuses on believing and behaving.

Verses 1–3 deal with believing. John stresses that to believe "that Jesus is the Christ" is to love God and that to love God is to believe that Jesus is the Christ. In 4:7–21, he pointed out the contradiction involved in claiming to love God while hating one's brothers or sisters (4:20). In today's reading he makes obeying God's commandments a test of our love of the children of God: "By this we know that we love the children of God, when we love God and obey his commandments" (v. 2). "By this we know" means "this is how we test the claim" that we love God (or whatever claim is being tested). Whoever believes that Jesus is the Christ is a child of God ("has been born of God") and "everyone who loves the parent loves the child" (v. 1). The primary point made in verses 1–3 is that (1) proper faith, (2) loving one's brothers and sisters, and (3) obeying God's commandments are the tests that let us know who the children of God really are. Children do not convince their parents of their love for them by declaring it; they convince them by loving each other. Nor do we convince God of our love for God by declaring it. We do it by loving our brothers and sisters.

The two loves—love of God and love of God's children—are coincident. Neither one precedes or is the cause of the other. Simply put, to love God is to love God's children and to love God's children is to love God. Our love for both is a response that is empowered by God's gracious love of us.

First John refers to God's commandments in 5:3 in the plural. John mentions only two—the commandment to believe that Jesus is the Christ and the commandment to love God and one another. That there are only these two may be what he means by saying that God's commandments are "not burdensome" [*bareiai*, "heavy"] (v. 3). Commentators sometimes take this statement to be a deliberate contrast with the commandments of Judaism, citing the remark that Matt. 23:4 attributes to Jesus that the Pharisees place "heavy burdens" on people. The total absence of any concern with Jews and Judaism in 1 John should, however, militate against any such interpretation as should the knowledge that the Pharisees and rabbis stressed that God's commandments are light (as when Matt. 11:29–30 uses the words of Woman Wisdom from Sirach to make that very point).

First John's own reason that God's commandments are not heavy is that "whatever is born of God conquers [*nikan*] the world" (5:4). In the Johannine literature the "world" is a place of antagonism toward John's community. His "world" was a Roman world, a world built on conquest. But that is not the world that will finally conquer. First John ironically uses the word "victory" (*nike*), which is also the name for the Greek goddess of victory, for "the victory that conquers the world, our faith" (v. 4). Thus he seeks to reassure his community that it can overcome the troubles amid which it lives.

Those who believe that "Jesus is the Son of God" will be vindicated at the parousia of Jesus. He came "by water and blood" (v. 6), that is, incarnationally; he was baptized (water) and crucified (blood) and is testified to by the Spirit who is the truth. Here John unpacks a bit of what is involved in 5:1, believing that Jesus is the Christ.

Ascension of the Lord/Years A, B, and C

Ephesians 1:15–23

Please see Ascension of the Lord/Year A for commentary on this passage.

Seventh Sunday of Easter/Year B

1 John 5:9–13

In today's reading John continues to reassure his community that it truly knows God in Jesus Christ and that those who have left the community (2:19) and "deny the son" (2:23) definitely do not know of whom they speak when they speak of God.

Verse 9 lays down the premise of John's argument: "the testimony of God is greater" than human testimony. Preachers should look at Jesus' remarks in John 5:31–38: "Not that I accept such human testimony . . ." (v. 34), and "The Father who sent me has himself testified on my behalf" (v. 37).

Verse 10 makes two statements and presents us with a difficulty that must be handled with some care. The first is that "those who believe in the Son of God have the testimony in their hearts." The point here is that the witness to Jesus was not only made in the past, whether that was by John the Baptist, or at Jesus' baptism, or at any other time. Because it is "the Father who . . . has himself testified on my behalf" (John 5:37), two things follow: first, this is an ongoing testimony, not an act completed in the past; and second, God's testimony now is heard in the heart. We do not know it by sense experience: "No one has ever seen God" (1 John 4:12). Rather, God is known in the heart.

The second statement is that "those who do not believe in God have made him a liar by not believing in the testimony that God has given concerning his Son." First John earlier used the same language: "If we say that we have not sinned, we make him a liar, and his word is not in us" (1:10). Whoever claims to know God but does not keep his commandments "is a liar" (2:4). Whoever denies that Jesus is the Christ "is the liar" (2:22). Those who claim to love God but hate their brothers and sisters "are liars" (4:20).

John's polarizing name calling is directed against the opponents of the community and is intended to reassure those who stayed in the community that the truth is in them. Such name calling can have disastrous consequences, and in the history of the church it often has. The other side of the problem is that such religious claims often conceal lies as, for example, when Christian teachings about humanity teach the inferiority of women to men or when the doctrine of God's radically free grace has been denied in the church's drive to make itself the broker of this grace and joining the church a condition of receiving God's unconditional love. This is why 1 John's language requires us to handle it with care. This test should become the occasion not for continuing the name calling but for self-criticism: how do we make God a liar?

Verses 11–12 reiterate and develop verse 9: "This is the testimony": the witness is that God "gave us eternal life, and this life is in his Son." For John this is a tautology. God's life is eternal; Jesus reveals God's life to us; therefore Jesus gave us eternal life, and he is the medium through which we receive it. To have the Son is to have the Father and vice versa. Hence, "whoever does not have the Son of God does not have life" (v. 12). Again, John's polarizing rhetoric is directed against his opponents. Its downside is that it can lead Christians to forget that God transcends the church and to deny God the freedom to love whomever God pleases to love. To do that is also to lie.

Verse 13 wraps up the reading (and in a way the whole letter) with the author's statement of his purpose in writing: so that you may believe in Jesus and "know that you have eternal life." His purpose is to reassure the troubled; the underlying pastoral intent should also be the spirit of sermons on this passage.

Day of Pentecost/Year B

Romans 8:22–27

In Romans 8:14–30, Paul expresses hope for the redemption that is to be consummated with the return of Christ but for which we now "wait . . . with patience" (8:25). Paul's theology of hope is worked out in spite of the suffering of his community: we are "heirs of God and joint heirs with Christ—if, in fact, we suffer with him so that we may also be glorified with him" (8:17). Paul is no fan of overly spiritualized faith that would claim that all our problems are behind us. He is saying, "Not so fast. We have a long way to go, and in our present situation we are groaning with the creation."[30]

Then Paul discusses three "groanings": "the whole creation has been groaning" (v. 22); we groan (vv. 23–25); and the "Spirit intercedes with sighs [*stenagmois*, groans] too deep for words" (v. 26). Redemption in any complete sense is still ahead of us. We discussed verses 18–22 on Proper 11/Year A; here we begin with verse 23.

One might hazard the generalization that for the community of faith, the times when things are going well produce a literature of despair but that, conversely, the times when things are going badly produce a literature of hope. However widely that generalization pertains, for Paul, groaning—expressing suffering—is grounds for hope. We, says Paul, are in a paradoxical situation: on the one hand, we have "the first fruits of the Spirit"; on the other, we "groan inwardly while we wait for adoption, the redemption of our bodies" (v. 23). Our hunger for redemption, for becoming more fully the children and heirs of God (the "adoption" for which we wait), is set within the framework of the hunger of "the whole creation [which] has been groaning in labor pains until now" (v. 22). We are not and will not be redeemed until all creation has been redeemed; everything is so deeply related to everything else that until we are all redeemed none of us is finally redeemed. Our redemption is known by and witnessed to by the Spirit (v. 16). God knows that we are justified, and in our present suffering, our faith that that is so gives us hope.

In verses 24–25, Paul does not assure his readers of their redemption; he reassures them. Their suffering has led them to question their original assurance. Yet this very suffering should lead them to hope, says Paul, for "hope that is seen is not hope" (v. 24). Their adoption is not terribly apparent to them; they are to hope in what they "do not see" (v. 25). There is a time to afflict the comfortable and a time to comfort the afflicted. Here Paul comforts the afflicted. Pastors know well of many afflictions among their congregants and can use Paul's message to comfort them.

Paul does say, "In hope we *were* saved" (v. 24; emphasis ours). Then he goes into his short discussion of hope. The logic here seems to be that were we not saved, we could not hope. It is the "first fruits of the Spirit" that enable us to hope for the whole bounty of the fruits of the Spirit yet to be revealed to us. Hence, we are empowered to "wait for it with patience" (v. 25). We can trust the promise God made to us in Jesus.

Verses 26–27 discuss the "groaning" of the Spirit, a groaning "too deep for words." It is not transparently clear that this refers to glossolalia. Paul is discussing prayer—"we do not know how to pray as we ought." In verse 34 he says that Christ "intercedes for us" with God. In verses 26–27 the Spirit "intercedes for the saints." The Spirit helps our praying. That the Spirit (roughly interchangeable with God or Christ in Paul) "groans" indicates that God is affected by us as we are affected (and effected—created) by God. God's passions can become our prayers, and our prayers can become God's passions.

Trinity Sunday/Year B

Romans 8:12–17

Paul concluded 8:1–11 (see Proper 10/Year A) with an astounding claim— "the Spirit of God dwells in you" (8:9). The Spirit of God (*ruach YHWH* in the First Testament) dwells in the community as YHWH's dwelling was with Israel, in their midst (Exod. 25:8). This is the people Israel's way of talking of God incarnate—God present in the people. "Salvation is of the Jews," says Michael Wyschogrod, "because the flesh of Israel is the abode of the divine presence in the world. It is the carnal anchor that God has sunk into the soil of creation."[31] For Paul, God's Spirit dwells in these

Gentile believers in Jesus and this very Spirit enables them to "cry, 'Abba, Father'" (8:15)!

Verses 12–13 of today's reading are persuasive speech. Paul reminds his readers that they are no longer debtors "to the flesh," to a life under the tyranny of sin, but to the Spirit and should live "by the Spirit" morally and hence eternally. The choice between two ways of living, that of the Spirit of life or that of sin and death (8:2), is a choice between life and death. This choice recalls the choice offered by YHWH to Israel after YHWH had given Israel the torah: "Today I have set before you life and death, blessings and curses. Choose life so that you and your descendants may live" (Deut. 30:19).

Verses 14–16 shift the metaphor from the indwelling of the Spirit or Christ to being "children of God." Again, Paul's metaphor of God's children draws on a rich vein of faith in the history of Israel. The people Israel itself is repeatedly referred to collectively as God's "son" or "child" (Isa. 1:2–4; 30:9; Hos. 1:10; Deut. 14:1; 32:5–6; Exod. 4:22–23). A relationship of confidence, of nearness and mutual love, is shared by God and Israel. An intensification of this relationship is promised and hoped for in the literature of Second Temple Judaism and was particularly to be the case in the eschaton (e.g., Ezra 6:58; *1 En.* 62:11). For Paul the eschaton is quite near (Rom. 13:11), and Gentiles also share in this close relationship with God.

The Spirit that Gentile followers of Jesus now have is not one of "slavery" but of "adoption," *huiothesia* (v. 15). In 9:4 Paul will say of the people Israel, "to them belong[s] the adoption." In other words, they are (not they *were*) God's children, which here Paul says Gentiles are. Paul lays claim for Gentiles the status that Israel enjoys, while affirming that Israel continues to enjoy it. Among Gentiles, the Spirit that has adopted them ("us") bears "witness with our spirit that we are children of God" (v. 16) when we cry "Abba, Father." Paul uses this Aramaic expression, apparently assuming that Gentiles in Rome are familiar with it, perhaps as it was used in the worship of the community (Gal. 4:6–7; Mark 14:36). Aramaic Targums (translations of Scripture into Aramaic) on the Psalms and Genesis have David and Isaac using "Abba." Various Galilean "mighty men of deeds" spoke to God as "Abba."[32]

Verse 17 deals with two themes: (1) Gentile children of God are "heirs" of God's promises and hence also children of the promise to Abraham. (2) God's Spirit of adoption will see them through their present sufferings so that they may be glorified with Christ. Difficulties are around and ahead, but hope is sustained by the Spirit. Paul will speak further of suffering and weakness in 8:18–39.

Proper 4 [9]/Year B

2 Corinthians 4:5–12

Please see the Ninth Sunday after the Epiphany [9]/Year B for commentary on this passage.

Proper 5 [10]/Year B

2 Corinthians 4:13–5:1

Paul now shifts his efforts to motivate the Corinthians to disregard the teaching of the super apostles who visited Corinth (2 Cor. 11:5; 12:11). He does this by abandoning the image of his ministry as a clay jar holding the treasure of the true gospel (2 Cor. 4:7–12) and presenting instead the dazzling promise of the new age (2 Cor. 4:13–5:5). Paul explains the hope the congregation can anticipate—if they embrace his understanding of the gospel.

In 2 Corinthians 4:13a, he affirms that those who follow his gospel have the same "spirit of faith" (or, better, "spirit of being faithful") as that found in Scripture, and in 4:13b he quotes the Septuagintal Psalm 115:1/English 116:10 to support this idea: "I believed and so I spoke." (The numbering of some of the Psalms differs between the English and the Septuagint). What did the psalmist believe and speak? The psalmist continued to trust in God's faithfulness even in affliction (Sept. Ps. 114:1–9/Engl. 116:1–9). The psalmist spoke by testifying to God's faithfulness in carrying the psalmist through difficulties (Sept. 115:3–10/Engl. 116:12–19). Paul's perspective is continuous with Israel's views on such matters. Paul and the Gentile Corinthians who believe and speak are doing in their day what the psalmists did in their earlier days.

Though the notion of suffering does not occur in today's lection, Paul presupposes it from 3:7–12. God's faithfulness to Israel in past afflictions is the basis for believing that God will prove faithful to the Corinthians who, like Paul, suffer for the gospel. Jesus, too, suffered, but God raised him from the dead and promises to raise those who witness to God's renewal of the world through Jesus and bring them "into his presence," that is, into the age to come when Jesus returns (4:14). According to 4:15, the purpose of Paul's ministry ("everything is for your sake") is twofold: (1) it allows the Gentile Corinthians to experience grace (*charis*, God's covenantal faithfulness), and (2) it increases thanksgiving to God. Though the false apostles provide experiences of glory through visions, their "glory" pales next to the eschatological presence of Jesus.

Paul then intensifies the readers' sense of the glory that is to come by contrasting present conditions with those that will prevail in the divine realm. Although Christians may be tempted to think of 4:16–5:4 as presenting a dualism in which the material body is inferior to the nonmaterial self, a more careful reading reveals that the dualism here is between the state of the embodied self in two ages, as in 1 Corinthians 15:35–57. Paul describes various negative characteristics of life that were common in first-century philosophical and religious literature: the self is wasting away, is afflicted, is temporary, is like a tent that can be destroyed, and is a time of groaning, nakedness, and morality. Several of these descriptors depict life in the painful tribulation right before the apocalypse.

By contrast, God is already at work among those who accept Paul's gospel, renewing them and preparing them for eternal "glory beyond all measure." God changes the body from an earthly tent into a resurrection body, here described as a "building from God, a house not made with hands, eternal in the heavens," a heavenly dwelling in which people are not naked but are "further clothed."

Paul brings this appeal to a theocentric climax. The God of Israel has prepared this eschatological world and has given the Spirit as a guarantee (5:5). In the background is a subtle criticism of the theology of the super apostles: ecstatic experiences of the Spirit are not an end but only assure the believer of the world to come. Those who wish to enter that world need to be faithful through tribulation in the same way as Paul, who, in turn, is simply being faithful in the tradition of Israel.

Proper 6 [11]/Year B

2 Corinthians 5:6–10, (11–13), 14–17

In the lesson discussed in Proper 5 [11]/Year B, Paul pressed language to its limits to draw the Corinthians to his vision of the coming eschatological world and away from the reduced vision of God's purposes advocated by the super apostles of 11:5 and 12:11. In today's reading, Paul explains how the hope for a resurrection body in the future world (4:16–5:5) energizes ministry in the present, even in the teeth of conflict and suffering.

The hope of living in the "house not made with hands, eternal in the heavens" (5:1), gives Paul confidence (*tharreo* = not just confidence but, even more, courage) for witnessing today (5:6a). This courage is operative "even though we know that while we are at home in the body we are away from the Lord" (5:6b). A caution that we uttered in connection with last week's reading applies to this part of the text for today. While it might seem convenient to take Paul's words as a body/spirit or material/nonmaterial dualism, the stronger dualism underlying today's lesson is between the two ages. Paul is currently at home in the body that is afflicted in the present age, and he is awaiting being in the presence of Jesus in the eschatological divine realm.

The difficult circumstances of the present mean that "we walk by faith and not by sight" (5:7). Jewish literature often employs the term "walk" (*peripateo*) to speak figuratively of one's conduct, especially of being faithful to God and manifesting covenantal values (Gen. 17:1; Deut. 10:12; Ps. 15:2). "Faith" (*pistos*) here, as is usual in Paul and in Jewish tradition, refers more to living faithfully in the covenantal ways of God than to the struggle to believe intellectual assertions about God. "Sight" (*eidos*) refers to what can be visually seen. Thus Paul again polemicizes gently against the super apostles. They urge the Corinthians to follow tangible (seeable) visions received in ecstatic experience whereas Paul urges the community to walk faithfully, in the Jewish way, toward an age whose glory is incomprehensible but not yet fully visible.

Paul is human, of course (5:8). The apostle would prefer for this present broken age to pass away, and the afflictions of the body with it ("we would rather be away from the body and at home with the Lord"). Nevertheless, he continues to live with confidence and courage, even in the chaos and suffering of the apostolic life. Whether in the chaotic present or the eschatological future ("whether we are at home or away"), Paul's goal is to "please" God. To please (*euarestos*) God is not just to make God happy but to walk or live in the way God wants—in covenantal relationship with God and the community (Gen. 5:22; Wis. 4:10; Sir. 44:16). Pleasing God often has an apocalyptic resonance (*T. Dan* 1:3; *T. Levi* 1:9; *T. Iss.* 4:1).

The latter association is specified in 5:10. Paul presumes the apocalyptic scenario in which God sends Jesus from heaven to invade the current evil world, destroy evil, raise everyone from the dead, and judge them. Each then "receives recompense" for what she or he has done "in the body," that is, in the present age. According to Paul, *all* (including those who follow Paul's gospel) will be judged according to whether they have done good (*agathos*) or evil (*phaulos*). Both of these terms have social dimensions: the good builds up covenantal community while the evil fractures it and creates injustice (2 Esd. 3:22; 8:26; 3 Macc. 3:6, 22, 26; 4 Macc. 2:23;

Let Aris 142; *Sib. Or.* 3:362). Paul's purpose, of course, is to bring the Corinthians face to face with the consequences of their not repudiating the spirituality of the super apostles. When standing before the cosmic judge, one wants to follow Paul in doing good.

Proper 7 [12]/Year B

2 Corinthians 6:1–13

Please see Ash Wednesday/Year A for commentary on this passage.

Proper 8 [13]/Year B

2 Corinthians 8:7–15

Many scholars think that 2 Corinthians 8 and 9 have been taken from another letter and inserted here in 2 Corinthians. Whatever the history of this correspondence, Paul seeks here to prompt the Corinthians to participate generously in an offering for the economically impoverished congregation in Jerusalem. He had collected a generous gift in Macedonia and is soon to pass through Corinth to receive their gift.

Underlying Paul's appeal are three values that derive from Judaism and from his experience in the church: First, responsibility for the poor is one of the core covenantal values of Judaism (Exod. 23:11; Deut. 15:11; Isa. 58:11). Second, the church is a partnership (*koinonia*; 2 Cor. 6:14; 8:4; 9:13; 13:13; 1 Cor. 1:9). Although the English versions typically render *koinonia* as "sharing" or "fellowship," in the Hellenistic age the term often designated a partnership in which multiple parties came together to pursue a common good. In the *koinonia* each party contributed something essential. According to Galatians 2:9, the Jerusalem congregation is in partnership with the Pauline congregations in that the Jerusalem congregation relates to the Jewish orb while Paul's congregations attend to the Gentile mission. And third, several Jewish thinkers anticipated the day when the Gentiles would bring offerings to Jerusalem (e.g., Isa. 60:4–16; 61:4–5). The community at Corinth is largely a Gentile group. By giving to the offering, the congregation expresses its continuity with Judaism and embodies a Jewish value; it reaffirms its part in the partnership with the Jerusalem congregation and Paul by contributing funds that are essential to the Jerusalem community; and it witnesses to the eschatological character of the time by sending its wealth to Jerusalem.

Paul begins the discussion of the offering by calling it a manifestation of grace (*charis*), that is, a part of covenantal faithfulness (2 Cor. 8:2). Unfortunately, the NRSV lessens the meaning of *charis* in this context, translating it as "generosity" rather than "grace" (2 Cor. 8:1, 4, 6–7, 9, 16, 19). At any rate, Paul emphasizes that, despite "a severe ordeal of affliction" and "their extreme poverty," the Macedonian believers have given generously (8:1–6), wanting to do their part in the *koinonia* (8:4).

In 8:7 Paul begins the appeal to the Corinthians by reminding them of the spiritual gifts that are important in the community, most of which were prominent in 1 Corinthians—faith (*pistos* = better "faithfulness"), speech (*logos*), knowledge (*gnosis*), eagerness (*spoude*—Rom. 12:8; 2 Cor. 8:11), and love (*agape*). By implication, generosity is a similar spiritual gift that the Corinthians can now manifest. Paul does not command the congregation to give but uses this occasion to "prove" or demonstrate (by testing, *dokimazo*), the depth of the Corinthian *agape* (8:8).

Jesus Christ is the definition of generosity/grace (v. 9). For (using terms from the economic world figuratively) he left the wealth of preexistence in heaven and became poor (entered into the sin-fractured world and suffered death) to facilitate the apocalypse so that the Corinthians and others could be rich (share in the divine realm). Paul advises the Corinthians now to do something similar by living out of the power bestowed upon them by the risen Jesus and giving generously (v. 10). They will bring their actions into line with their eagerness (and thus manifest integrity) if they finish collecting the offering they had begun (v. 11).

In 8:12–15, the apostle implicitly draws on the notion of partnership. The Corinthians have greater financial resources than the Macedonians and, in the interest of a "fair balance," are expected to give more. However, the Macedonian (and Jerusalem) *needs* are a contribution to the *koinonia* with the Corinthians. For the need gives the Corinthians an opportunity to express their commitment to the *koinonia*.

Paul's point becomes clear when he cites Exodus 16:18: the hunger of the people in the wilderness gave God the opportunity to demonstrate the reliability of providence by providing abundantly for all (2 Cor. 8:15). Through the need in Macedonia and Jerusalem, the Corinthians can experience God's grace at work as the Corinthians contribute to the offering.

Proper 9 [14]/Year B

2 Corinthians 12:2–10

In 2 Corinthians 10–12, Paul gives his fullest interpretation of the false apostles who caused a breakdown in his relationship with the congregation at Corinth: they, foolishly, compare themselves with one another (2 Cor.

10:12). They came from outside of Corinth (11:4) and interpret Jesus differently from Paul (11:4–5). They received money but became a financial burden (11:7–12). Although of Jewish origin (11:22–23a), there is no evidence they are from Jerusalem, or that they persuade Gentiles to adopt Jewish practices. Paul objects not to their Jewishness but to the degree to which their religious vision is not faithful to the deepest insights of Judaism. Their central religious experiences are ecstatic visions (12:1–4) and dramatic signs such as miracles (12:12). Like many religious figures in the Hellenistic world, they likely tried to impress people around them with their dramatic style. The reading assigned for today is an integral part of Paul's defense of his ministry that is intended to reclaim his warm relationship with the Corinthians.

In 12:1–4, the apostle uses language reminiscent of widespread practices in first-century Judaism. He does this to establish common ground with the super apostles and their followers by showing that, like them, he has had visions and revelations. In 12:2–4 Paul speaks of himself in the third person ("I know a person in Christ"), perhaps recalling a rabbinic way of speaking of "this man" instead of "I." Paul reports that fourteen years previously, he was "caught up to the third heaven," "to paradise" (12:2, 4). The specific mention of fourteen years is not significant. The notion of the "third heaven" and "paradise" derives from widespread perceptions in Judaism that the heavenly world was divided into different areas and that God could give people visions of them. Jewish sources contain different nuances regarding the number (three? seven?) and relationship (different spheres on the same plane? hierarchically ordered?) of these spheres (e.g., 2 Esd. 4:7–8; *1 En.* 39:3–4; 52:1; 60:7–8; *T. Levi* 13:1). For the preacher's purpose, it is enough to note that Paul reports similar heavenly journeys (as a seer) and similar experiences and credentials as the super apostles.

However, in 2 Corinthians 12:5–10, Paul rejects the criticisms made by the super apostles and writes that the basis for religious life is awareness of God's sustaining grace—not ephemeral visions. Indeed, Paul boasts not over his impressive visionary experience but over his own weakness, for it is in weakness that God's power is truly revealed and proven trustworthy (12:5). This is true "even considering the exceptional character of the revelations" (12:7a).

The apostle believes that to keep him "from being too elated," that is, too caught up in ecstasy (and unfocused on the world), God gave him "a thorn in the flesh." Although preachers have speculated about what this difficulty might be, Paul offers no specific information, simply making readers aware that it is part and parcel of life in the broken and evil present age, for it came from "a messenger of Satan" (12:7b).

Three times Paul asked God to take away this thorn but was turned away with the message "My grace is sufficient for you, for power is made perfect in weakness." As we have frequently pointed out, grace (*charis*) resonates with God's covenantal faithfulness as made known in Israel and confirmed through Jesus Christ. The verb translated "made perfect" (*teleioo*) evokes the idea of reaching its purpose: God's power achieves it purpose when it is manifest through circumstances that people would ordinarily interpret as weak. For Paul the death (weakness) and resurrection (sign of power) of Jesus is such a demonstration. Further, the goal of God's power is to end the present age (with its agents of death) and manifest the divine realm. Prior to the apocalypse the faithful will suffer, but in this weakened state they have an opportunity to witness to their trust that God is coming with the new world. That is why Paul "boasts all the more gladly" not only of the thorn in the flesh but also of all "my weaknesses," for they provide an opportunity "to show that the power of Christ [agent of the coming age] dwells in me." This power can also dwell in the Corinthians if they embrace it after the fashion of Paul and not the super apostles.

Proper 10 [15]/Year B

Ephesians 1:3–14

Please see the second Sunday after Christmas Day/Year A for commentary on this passage.

Proper 11 [16]/Year B

Ephesians 2:11–22

Today's reading takes up, for a later generation, the topic discussed in Romans 9–11: how Gentile Jesus followers should understand their relation to Jews. Paul urged Gentiles not to "boast" over Israel but to remember that "it is not you that support the root, but the root that supports you" (Rom. 11:18). Apparently, what Paul warned Gentiles against has occurred in Asia Minor; so Ephesians reminds Gentile believers that they are "no longer strangers and aliens, but . . . citizens with the saints and also members of the household of God" (2:19). After two millennia of the "teaching of contempt" for Jews and Judaism, this reminder is more than ever in order today.

Verses 11–12 call readers to "remember that at one time you Gentiles by birth . . . were at that time without Christ, being aliens from the commonwealth of Israel, and strangers to the covenants of promise, having no hope and without God in the world." Ephesians addresses Gentiles, although the community was probably a mix of Gentiles and Jews. The concern of 2:11–22 is what salvation means for social relations between Jews and Gentiles. Verses 11–12 describe Gentile existence, prior to reconciliation with God and Israel, in the gloomiest of terms: you were aliens from Israel, strangers to God's promises expressed in the covenants, without hope and without God (*atheoi*). "Aliens" is the opposite of "citizens" (v. 19). Through Christ, however, God has reconciled Jew and Gentile: "You who once were far off have been brought near" (v. 13). "Peace, peace, to the far and the near, says the Lord; and I will heal them" (Isa. 57:19).

Verses 14–18 describe what God has done in Christ. First, "he is our peace" (*eirene*). He has "broken down the dividing wall, that is, the hostility between us." Much ink has been spilled trying to identify this wall. Was it the wall between the Gentile area of the Jerusalem temple and the area to which only Jews were admitted? This effort is odd in light of Ephesians's straightforward identification of the wall: "the hostility between us." Its plain sense is that the wall is a metaphor for intergroup animosity. If Christ is indeed our peace, all such walls need to be destroyed. Second, Christ has "abolished the law" (obviously not in all senses, unless we are now free to commit murder and idolatry) to "create one new humanity in place of the two, thus making peace." Our war-torn world needs more than ever to hear that he "proclaimed peace" to all of us, granting all "access in one Spirit to the Father."

We have this peace "in one body" (v. 16). "Body" is one of Ephesians's two metaphors for the church; the other is "building" (v. 20). The concern is for Jews and Gentiles in the church; Paul's concern with Gentile attitudes toward Jews not in the church seems to have disappeared. In this sense, Ephesians cuts short its own argument in 2:11–14. A contemporary discussion responsive to the post-Shoah (Holocaust) teachings of the churches will want to keep in mind Paul's wider sensibility.

Verses 19–22 portray the new reality that Christ created. We Gentiles are "no longer strangers and aliens," but . . . cocitizens (*sympolitai*) and also members of the household of God. An excellent antidote to "boasting" over Israel is to remember that we are the "also-members," not the only members, of God's family. The "saints" (v. 19) are *all* members of the household. The new reality is built on the "foundations" of the apostles and prophets with Christ as the "cornerstone" and the community as the "temple." Many a group in first-century Judaism, for example, Qumran, regarded itself as the true "temple." "You also," says Ephesians, "are built together as a dwelling place for God." Note that Ephesians speaks of "a" dwelling space, not "the" dwelling place. We are not the only such dwelling place, but we are "also" God's dwelling place.

Proper 12 [17]/Year B

Ephesians 3:14–21

This passage is the second half of a chapter on Paul's authority (3:1–12 is discussed on Epiphany of the Lord/Years A, B, and C). Ephesians 3:14–21 is a prayer of Paul's on behalf of the community to which he is writing. Paul, an authority figure of an earlier generation for Ephesians, is the one to whom "the mystery" unknown to earlier generations was revealed (3:3–5). This respected teacher bows down "before the Father" (v. 14). Many find the "father" metaphor for God problematic, but Paul used it to distinguish the God of Israel from the "gods many and lords many" (1 Cor. 8:5) of first-century polytheism. In keeping with the universal thrust of Ephesians and its insistence that God through Christ made "one new humanity" of Jews and Gentiles, the text makes it clear that "every family on earth takes its name" (v. 15) from God the Father. There is a play on words in the Greek: *pater* is the word for "father" and *patria* the word for family; every family takes its name from God.

Paul petitions God three times in his prayer. First, he asks that God "may grant that you may be strengthened in your inner being with power through his Spirit" (v. 16). The role of the Spirit is to strengthen. In Latin the Spirit is often called the "Comforter," a term deriving from *cum*, meaning "with," and *fortis*, meaning "strength." God is asked to do this "according to the riches of his glory." If the community being addressed needs to be strengthened for some particular reason, that reason is not made clear; no specific problems of the community are cited in the letter. Nevertheless, communities of faith are persistently in need of strength against various kinds of adversity. This petition also asks "that Christ may dwell in your hearts through faith, as you are being rooted and grounded in love" (v. 17). The Spirit is to be understood as the indwelling of Christ in the heart. "Spirit" is a notoriously vague word and is always accompanied by the preposition "of"; hence, people have spoken of "spirit of teamwork"; there is the "spirit of Sigma Chi"; and the Nazis spoke of the "spirit of the Leader." Ephesians makes clear that it speaks of the "Spirit of

Christ" as the Scriptures of Israel spoke of the *ruach YHWH*, the "spirit of the Lord." The "heart" is to be strengthened; we are to "take heart" or to have a heart for love—rooted and grounded in love, one of Ephesians's frequent themes.

The second petition asks that the community "may have the power to comprehend . . . what is the breadth and length and height and depth, and to know the love of Christ" (v. 18). Scholars frequently scratch their heads over the meaning of "breadth and length and height and depth." Many groups in the ancient world used this expression, but in a multiplicity of ways. We suggest that it refers to the vast extent of God's grace and love, which Ephesians has insisted throughout are all-embracing and extend even above the rulers and authorities in "the heavenly places." It is, after all, that very love which this petition asks that we may "comprehend" and "know." Ephesians has so far prayed that we may love God and each other with "all our strength" and "all our mind" (Mark 12:30; Luke 10:27).

The third request (v. 19b) is "that you may be filled with all the fullness (*pleroma*) of God." "May be filled" is expressed in the divine passive; God is the one who fills us with all God's fullness. Earlier, 1:23 spoke of the church as Christ's "body, the fullness of him who fills all in all." Colossians, which is closely related to Ephesians, writes of Christ, "In him all the fullness of God was pleased to dwell" (1:19). Hence, 3:19 most likely repeats and interprets the request that Christ "may dwell in your hearts" (3:17). The reading ends with a doxology of praise and glory to God (vv. 20–21).

Proper 13 [18]/Year B

Ephesians 4:1–16

Today's reading begins the ethical part of Ephesians; it follows the gospel of God's gracious inclusion of Gentiles that was the earlier topic of this letter. The structure of Ephesians is the typical biblical and Pauline structure in which the indicative of what God has done for us precedes the imperative of what we should, therefore, do.

In verses 1–3 Ephesians "begs" (*parakalo*) its readers "to lead a life worthy of the calling to which you have been called." This language is characteristic of Israelite faith—"lead a life" translates *peripateo*, "walk." Contrary to traditional interpretations, Israel did not justify itself by keeping the law. God had taken care of that quite nicely in the election. Rather, the commandments (*mitzvoth*) were given to Israel as guides for walking a way (*torah*) of life and blessing (well-being). In chapters 4–6 Ephesians provides its own such commandments, after clearly insisting that the Gentiles were "righteoused" as a matter of God's mercy: "By grace you have been saved through faith" (2:8). We have been "called" by God—chosen in and for blessing (1:3–14). For blessing to be actualized, however, we must act appropriately to our calling.

Certain character traits are crucial to communal well-being: humility, gentleness, patience, bearing with each other in love. Being humble does not mean being servile, as in the Roman/Hellenistic world. It means that in the church, the cutthroat spirit of competition has no place. We should acknowledge each other's gifts (vv. 7, 11–13) and not compete with each other for pride of place: "Whoever wishes to be first among you must be slave of all" (Mark 10:44; cf. Matt. 20:27). "Bearing with one another" (v. 2) means that status differences must be set aside. Being "eager" (*dazontes*) "to maintain the unity of the Spirit in the bond of peace" (v. 3) means being active about it, not merely reactive. Verses 4–6 are a graceful celebration or confession of the unity of the church.

Verses 7–16 have to do with grace and gifts—who gives them and their purpose: "Each of us was given grace according to the measure [*metron*] of Christ's gift" (v. 7). Paul had spoken of "measures" of faith and gifts (Rom. 12:3–8). But whereas Paul thought of each member as having a distinct gift, Ephesians thinks of gifts allotted by Christ differently: "The gifts he gave were that some would be apostles, some prophets, some evangelists, some pastors and teachers" (v. 11). The intervening remarks about Christ's ascending and descending (vv. 8–10) are pertinent in this way: Moses had ascended and descended Sinai to give gifts—the *mitzvoth* —to Israel; his ascent was interpreted as into "heaven" (*Avot R. Nat.*, 2.2). So Christ's "descending" into incarnation brings gifts to humanity. "Into the lower parts of the earth" likely is not a reference to Hades; nowhere else does Ephesians refer to hell. Most likely it has to do with his descent even unto crucifixion (see Phil. 2:10).

Christ "gave" gifts to the church "to equip the saints for the work of ministry, for building up the body of Christ" (vv. 11–12). All the gifts and qualities of character aim at building up the community of faithful people. The purpose of "pastors and teachers" is "to equip the saints for the work of ministry." Believers need to be brought to "unity of the faith," to "knowledge of the Son of God, to maturity."

Of all the functions of ministry, teaching too often receives short shrift in the churches. But it is teaching that will "equip the saints" so that they are no longer "children, blown about by every wind of doctrine" (v. 14).

If the community is to be built up, we may not deceive one another (v. 14), but must "speak the truth in love" to one another. Only so can the community grow "in building itself up in love" (v. 16).

Proper 14 [19]/Year B

Ephesians 4:25–5:2

Today's reading picks up where last week's ended, admonishing the community to speak the truth in love because we are members of Christ's body (4:15–16). The lectionary drops 4:17 in which Ephesians beseeches Gentiles "no longer [to] live as the Gentiles live, in the futility of their mind." The Protestant tradition has unfortunately tended to regard the ethical sections of the epistles as unimportant. However, we should note the hint in 4:17 that the early church grew as it did among Gentiles because it provided sound moral guidance amid the moral chaos of the Roman/Hellenistic world. We have much to learn from the ethical reflections of the early church, as it did from Judaism.[33]

The passage is bookended by discussion of how followers of Jesus are to "walk" (*peripateo*): "no longer . . . in the futility of their minds" (v. 17) but "in love" (5:2). Walking in love and walking intelligently go together. Verses 25–29 delineate the difference between these two "ways" by urging upon the community five virtues, each of which is contrasted to a particular vice. "Putting away falsehood, let us speak the truth to our neighbors" (v. 25). Says Zechariah, "Speak the truth to one another, render in your gates judgments that are true and make for peace" (8:16). We do not lie, says Ephesians, because "we are members of one another." We speak the truth kindly, in love, for the same reason. The reason is important. We cannot build a genuine community on a tissue of lies.

Verse 26 says, "Be angry but do not sin; do not let the sun go down on your anger." Like the Sermon on the Mount (Matt. 5:22), Ephesians concedes that people do feel anger but counsels us not to act in anger. We can express anger constructively. And we should not carry it over, even to the next day. Carrying a grudge for the rest of life, never forgetting a slight, prevents the building up of a community of love. Doing so makes "room for the devil" (*diabolos*); a room is a "dwelling," and the community is supposed to be the dwelling of Christ or the Spirit, not the demonic, which always destroys community.

Verse 28 admonishes, "Thieves must give up stealing; rather let them . . . work honestly . . . so as to have something to share with the needy."

Again, the reason is communal—to be able to share with "the least of these" (Matt. 25:45). Paul, the authority figure of Ephesians, worked with his hands as a tent maker (Acts 18:3) and urged his followers to contribute to the poor (Rom. 12:13; 2 Cor. 9:6–12).

Verse 29 says, "Let no evil talk [*logos sapros*, foul language] come out of your mouths, but only what is useful for building up." Talking is one of the most important things that we do. How we talk is a matter of moral responsibility; how we talk about women, Jews, and racial and ethnic minorities all have grave consequences. Language can both reflect and reinforce prejudices that have become ingrained in unjust practices. Our speech can either serve to enhance community or destroy it; our talk should contribute constructively to the common life.

Finally, verse 30 advises, "And do not grieve [*lypeo*] the Holy Spirit." Our behavior and talk can "pain" God, the holy One who lives in the midst of the people, the Christ whose body we rend apart with "bitterness and wrath and anger and wrangling and slander" (v. 32). Why not, indeed, "be kind to one another, tenderhearted, forgiving one another as God in Christ has forgiven you" (v. 32)? "Live in love, as Christ loved us" (5:2).

Proper 15 [20]/Year B

Ephesians 5:15–20

Today's reading continues Ephesians's reflections on how followers of Jesus are to live graceful lives, lives that reflect the grace by which they have been called and claimed by God through Jesus Christ. Earlier, Ephesians had insisted that we are saved by grace through God's faithfulness (2:5). Having been transformed by grace, however, we are to live as the people we are—those who now walk in the light instead of in the darkness of our former ways. Ephesians 2:11–22 spelled out clearly the then/now contrast in the lives of the Gentiles (2:11) to whom it was addressed.

Verse 15 says, "Be careful [*blepo*] then how you live [*peripateo*, walk], not as unwise people but as wise [*sophoi*]." *Blepo* means "look, pay attention." We are to live attentively—being aware of the impact of our behavior on others, paying attention to the needs of the neighbor and of "the least of these" and being aware of the context in which we now live and which is the framework for dealing with problems that we cannot responsibly avoid. Paying attention is the heart of spirituality—as, for example, in paying attention to a biblical text for what it actually says instead of reading it as if we already know.

We are to pay attention to how we "walk," an inherited biblical way of talking about how we live life and of the Scriptures as showing us the "path of life" (Ps. 16:11). Ephesians takes over this Israelite heritage and exercises its responsibility to its readers by suggesting to them how followers of Jesus should walk the way of life and blessing instead of the way of death and destruction walked by those who live "in darkness" rather than in the "light." If we walk according to the instructions of Scripture we will walk "as wise" people. Wisdom here is practical wisdom, wisdom for living a useful life rather than one wasted in self-centeredness and self-indulgence or mere triviality and boredom.

Verse 16 says we should make "the most of the time [*kairos*], because the days are evil." In Paul, *kairos* is used to speak of the shortness of time between now and the return of Christ with the kingdom or rule of God. Ephesians has little sense of the imminent return of Jesus, having said instead that we are already seated with Christ in heaven (2:6), as if hope for the "second coming" of Christ is fading from significance by its time. Hence, "making the most of the time" in Ephesians means something like seize the day, make the most of the opportunity to do "what is pleasing to the Lord" (5:10) and to "expose," bring to light, "the unfruitful works of darkness" (5:11). Whatever our views of eschatology, we have one short life to live; we can make it a useful life one day at a time by seizing the opportunity to do so. *Opportunitas* is the Latin equivalent of *kairos*.

"So do not be foolish, but understand what the will of the Lord is" (v. 17). Foolishness is the opposite of wisdom. "Do not get drunk with wine, for that is debauchery; but be filled with the Spirit" (v. 18). The Jewish tradition had a healthy attitude toward wine, praising God for bringing it forth from the earth "to gladden the human heart" (Ps. 104:15). Still, it cautioned against drunkenness and associated it with licentiousness (*asotia*). Local religions such as the cult of Dionysius worked followers into wine-induced excitement, and there was every risk that recently converted Gentiles could confuse the working of the Spirit in the church with Dionysian ecstasy.

Verses 19–20 treat worship as formative of the life of Jesus' followers. It shapes our character as much as do moral instructions; the two are hardly incompatible. Behavior during worship shapes behavior outside of worship.

Proper 16 [21]/Year B

Ephesians 6:10–20

There is a sense of foreboding in this reading, of threat from "the cosmic powers of this present darkness" (v. 12). The church lived in an anxious time. Because the church and the world have seldom not lived in fear-inducing times, today's reading is ever pertinent. It forces us to ask the question, How shall we deal with such threats in our time? And it helps us to answer that question in a way too seldom considered.

Scholars widely agree that Ephesians perceived the source of the threat to the community as entirely spiritual and not animosity from this-worldly agents. They point to the comment that "our struggle is not against enemies of blood and flesh, but against the rulers, against the . . . spiritual forces of evil in the heavenly places" (v. 12). However, matters may have been more complicated than that. In Ephesus a new city center had been built to the cult of the emperor (including the then-ruling emperor). A temple to Augustus lay at the heart of this center, added to an older temple to Artemis, a virgin goddess of the hunt. Statues and temples to Tiberius and Domitian were later included in this city center.[34] The imperial cult affirmed that emperors, once they died, ascended to join the other gods in heaven. Clearly these "forces of evil" were not merely spiritual. These "rulers . . . in the heavenly places" had earthly counterparts.

Our passage encourages the Ephesians to "put on the whole armor of God" (v. 11). This "armor" is metaphorical; the real armor of the community is spelled out in verses 14–20: truth, righteousness, proclamation of the gospel of peace, faith, confidence of salvation, the Spirit, and prayer. The appropriate way to fight against the demonic forces of evil is to preach the gospel of peace. We should not misuse the armor metaphors by encouraging militarism among Christians. The purpose of the armor is not to enable the Ephesians to be aggressive. It is to empower them to "stand against the wiles of the devil" (v. 11). Preaching the gospel, being righteous, having faith, working for peace, and praying for ourselves and our neighbors are our best defense.

Metaphorical armor imagery is hardly unexpected in Ephesians's time; the Roman army was one of the major tools of Roman rule in conquered provinces, of which Ephesus was one. In our passage the "armor" metaphor is elaborately articulated. Twice readers are told to put on the "whole armor" (*panoplia*, vv. 11, 13). This includes the "breastplate," a belt, proper shoes for battle, a shield, a helmet, and a sword. Familiarity with how Roman soldiers were fitted out for battle is assumed.

What is striking about our passage is the difference between the armor of a Roman soldier and that of the church. We can read Ephesians as a parody of militarism. Imagine a people, living in fearful times, willing to take seriously the suggestion that they arm themselves with truth, righteousness, the gospel of peace, faith, salvation, the Spirit, and prayer. Throughout its ethical section, Ephesians has been urging its readers to "put away your former way of life" (4:22), to "expose" the unfruitful works of darkness (5:11), and "no longer [to] live as the Gentiles live" (4:17). In this parody of Caesar's army and this recommendation as to how they should defend themselves against the forces of destruction, Ephesians makes its contrast perfectly clear.

Preachers have here an ever-pertinent passage. In times of trouble, all of us are too ready to resort to bombing and maiming. Why not preach the gospel?

Proper 17 [22]/Year B

James 1:17–27

James is addressed to "the twelve tribes in the Dispersion" (v. 1), indicating that it is sent to Jewish followers of Jesus throughout the Roman Empire. As Jesus' ministry, according to Matthew, was limited to the people Israel (Matt. 10:5–6; 15:24), James's was directed to Israelite followers of Jesus. The twelve tribes symbolism shows James's eschatology: "Be patient, therefore, beloved, until the coming of the Lord" (5:7).

"Every generous act of giving, with every perfect gift, is from above, coming down from the Father of lights" (v. 17). James has been characterized as "works-righteous," a view that this verse refutes. Our good acts of giving to "orphans and widows in their distress" (v. 27) are gifts from God. That God is "the Father of lights" stems from God's creation of the sun, moon, and stars (Gen. 1:14–18; Ps. 136:7). That in God there is no "shadow due to change" (v. 17) testifies to God's faithfulness.

"In fulfillment of his own purpose he gave us birth by the word of truth, so that we would become a kind of first fruits of his creatures" (v. 18). God's giving us "birth" is a female image of God. That we are the "first fruits" reminds us of Paul's claim that Christ was "the first fruits of those who have died" (1 Cor. 15:20).

Verses 19 and 20 deal with anger: "Let everyone be quick to listen, slow to speak, slow to anger." This is straight out of the wisdom tradition of Israel: "Be quick to hear, but deliberate in answering" (Sir. 5:11). Proverbs 29:20 says that those who are "hasty in speech" are foolish. Anger is condemned as well: "Unjust anger cannot be justified, for anger tips the scale to one's ruin" (Sir. 1:22). "Anger does not produce God's righteousness" (v. 19). Because God is faithful, God is slow to anger (Deut. 34:6; Num. 14:18); God's faithfulness is the model for ours. That we should "rid" ourselves of wickedness (v. 21) recalls our ridding ourselves of the old self in baptism.

Verses 22–25 deal with being "doers of the word." The word of the gospel was "implanted" (v. 21) in us through preaching; now we are to become doers of it. This echoes Paul: "For it is not the hearers of the law who are righteous in God's sight, but the doers of the law who will be justified" (Rom. 2:13). Instead of looking at a mirror, we are to "look into the perfect law . . . and persevere, being not hearers who forget but doers who act—they will be blessed in their doing" (v. 25). The "perfect law" is the gospel, the teachings of Jesus, and the Torah. James does not separate these. His attitude toward torah is like that of Jesus in Matthew 5:17. Note the contrast between looking "at" and looking "into"; we are to look deeply into the perfect law, not merely glance at it.

Verses 26–27 deal with the distinction between "worthless religion" and "pure religion." Responsible use of language is one of our most important religious obligations. Several Second Testament authors agree, as seen in "Let your speech always be gracious, seasoned with salt" (Col. 4:6).

James concludes, "Religion that is pure and undefiled before God, the Father, is this: to care for orphans and widows in their distress, and to keep oneself unstained by the world" (v. 27). The purity rules by which the community is to live are matters of social action, chief among which is care for orphans and widows. In the Torah, God was the defender of widows and orphans (Exod. 22:22–23; Deut. 24:17–18); "Father of orphans and protector of widows is his holy habitation" (Ps. 85:5). The church's faith is shown in its active care for the most vulnerable members of the society.

Proper 18 [23]/Year B

James 2:1–10, (11–13), 14–17

James was committed to egalitarianism, a commitment made clear in today's argument against favoritism toward the rich typified by "a person with gold rings and in fine clothes" (v. 2). He bases his argument on "our glorious Lord Jesus Christ" (v. 1). The Greek asks, "Have you the faith of our Lord [*pistin tou kuriou*] Jesus Christ of glory?" (authors' translation). This subjective genitive grounds the argument in Jesus' faithfulness, not ours. Christ's faithfulness is a prototype for ours.

In verses 2–4, James gives an example of the prejudicial treatment that he opposes: the rich person is offered a seat, while the poor one (*ptochos*) is told to "stand" or to sit in a place of abasement—"at my feet." If you do this, asks James, "have you not made distinctions among yourselves, and become judges with evil thoughts?" (v. 4). Translations hide the fact that the "assembly" is a synagogue (*synagoge*), a clue that this is a community of Jewish followers of Jesus. The poor person is destitute, wearing "dirty clothes." The story calls to mind Jesus' parable of the Rich Man and Lazarus (Luke 16:19–31). The question about making "distinctions among yourselves" has the sense of "are you not split within yourselves?" That is, does not such behavior contradict the gospel that was implanted in you (1:21)? Are you not denying who and whose you are?

In verses 5–7, James supports his claim that the community should practice egalitarianism and avoid discrimination. He begins with one word: "Listen." Readers should recall the Shema, "Hear, O Israel: the Lord is our God, the Lord alone. You shall love the Lord your God with all your heart, and with all your soul, and with all your might" (Deut. 6:4–5). They should also recall that Jesus began the great commandment with the Shema (Matt. 22:37). God, says James, has "chosen the poor in the world to be rich in faith and to be heirs of the kingdom" (v. 5). As God elected Israel, so God elects the poor. They are the heirs of the kingdom, as Jesus said: "Blessed are the poor [*ptochoi*] in spirit, for theirs is the kingdom of heaven" (Matt. 5:3). Little wonder that in dishonoring the poor (v. 6), the community pays homage to the rich who "oppress" them and "blaspheme the excellent name that was invoked over you" (v. 7).

Verses 8–11 constitute a second argument from "the royal law according to the scripture" (v. 8) or "the law of liberty" (v. 12), the law of the Torah and of Jesus' teachings. Nothing was closer to the heart of the Torah than protecting the poor: "You shall not be partial to the poor or defer to the great" (Lev. 19:15). Failing in this, says James, is equivalent to committing adultery or murder (v. 11). That is, "whoever . . . fails in one point [of the law] has become accountable for all of it" (v. 10). To James, nothing was more important than care for the poor.

Verses 12–13 conclude that "judgment will be without mercy to anyone who has shown no mercy; mercy triumphs over judgment." This recalls Jesus' words "If you do not forgive others, neither will your Father forgive your trespasses" (Matt. 6:15). These statements should be taken as stressing the seriousness with which mercilessness is regarded, not as describing God's harshness. Instead, our compassion to the poor is modeled on God's and Jesus' faithfulness and *hesed*, steadfast love, toward us.

Verses 14–17 shift the emphasis slightly, contrasting faith without works with faith that has works. The emphasis on care for the poor continues in the example of a "brother or sister" (*adelphos* or *adelphe*) in need of clothing and food. We are not to bless them and send them on their way without supplying "their bodily needs." The contrast is not between faith and works but between living faith and lifeless faith.

Proper 19 [24]/Year B

James 3:1–12

Today's reading discusses the need to be responsible for what we say and how we say it. Too many congregations today are dysfunctional because some members fail to control their tongues, and this section of James is pertinent today for pastors in that situation.

Verse 1 states the subject matter: "Not many of you should become teachers [*didaskalos*]." Teachers played a critical role in the early church (Acts 13:1; 1 Cor. 12:28–29; Eph. 4:11), and congregations need responsible teaching to be healthy.[35] James is not rejecting teaching; he is stressing the responsibility of teachers. Yet his point also applies to all of us. *Didaskolos* translates "rabbi" into Greek. In the Gospels, Jesus is called "teacher" or "rabbi" over forty times. Teachers will be judged by a higher standard because they are supposed to understand more profoundly.

Verse 2 tells us why not many should become teachers: "For all of us make many mistakes." We all "stumble," says the Greek. Previously James advised us to be "quick to listen, slow to speak" (1:19). Teachers, however, talk a lot. We should speak with integrity of mind and mouth.

Verses 3–10 illustrate the power of the tongue and its attendant perils. The tongue is like a bridle put into the mouth of a horse—"we guide their whole bodies" with it. The bridle is small, the horse large, yet the bridle controls the horse. A small rudder can guide a large ship, even though it takes strong winds to move the ship. That the small tongue "boasts of great exploits" (v. 5) recalls Paul's arguments against boasting—it is a sign of trust in our own capacities instead of in God's grace.

The perils of the tongue are exemplified by a small flame that sets a large forest on fire (v. 5b). Psalm 39:1–3 says

> . . . "I will guard my ways
>   that I may not sin with my tongue;
> I will keep a muzzle on my mouth
>   as long as the wicked are in my presence." . . .
>   my heart became hot within me.
> While I mused, the fire burned;
>   then I spoke with my tongue.

Sirach 28:18 comments, "Many have fallen by the sword, but not as many as have fallen because of the tongue." The tongue is the "world of iniquity"

(v. 6) inhabiting our bodies; it is the "world" in the sense of the sinful world internalized in us. Human beings, says James, have tamed "every species of beast and bird, of reptile and sea creature . . . but no one can tame the tongue" (vv. 7–8). With the tongue we bless God and curse those made in God's image (v. 9)! James taps into a deep biblical theme: "I have set before you life and death, blessings and curses. Choose life so that you and your descendants may live" (Deut. 30:19). That blessings and curses come from the same mouths is a sign of persons divided against themselves (see 2:4).

Verses 11–12 are James's wrap-up of his argument that all of us need to be responsible for and in our talking. A spring is not the source of both fresh and brackish water, nor can a fig tree yield olives or a grapevine, figs. James points us to Jesus' teaching: "You will know them by their fruits. Are grapes gathered from thorns, or figs from thistles? In the same way, every good tree bears good fruit, but the bad tree bears bad fruit" (Matt. 7:16–17; see Luke 6:43–44). What is preposterous for a fig tree should be equally preposterous for us.

Proper 20 [25]/Year B

James 3:13–4:3, 7–8a

Today's reading falls into two parts: an admonition against "envy and selfish ambition" (3:13–4:6) and a call to transformation of the way of life (4:6–8a). James's concern with envy is comprehensible in light of the broker-client structure of Mediterranean society. Given the scarcity of all goods and the need of peasant clients to compete for access to brokers who could provide these goods, envy was widespread and generated conflict and friction in society.

Verse 13 sets the tone for the discussion. Readers are asked to "show by your good life that your works are done with gentleness [*prautes*] born of wisdom." Biblical teaching had long claimed that we should show the wisdom that comes from torah in our conduct. "Gentleness," literally, is "meekness," trusting in God rather than in ourselves. For Paul it is one of the fruits of the Spirit (Gal. 5:23).

Even if we harbor envy and ambition in our hearts (v. 14), we should not let them find expression ("do not be boastful"). Doing so would be "false to the truth," to the practical wisdom that we heard in the preaching of wisdom (2:21–22). Envy produces "disorder and wickedness of every kind" (v. 16; see the first paragraph above).

By contrast the gracious wisdom from above produces seven qualities (v. 17) that characterize a person's life: purity, peacefulness, gentleness, willingness to yield, mercifulness, impartiality, and integrity. These have to do with sustaining relationships with God and the neighbor. Purity and righteousness are about making concern for one's relationships with one's neighbors and with God a matter of central importance. Being "willing to yield" means listening to the neighbor, taking that person's view into account. We are not being told to be servile. Wisdom makes for peace: "Her ways are ways of pleasantness, and all her paths are peace" (Prov. 3:17). It creates community.

Verses 4:1–6 contend that "conflicts and disputes . . . come from your cravings that are at war within you" (v. 1). James frequently makes the point that our problem is that we are double-minded, divided within ourselves, torn between contradictory impulses. Paul says, "I see in my members another law at war with the law of my mind" (Rom. 7:23). Because we "want" and "covet" (desire and envy), we "commit murder" and "engage in disputes and conflicts" (v. 2). We "ask," that is, we pray, "and do not receive," because we "ask wrongly" (v. 3). James knew the tradition: "Ask, and it will be given you" (Matt. 7:7; Luke 11:9); but with experience he sagely noted that it depends on what we ask for and how we ask. God is the giver of all "good" gifts; it is these for which we should ask: meekness, patience, mercy, peace, willingness to listen.

We seek "friendship with the world" (v. 4) whereas we should seek friendship with God and the neighbor. The "world" is a world of limited goods, the dependence of peasant clients on brokers, and the resultant envy and conflict. Being a "friend" at the time meant seeing things in the same way that the friend does. Hence, being a "friend of the world" meant being an "enemy of God" (v. 4).

But in contrast to the broker/client world with its economy of scarcity, God's grace is lavishly, generously given to us: God "gives all the more grace"; "'God opposes the proud, but gives grace to the humble'" (v. 6). It is the humble—"orphans and widows" (1:27), the "poor person in dirty clothes" (2:3)—who are James's main concern. Our envy for the goods of the world blinds us to their condition. But if we "draw near to God" (v. 8), God will "purify our hearts."

Proper 21 [26]/Year B

James 5:13–20

James pays attention to prayer and the question of (apparently) unanswered prayer. In 4:3, he remarked, "You ask and do not receive, because you ask wrongly, in order to spend what you get on your pleasures." His point is that we must know what is proper to pray for and what is not. Now, in 5:13–18, James again turns his attention to prayer.

He deals with three situations to which prayer is the appropriate response. In v. 13 he asks, "Are any among you suffering [*kakopathei*]? They should pray." The verb for "suffering" points us less to what causes suffering than to how suffering taxes the human spirit, gets us down in the dumps. Prayer, James suggests, can help us live faithful lives in spite of bad circumstances, by allowing us to open ourselves to God's grace and love.

He then asks, "Are any cheerful? They should sing [*psalleto*] songs of praise" (v. 13). A literal translation would read, "sing a psalm," although the NRSV conveys James's meaning. The psalms were the hymn book of the temple and contained many psalms of praise. It is when we are cheerful that we are most prone to forget God and presume that we are self-sufficient; at precisely such times, therefore, we should sing psalms of praise—to remind ourselves that we live by virtue of God's love and grace.

Finally, he asks, "Are any among you sick? They should call for the elders of the church and have them pray over them, anointing them with oil in the name of the Lord" (v. 14). Elders were leaders in the tradition of Israel and early communities of Jesus' followers (Acts 11:30; 14:23; 1 Tim. 5:17–19). The ancient world believed that oil had healing properties. The Good Samaritan poured "oil and wine" on the wounds of the man who was mugged and left lying on the side of the road (Luke 10:34). The alcohol in the wine served as a disinfectant, and the oil soothed his pain. James suggests that the elders do two things: provide medical care and pray for the sick. Neither one, by itself, is sufficient. Sickness is not caused by sin in James's understanding; the gifts that come from God are good (1:17), not evil.

James next says, "The prayer of faith will save the sick, and the Lord will raise them up; and anyone who has committed sins will be forgiven" (v. 15). We should note the future tense in this comment; healing takes place both in the present and at the second coming of Jesus when we will be raised up and our sins will be forgiven.

The focus then shifts to the whole community. James urges his readers to "confess your sins to one another [*allelois*], and pray for one another, so that you may be healed" (v. 16). Confession of sins and prayer are to be engaged in by all members of the community, not merely in private. True followers of Jesus will confess their sins to one another and pray for one another. In most congregations, one person prays publicly and the rest listen and pray privately; this leads to the assumption that only the pastor can pray publicly. James makes us ask whether this is a healthy development.

The next line, "The prayer of the righteous is powerful and effective" (v. 16), might be taken to mean that the prayers of some people are more effective than those of others. Untangling the Greek is difficult; James speaks of the prayer of the righteous "being made effective." His emphasis, hence, is on God's making prayer effective by God's grace.

After lifting up Elijah as "a human being like us" (v. 17) and a person of prayer, James encourages members of the community to extend their responsibility for each other to the extent of bringing back "a sinner from wandering" (v. 20).

Proper 22 [27]/Year B

Hebrews 1:1–4; 2:5–12

In 1:1–4, Hebrews elegantly presents the central motifs that structure the entire letter. The two most important themes are (1) that in self-disclosing God's self, God "in these last days . . . has spoken to us by a Son" (v. 2) and (2) that this Son "had made purification for sins" before sitting down "at the right hand of the Majesty on high" (v. 3). Who Christ is— the ascended Son—and what he did—having made atonement for sins— are at the heart of Hebrews's message.

"Of old" (*palai*), says Hebrews, God spoke to our forebears "in many and various ways, but in these last days he has spoken to us by a Son" (v. 1). Christians have taken this to mean that God's latest self-disclosure is superior to God's earlier effort. We should note, however, that "but" is not in the Greek. The relation between the old and the new is central to Hebrews; without God's prior self-disclosures, the latest would have made no sense. Throughout Hebrews, the author presents the work of Christ as the perfection of the Yom Kippur (Day of Atonement) sacrifices in the desert sanctuary; what the priests did annually, Christ has done once and forever—he has made "cleansing," *katharismon*, for sins.

Hebrews thinks that the revelation in Christ is God's last revelation to human beings; literally it comes "in the last days" (v. 2). The world is redeemed by the One through whom it was created—salvation and creation may not be separated. As in Sophia, of whom Wisdom 7:26 speaks as the "radiance" of God's glory, so Hebrews uses the same term of Christ (v. 3). This is high wisdom Christology. Glory is standard Jewish speech of God. God and Christ not only created all things but also sustain them. That Christ "sat down at the right hand of God" (v. 3) echoes Psalm 110:1, a text that is critical to Hebrews. His superiority to the angels (v. 4) will be important to Hebrews's later argument. His "name" is "Son," as was made clear in verse 2.

Hebrews 2:5–12 deals with the subjection of the Son, his crowning with glory and honor, and his high-priestly perfection. Note that God did not "subject the coming world . . . to angels" (v. 5). Rather, the world to come was begun by Christ's suffering and ascension to the right hand of God. Verses 6–8a quote Psalm 8:4–6, a psalm that praises the majestic name of God and wonders "what are human beings that you are mindful of them." Hebrews imaginatively interprets the psalm not simply as the exaltation of Christ but as his subjection: "Jesus, who for a little while was made lower than the angels" (v. 9) and, subsequently, who was "crowned with glory and honor because of the suffering of death" (v. 9). He tasted death, on our behalf, "by the grace of God."

Hebrews stands within a pattern of Jewish thinking about redemption, a pattern in which the classic Exodus story of liberation from slavery became transformed in the Hellenistic age to an archetype of release from the captivity of this world to the freedom of "heaven" (a roundabout way of saying "God"). The Wisdom of Solomon says,

> . . . love of her [wisdom] is the keeping of her laws,
> and giving heed to her laws is assurance of immortality,
> and immortality brings one near to God.
> (6:18–19)

Hebrews wants to make it as clear as possible that Christ shares fully in the human situation; as he tasted the bitterness of death (2:9), so in verses 10–11 the "one who sanctifies" and is the pioneer of our salvation is made "perfect through sufferings." Hence the one who sanctifies and the sanctified "all have one Father" and Jesus "is not ashamed to call them brothers and sisters" (v. 11). God's plan is to consummate God's creation by bringing "all things" to glory, "many children," not just a few. Hence the Son, understood as speaking in the words of Psalm 22:23, praises God "in the midst of the congregation" (*ekklesia*). We will see later that Hebrews is deeply troubled by defections from the congregation (10:35).

Proper 23 [28]/Year B

Hebrews 4:12–16

Please see Good Friday/Year A for commentary on this passage.

Proper 24 [29]/Year B

Hebrews 5:1–10

Please see the Fifth Sunday in Lent/Year B for commentary on this passage.

Proper 25 [30]/Year B

Hebrews 7:23–28

When the first word in a reading is "Furthermore," we know that it presumes what went before. In this case, that is the first twenty-two verses of chapter seven that deal with the elusive figure of Melchizedek, who was introduced in 6:20. The whole chapter is a *midrash* on Psalm 110:4: "The Lord has sworn and will not change his mind, 'You are a priest forever according to the order of Melchizedek.'" Verses 1–10 expound Psalm 110:4 and Genesis 14, the two places in Scripture where Melchizedek is mentioned. Hebrews suggests that Melchizedek is greater even than Abraham and Levi (and hence the levitical priesthood) because they paid tithes to Melchizedek (vv. 6–10). Verses 11–19 argue that the priesthood of the order of Melchizedek is a cut above the levitical priesthood because the latter, established by the law and not by "the power of an indestructible life" (v. 16), "made nothing perfect" (v. 19).

Today's reading effectively begins with verses 20–25, which argue (and Hebrews is making a case) that the new priesthood's supremacy is grounded in Hebrews' interpretation of Psalm 110:4. Verses 20–22 contend that Christ's new priesthood is confirmed by the oath that God swore in Psalm 110:4 (v. 20). Originally, Psalm 110 was a psalm "of David," hymning God's pledge of loyalty to the king of Israel, but Hebrews takes it as though it is addressed to Christ and concludes from it that his priesthood has preeminence over that of the Levites because theirs was not grounded in God's oath. Our text further concludes that "Jesus has also become the guarantee [*egguos*] of a better covenant" (v. 22), a comment on which Hebrews will expand in 8:8–13 in a *midrash* on Jeremiah 31:31–32. Hebrews's use of *egguos* shows the writer's indebtedness to legal metaphors circulating in the Hellenistic world; it is not a typical biblical term used in reference to covenants where covenant making is a sign of God's graciousness (and some covenants are purely gracious).

Verses 23–25 move in a new direction and put forward another set of reasons that Christ's priesthood is greater than that of the Levites: they were "many in number," while Christ, the inference is, is one. Further, they were many because they died and were thus "prevented . . . from continuing in office" (v. 23). Christ, by contrast, "holds his priesthood permanently, because he continues forever" (v. 24). Here Hebrews's philosophical preference for a form of Platonism shows itself: the immutable, everlasting, and unchangeable is "better" than that which grows, becomes, and perishes, giving way to the new. This view is somewhat at odds with the biblical notion of God who interacts with God's creatures and even suffers for and with them, although Hebrews certainly affirms the latter in his discussion of Jesus' suffering. The question of the coherence of these two claims alongside each other will later make problems for the church. "Consequently," says Hebrews, "he is able for all time to save those who approach God through him" (v. 25). The Greek does not mention "time" but says that he is "able to save entirely [*panteles*] the ones approaching through him to God" (authors' translation). He can do this because he "always lives to make intercession for them" (v. 25).

Verses 26–28 are a closing expression of rapture "that we should have such a high priest" (v. 26). He is holy, blameless, pure, separated from sinners (that is, not from ordinary sinners but from those who deny him). He made his offering "once for all" and does not need to repeat it, as did the Levites. In short, he is "a Son . . . made perfect forever" (v. 28). Mainly, however, he sympathizes with our weaknesses (4:15).

Preachers and teachers will find that Hebrews's emphasis on God's empathy with us is a strong point worthy of unpacking for those whose view of God is mainly that of a stern judge. At the same time, they should be aware that this emphasis on God's compassionate love for the weak and the wayward is itself profoundly Jewish and hardly unique to Christianity.

Proper 26 [31]/Year B

Hebrews 9:11–14

Please see Monday of Holy Week/Year A for commentary on this passage.

Proper 27 [32]/Year B

Hebrews 9:24–28

Today's reading should begin with verse 23, which recaps Hebrews's argument in 9:15–22 leading to the conclusion that Christ's sacrifice "was necessary." Our author had just argued that "where a will [*diatheke*] is involved, the death of the one who made it must be established" (9:16). Hebrews sometimes uses *diatheke* to mean "covenant" (9:15) and sometimes to mean "will," as in "last will and testament" (9:16–17). The latter sense is derived from the legal culture of the Hellenistic world. Clearly, when God made the various covenants in Scripture, God did not have to die.

Today's reading pushes Hebrews's argument further, asserting (v. 23) that even the "heavenly things" needed to be "purified," that is, cleansed. Hence, they need "better sacrifices" than those that merely cleansed the tent and "vessels used in worship" (v. 21). What is meant by claiming that the heavenly things needed cleansing has been much disputed. Does this refer to evicting Satan from heaven, the cosmic eradication of sin, or something else? The likely answer is that it refers to the minds and hearts of Christ's followers. High-flown theological and philosophical language often is a manner of talking about existential matters: it takes this to cleanse your heart.

Verse 24 interprets the way in which the heavenly things are cleansed by returning to the Yom Kippur similes to compare sacrifices offered in the sanctuary "made by human hands" with those offered "in heaven itself." The earthly temple, in platonic fashion, was "a mere copy of the true one," as for Plato all earthly realities are mere copies of their eternal ideal forms. The point is that Christ entered "the presence of God in our behalf," and there he intercedes "on our behalf" (see 7:25).

Verse 25 similarly contrasts Christ's offering with that of the high priests; the latter had to make the Yom Kippur offering "again and again," and with blood not their own. Christ offers himself. Verse 26 continues to describe, depreciatively, the desert tabernacle and its lack of efficacy as contrasted with Christ's entry into heaven. Had Christ been like the priests, "he would have had to suffer again and again since the foundation of the world." Instead, he "appeared once for all at the end of the age to remove sin [*athetesin*, annulment] by sacrifice of himself." The phrase "at the end of the age" (*ton aionon*) shows Hebrews's eschatological conviction that the time is short until Christ's return (see v. 28).

Verses 27–28 conclude today's reading. Verse 27 begins with "just as" and is one of Hebrews's typical uses of comparison; the phrase "just as" (*kath hoson*) occurs also in 3:3 and 7:20 (although not in the NRSV in 7:20). Just as human beings "die once," so Christ was "offered once to bear the sins of many" (v. 28). Hebrews keeps its focus on Christ's offering as once for all. How the claim that Christ "will appear a second time" fits the comparison with ordinary mortals is not transparently clear; what is clear is that this is part of the early church's eschatology.

It is striking that Christ's return, unlike his first appearance, will not "deal with sin [*choris hamartias*, without sin]" (v. 28). It will not have the reconciling, forgiving character of his first appearance. Instead, it will be "to save those who are eagerly waiting for him." Later the author of Hebrews will warn his readers not to persist in sin, because if they do "there no longer remains a sacrifice for sins, but a fearful prospect of judgment and a fury of fire that will consume the adversaries" (10:26–27). This is the portentous downside of Hebrews's view that Christ offered his sacrifice once: it will not be repeated.

Proper 28 [33]/Year B

Hebrews 10:11–14, (15–18), 19–25

Please see Good Friday/Year A (alt) for commentary on this passage.

Reign of Christ (Proper 29 [34])/Year B

Revelation 1:4b–8

The book of Revelation was written in the early to mid 90s CE when John, its author, was imprisoned by the Roman Empire "because of the word of God and the testimony" of Jesus on the island of Patmos (Rev. 1:9). The church was either being persecuted or perceived itself about to be persecuted, and John writes to encourage the church to endure difficulty (Rev. 1:9; 13:10; 14:12). Apocalyptic writers believed they were living in or near the last days of the present evil age that God would destroy with a cataclysm, after which God would fully manifest the divine realm (NRSV: kingdom). John believed God used Jesus Christ as the agent of apocalyptic transformation. Apocalyptic theologians seek to assure the community that God will triumph over evil and establish justice. For John, the Roman Empire is the embodiment of Satan and will soon be destroyed in the final apocalypse. The book of Revelation frequently implies a contrast between idolatrous, exploitative, and savage Rome with the one, true, living God who wishes justice and peace. While Caesar is temporarily on the throne of the empire, God rules the world and will soon finally and fully manifest that rule.

Today's passage employs a letter format of sender, addressees, and greeting to set out main themes in the book. While some think the author (1:4) was the apostle, most think that John (a common name) was an apocalyptic prophet who received and transmitted the vision. While the seven churches are named (1:11), many scholars think the number functions here (and elsewhere in the book) to signify God's control over events. The churches are located in the part of "Asia" that is western, modern-day

Turkey. (On the formula "grace and peace," see the Second Sunday after the Epiphany/Year A.)

The letter is from three entities (1:4–5a): First, there is the one "who is and who was and who is to come." This is a subtle critique of a popular Greek designation of deity as one who "is, was, and will be." The Jewish God does not simply exist ("shall be") but "comes" to end evil and establish peace and justice. Second, there are seven spirits. These are the seven archangels, who stand before God's throne to do God's will (Rev. 4:5; 5:6; Tob. 12:15; *1 En.* 20:1–7). And finally there is Jesus. John identifies Jesus in three ways. As "faithful witness" he faithfully announced the coming apocalyptic transformation even though put to death. As "firstborn of the dead" God raised him for life in the divine realm to demonstrate that the season of apocalypse was imminent. As "the ruler of the kings of the earth" he is sovereign of all earthly rulers—including Caesar—and in the new world his rule will replace theirs.

In the doxological 1:5b–6 Jesus loves (*agapao*) the community with the same love with which God loves Israel (Deut. 4:37). In apocalyptic theology, sin is often an enslaving power from which the community needs liberation. The notion of "blood" appears here figuratively to speak of death: his death allowed God to raise him to show that the community would soon be free from enslaving powers. Jesus gave the community a priestly character (per Exod. 19:6) that mediates the assurance of God's presence and coming. These various aspects of the work of Jesus point not to Jesus himself but to God (1:6b).

Drawing on Daniel 7:13 and Zechariah 12:10–12, the author depicts Jesus returning on a cloud as apocalyptic judge and redeemer in a massive public event ("every eye will see him") visible even to the Romans who put him to death ("pierced him") (Rev. 1:7). When the people realize that this is the moment of cosmic judgment ("on account of him"), they will "wail." The word "wail" (*kopto*) indicates not simply sadness but mourning the brokenness of the present evil age, and often one's own complicity in that age (Joel 2:12; Zech. 12:10; 14:12; 2 Esd. 16:2).

The "Alpha" and "Omega" of 1:8 are the first and last letters of the Greek alphabet and function here similarly to the formulae "the first and the last" (Isa. 41:4; 44:6; 48:12; cf. Rev. 1:17; 2:8; 22:13) and "the beginning and the end" (21:6; 22:13) to indicate the sovereignty of the God of Israel who created the present world and will bring it to its apocalyptic conclusion. God is almighty (*pantokrator*), the divine warrior who is more powerful than any other deity (Zech. 9:14–15). The contrast is palpable between the Almighty and Caesar who has temporary and misguided control over a few things.

All Saints/Year B

Revelation 21:1–6a

In the immediate background of the biblical passages for today and the next two weeks is the foundation of apocalyptic thinking—the notion that God is about to end the present evil age with an apocalypse that simultaneously brings the world to full and final manifestation. The Scripture texts assigned for these weeks interpret the new universe, as it will be after the apocalypse, in expressions that move across a spectrum ranging from straightforward to figurative.

Prior to today's reading, the prophet was given a vision that assures readers of the apocalyptic destruction of the present evil age, the "first earth" (Rev. 21:1). Different apocalyptic theologians offered differing time lines of such events. God ends a social form of evil—Babylon/Rome (18:1–24)—which is followed by rejoicing over the fall (19:1–10), the interim defeat of the evil cosmic forces who empowered Rome and their consignment to a lake of fire (19:11–20:3), the reign of the saints for a millennium (20:4–6), the final defeat of Satan (20:7–10), and the judgment of all the dead, climaxed by Death and Hades being thrown into the fire (20:11–15).

Revelation 21:1 alludes to the common belief in Judaism of John's day that the apocalypse would remake not only the earth but heaven as well (Isa. 65:17; *1 En.* 45:4; *Sib. Or.* 5:212; *2 Bar.* 32:6). The sea—a representation of chaos—is "no more," that is, chaos no longer exists. Beginning in 21:1, the writer details the great change.

The new Jerusalem, an image that John gets from Isaiah 65:17–20, is "holy," that is, manifesting God's purposes (21:2). The fact that it "comes down" reminds the reader that Revelation 21–22 does not describe "heaven" as a realm above the earth as conventional Christian piety imagines it but envisions instead the replacement of the present world. By comparing the new Jerusalem to a beautifully dressed bride, John evokes one of the most joyous associations in the ancient Near East.

The home of God is now with human beings: God dwells with them, and God is with them in an unmediated way (21:3). The "home" (*skene*) alludes to Ezekiel 37:27 and 43:7; and the tradition that God "tents" or "dwells" (*sknenoo*) with people refers to Exodus 29:45; Leviticus 26:11–13; and Zechariah 2:10–11. The new city does not contain a temple because the immediate presence of God takes over the function of the temple (21:22). When Jewish texts speak of God being "with people," they usually mean not simply that God is present but that God's presence brings victory or other positive change (Exod. 3:12; Deut. 7:21; Isa. 8:10; Zeph. 3:17; Zech. 8:23).

The seer turns to Isaiah 25:8 to describe important qualities of life in the new age (21:4). The text is concerned not simply with specific circumstances of sadness (such as death) but with the fact that the present is fundamentally adrift from God's purposes and is consequently a realm of unrelenting exploitation, oppression, and violence. "Mourning and crying and pain" are more than reactions to isolated events; they characterize experience in the present. Death is the archetypal representative of life in the present. However, at the apocalypse, this quality of existence passes away. The prophet alludes to Isaiah 43:19 to reinforce the notion that God remakes "'all things'" (Rev. 21:5), which is why God can "'wipe away every tear from their eyes'" (v. 4).

In 1:6, the author hears God say, "'It is done'" (*gegonan*), that is, the train of events leading from the end of the old world to the beginning of the new. The verb is in the perfect tense meaning that the action (of remaking the world) is finished but the effect abides (the new world). When John returns to earth from the vision in heaven, Rome is still in operation, but John has seen what will soon happen, so the congregation can better endure the affliction pressed upon them in the present evil world. (See Proper 29/Year B and the Fourth Sunday after Easter/Year C for our comments on the expression "I am the Alpha and the Omega, the beginning and the end" and the notion of the water of life.)

Thanksgiving Day/Year B

1 Timothy 2:1–7

Today's reading consists of teachings on prayer sent to Timothy on behalf of the *ekklesia* in Ephesus (1:3). They are some of the most beautiful teachings on prayer in the Second Testament.

In verse 1, Paul appeals (*parakalo*) "that supplications, prayers, intercessions, and thanksgivings be made for everyone [*panton anthropon*]." Immediately, a universal note is struck; we are to pray not for some but for all. "Supplications [*deeseis*], prayers [*proseuchas*], intercessions [*enteuxdis*], and thanksgivings [*eucharistias*]" refer to different kinds of prayer. Intercessory prayer for others expresses understanding of neighbors as those whom we are given to love; petitionary prayer for ourselves expresses understanding of ourselves as relying on God; and prayers of thanksgiving give voice to proper understanding of God as the One from whom all things come.

Included among all people for whom we are to pray are "kings [*basileon*] and all who are in high positions" (v. 2). Some churches continue this practice today, praying for presidents, governors, members of the legislature, and other public servants. Here it is important to remember the world of difference that a preposition makes: we are to pray for, not to, those in high positions. In an empire where the emperor was regarded as God, praying for rather than to the emperor at least tacitly undercut such an idolatrous claim. In the return from exile, Ezra 6:10 notes that in the Second Temple prayer was to be offered "for the life of the king and his children." While the Roman Empire was generally tolerant of all religions, it could also crack down severely on one that was regarded as a threat to public order, an order sustained as much by the emperor cult as by the patron-client system and the army. Hence prayer for the king is offered "so that we may lead a quiet and peaceable life." First Timothy's mention of Pontius Pilate in 6:13 shows that Paul is aware of the oppressive side of the Roman Empire.

Verses 3–4 strike the second all-inclusive note in this set of teachings on prayer: "This is right and is acceptable in the sight of God our Savior [*tou soteros hemon theou*], who desires everyone [*pantas anthropous*] to be saved." It is God who is explicitly our savior, a point that is clear in other Pauline language about God's salvific activity: "In Christ God was reconciling the world to himself" (2 Cor. 5:19). And God wants all to be saved. Later in 4:10, 1 Timothy describes God as "the Savior of all people." God wants all "to come to the knowledge of the truth [*epignosis aletheias*]." God wants all to "recognize" the truth of the gospel, specifically Paul's understanding of it as the unconditional gift of God's gracious love freely offered to each and all.

Verses 5–6 strike two more all-inclusive notes:

> For
> there is one God;
> > there is also one mediator between God and humankind,
> Christ Jesus, himself human,
> > who gave himself a ransom for all.

That God is one recalls again the *Shema Israel's* affirmation that God is one (see Rom. 3:30). Christ is the one mediator (*mesites*) between God and human beings (*anthropon*), not just our mediator, but everyone's, a point reaffirmed in the statement that he gave himself a ransom for all (*antilutron hyper panton*).

The remark that this testimony was given *kairois idiois*, "at the right time" or when the time was ripe has to do with Paul's eschatology—now, in these last days before the turning of history, the good news is timely.

This is the gospel, properly understood, for the spreading of which Paul "was appointed a herald [*keryx*] and an apostle" (v. 7); Paul is a herald of the *kerygma*. As such he is "a teacher of the Gentiles in faith and truth," carrying out his all-inclusive mission to all people, precisely all those for whom we are asked to pray.

Year C

First Sunday of Advent/Year C

1 Thessalonians 3:9–13

In connection with Proper 26/Year A, we noted the importance in 2:11–12 of Paul's language of family in 1 Thessalonians, a force that intensifies in 2:17–3:5. The ties between the apostles and the congregation are so strong that, when separated, the apostles became "orphans" (2:17), without the identity, support, and social standing that came from the community.

Paul wanted to see the Thessalonians face to face but was prevented by Satan. In apocalyptic Judaism, Satan was "power," a suprahuman entity who sought to wrest the world away from God and was in league with the demons and the principalities and powers. He made the age a realm of fractiousness, poverty, violence, sickness, and death. Paul does not specify the mechanism by which Satan blocked his movement (2:18), but as frightful as is the power of Satan, the apostle does not flinch because of confidence in the return of Jesus where the Thessalonians will be the apostle's joy (2:19–20).

The apostles understand the separation as "persecution" (*thlipsis*), a word that might better be translated "tribulation," because in apocalyptic literature it often indicates the tribulation or intensification of suffering during the last days (2 Esd. 13:16–19; *2 Bar.* 25:1–4). Paul follows several other apocalyptic theologians in thinking that such suffering is part of God's plan ("what we are destined for. In fact, . . . we told you before hand that we were to suffer" 3:4–5). More grievous than the apostle's own suffering was the fear that the Thessalonians might have been tempted by Satan to cease their faithfulness.

Across the centuries we can feel the force of the apostle's joy that Timothy has brought "the good news" of the congregation's "faith and love," or better "faithfulness [*pistos*] and love [*agape*]" (3:6a), key qualities of life in covenantal community. As we learn from 3:6b, the relationship between the apostles and the congregation is reciprocal: the congregation remembers the apostles (especially in prayer, per 1:2) and longs to see them.

The reciprocity of relationship continues in 3:7 as the apostle indicates that the congregation's faithfulness has been encouraging to the apostles during their season of "distress and persecution." The doctrine of the priesthood of all believers was formulated much later in the church's life, but its spirit is evident here. When Paul says, "We now live" (*zao*) because the Thessalonians "continue to stand firm in the Lord," he certainly means that their continuing relationship is a blessing in the sense of life in covenant as God intends (Sir. 7:33; Tob. 12:17), and he perhaps anticipates the life eternal in the community of the eschatological world (Dan. 12:2; *T. Jud.* 25:1). The spirit of interconnectedness between apostles and people increases again in 3:9.

In 3:10, the writers want to help the Thessalonians "restore [*katartizo*] whatever is lacking [*ta husteremata*] in your faith" (that is, in your practice of faithfulness). *Husterema* occurs in 2 Esdras 6:9 in reference to the end of an age, which may mean that Paul is thinking that the Thessalonians "lack" could have consequences at the end of the present age. In support is 3:11–13 in which Paul and his companions invoke God's help in getting to Thessalonica and pray that God will cause their love for one another as an eschatological family to increase to the same intensity as the love of the apostles for the community. Paul further prays that the community will be prepared for the moment of judgment in connection with the coming of Jesus with "all [the] saints" by being strengthened in holiness (*hagiosune*) and by being "blameless" (*amemptos*; 3:13), both terms from Judaism for living in community as God desires. The former is a key quality of both God and the Jewish community: just as God is sovereign and separate from all other powers, so the community is to live according to God's design and not in accord with other deities and values. (On *amemptos*, see Proper 25/Year A.)

A preacher might reflect on the character of relationships in the congregation and on the character of congregation as community. To what degree—and for what purposes—are we bound with one another today? What would it take for a congregation today to develop bonds that are similar to the ones between the apostles and the Thessalonians?

Second Sunday of Advent/Year C

Philippians 1:3–11

Paul wrote this letter while in prison, though he does not indicate his location (1:7, 13–14, 17). The congregation responded to his imprisonment with prayers for his release and with supplies (1:19; 4:17–18). Despite his imprisonment, Paul's tone is largely joyful, in part because he is confident that the day of Christ is coming (see below) and will bring redemption with it. Unfortunately, he observes, some missionaries preach from regrettable motives (1:15, 17), and others misinterpret circumcision and the law (3:2–3, 7–11, 19). Regrettably, Paul refers to them as "dogs" and "evil workers" (3:2) as well as "enemies of the cross of Christ" (3:17). Their fundamental problem is, however, not that they are Jewish but, that they misunderstand and misuse Jewish tradition. Indeed, they are likely Gentiles who, as adults, came into the church and assimilated aspects of Jewish tradition without fully converting to Judaism or fully understanding Jewish tradition.

A thanksgiving paragraph was a standard part of ancient letters. A letter penned by a pagan Gentile usually contained a sentence or two of appreciation to idols or other deities. Like some other Jewish writers (e.g., 2 Macc. 1:2–6), Paul's thanksgivings are more personal. They also set the tone of the letter and preview major themes.

The tone of Paul's thanksgivings echoes that of the thanksgiving Psalms (e.g., Pss. 105, 106, 135, 136) as the apostle recalls God's faithfulness and acts of deliverance. The opening words, "I thank" (*eucharisteo*) echoes "grace" (*charis*). Paul remembers the covenantal quality of the community and its hospitality. The apostle recalls these elements of their history to refresh the congregation's connection with the apostle (1:5, 7–8). Paul encourages the church to continue to grow in Christ so that it will be prepared for his return (1:6, 10–11).

A key motif in the thanksgiving paragraph is that the apostle is in a *koinonia* with the Philippians, a word usually translated "fellowship" or "sharing" (1:5, 7; 2:1; 3:10; 4:14, 15). A better rendering is "partnership," for *koinonia* was often used of a voluntary partnership formed to achieve a common goal. In this spirit, the Philippian Christians are partners in Paul's imprisonment. The congregation contributes prayers, faithfulness, financial resources, and their witness in Philippi. Paul is thankful that the Philippians are reliable partners.

Paul uses technical legal language in 1:7 to say that he has made, or is about to make, a defense in court, but regrettably (in our view) he does not state the charges against him.

Paul feels for the Philippians "with the compassion of Christ Jesus" (1:8). "Compassion" (*splangchnon*) refers to bowels, which in Hebrew symbolize feeling. To have compassion is to feel the sufferings of another and to respond. God compassionately feels the fractiousness of the present evil age and aims to replace the world (*T. Zeb.* 8:2; 9:7–8; *T. Nap.* 4:5). Through Christ, the Philippians experience the compassion of the God of Israel.

The Philippians need love, knowledge, and insight "to help them determine what is best" as they contemplate how to respond to the "dogs" and how to produce "the harvest of righteousness."

The "day of Christ" is the apocalyptic return of Jesus. The term is a spin-off of the "day of the Lord." Apocalyptic theologians viewed the day of the Lord as a cosmic cataclysm when God ends the present evil age, judges the wicked, and conforms every person, relationship, and element of the world—including nature—to the divine purposes. (e.g., *1 En.* 83–90, 2 Esd. 6:35–9:25, *2 Bar.* 20:5–30:5).

Third Sunday of Advent/Year C

Philippians 4:4–7

Please see Proper 23 [28]/Year A for commentary on this passage.

Fourth Sunday of Advent/Year C

Hebrews 10:5–10

Please see Annunciation/Year A for commentary on this passage.

Christmas Day/Years A, B, and C

Titus 2:11–14

Titus 3:4–7

Hebrews 1:1–4, (5–12)

Please see Christmas Day/Year A for commentary on this passage.

First Sunday after Christmas Day/Year C

Colossians 3:12–17

Today's reading is a list of character strengths that describe the way of life of those transformed by the gracious love of God in Jesus Christ. Because they are usually called a "list of virtues," in contrast to the "list of vices" found in 3:5–11, it is helpful to remember that virtues were understood as "strengths." These are not arbitrary commandments imposed hetero-nomously on people. Instead, they describe who the followers of Jesus already are as transformed by God's love. We are asked to become who we are, called to become what God has given us to be.

Verse 12: "As God's chosen ones, holy and beloved, clothe yourselves with compassion, kindness, humility, meekness, and patience." "Clothe yourselves" alludes to baptism in which Jesus' followers "put on" the new self, symbolized by donning new clothes. We do this because we have been "chosen" and "beloved," not in order to be loved by God. Note that humil-ity is not self-abasement, which is condemned in 2:18 and 2:23. Humility is willingness to be a servant; it is not slavishness. Compassion is "feeling with" others, as the good Samaritan "felt with" the man in the ditch.

Verse 13: "Bear with one another and, if anyone has a complaint against another, forgive each other; just as the Lord has forgiven you." This is reminiscent of the teaching of Jesus concerning worship in Matthew 5:23–24: "If . . . your brother or sister has something against you, leave your gift there before the altar and go; first be reconciled to your brother or sister." Reconciliation with God is spurious apart from reconciliation with the neighbor. It also recalls the Lord's Prayer: "Forgive us our sins, for we our-selves forgive everyone indebted to us" (Luke 11:4). Seeking forgiveness is a strength; it presupposes our awareness that we are loved and frees us to be honest with ourselves. That we have been forgiven empowers us to be forgiving.

Verse 14: "Above all, clothe yourselves with love [*agape*], which binds everything together in perfect harmony." "Above all" indicates that of all the virtues, love is the principal one, and the others unpack its meaning. For the early church, love was not first a matter of the individual heart, as it has become, but a communal attribute. Love has to do with what "binds everything together in perfect harmony."

Verse 15: "And let the peace [*eirene*] of Christ rule in your hearts. . . . And be thankful [*eucharistos*]." Peace is first what Christ gives to us; he gives us *his* peace. Because it is graciously given we are to "let" it rule in our hearts. We do not have to strive for it; we have only to get out of its way. Being "thankful," grateful, is the only appropriate response to grace. We are not to feel superior to others (remember humility) but thankful to God for the transforming grace that has been extravagantly given to us.

Verse 16: "Let the word of Christ dwell in you richly; teach . . . admonish . . . sing." This both describes worship in the early community and makes it clear that worship shapes the way of life of Jesus' followers. In worship we practice being the community we are given and called to become.

Verse 17: "And whatever you do, in word or deed, do everything in the name of the Lord Jesus, giving thanks to God the Father through him." Here we are reminded of the commandment that we are to love God with all our selves, that commitment to God is an ultimate commitment. In Jesus, whose name means "YHWH saves," the grace of God has set us right in relation to God and the neighbor and for that we give thanks to God through him.

Second Sunday after Christmas Day/Years A, B, and C

Ephesians 1:3–14

Please see the Second Sunday after Christmas Day/Year A for commentary on this passage.

Epiphany of the Lord/Years A, B, and C

Ephesians 3:1–12

Please see Epiphany/Year A for commentary on this passage.

First Sunday after the Epiphany/Year C

Baptism of the Lord

Acts 8:14–17

Although the book of Acts is not a letter, the lectionary assigns the text for today to the place usually occupied by the letter in the sequence of readings. Like many other writings in the Second Testament, the Gospel of Luke and the book of Acts presume the apocalyptic belief that God is about to bring the current evil era of history to a close and to unfold a new realm in which all things conform in every way to the divine purposes. For

Luke, the birth, life, death, resurrection, and ascension of Jesus Christ reveal that the turning of the ages is at hand.

Two themes from this world of thought are important for understanding Acts 8:14–17. One is the expectation that God would regather Jewish and Gentile peoples into one human family in the new world. The other is that people anticipating the coming would experience the fullness of the Spirit as both ecstatic presence and as force creating the new community. Indeed, for Luke a work of the Spirit is to manifest the qualities of the divine realm in the present.

Luke carefully shows that the Spirit guides all significant aspects of the work of Jesus, the apostles, the Jersualem community, and other early communities. The Spirit is responsible for the births of John the Baptist and Jesus (Luke 1:15, 35, 41, 67), and the witness of Simeon and Anna (Luke 2:25–27). The Spirit guides the ministries of John and Jesus (Luke 3:17, 21–22; 4:18; 11:1–13) and particularly guides the apostles and the wider group of followers as well as the Gentile mission (Luke 24:44–49; Acts 1:5, 8; 2:1–4, 17, 38, 42–47; 4:8, 25, 31; 6:3, 5, 10; 7:59; 8:29; 9:17; 10:19, 34–44; 11:12, 24; 13:52; 15:8, 29; 20:28).

In Acts 1:8, the risen Jesus promises the Spirit to the followers and commissions them to spread the news of the coming realm in Jerusalem and Judea, then through Samaria, and to the ends of the earth. It is important for the preacher to stress that the early witnesses were not inviting Jewish people to leave Judaism and affiliate with the alternative religion of Christianity. At the time of Luke, Judaism and Christianity were not two religions; although tensions were increasing, the community of Jesus' followers was still closely related to Judaism. The witnesses were to invite others to recognize that the God of Israel was about to use Jesus Christ as the agent of cosmic transformation.

This news is first distributed in Jerusalem and Judea—significant symbols of Judaism in antiquity. Samaria was the home of Samaritans, who were considered Jewish until the Babylonian exile. In the vacuum of Jewish leadership during the exile, the Samaritans adopted Gerizim (not Jerusalem) as their place of worship and turned to the writings attributed to Moses (the Pentateuch) as their sacred Scriptures. Relationships between Jewish and Samaritan communities were generally friendly but marked by some tension and occasional hostility.

Acts 1:12–8:3 tells the story of the Spirit-led witness in Jerusalem and Judea. Acts 8:3–25 continues the story into Samaria. The coming of the gospel to the Samaritans is a kind of a bridge from the Jewish world to the Gentile mission. In today's text, we encounter a group of Samaritans who had been baptized; that is, they had repented of complicity with the broken present age and had turned towards the coming of the realm of God. The main point of Acts 8:14–17 is to confirm that the Samaritans also received the Spirit and thus are fully members of the eschatological community.

Preachers and laypeople sometimes get exercised over the question of whether baptism and the coming of the Spirit are two distinct experiences. Luke pictures baptism and the manifestation of the Spirit occurring both simultaneously and at separate times. For Luke, the issue is not whether the two are distinct experiences, nor is one more important than the other. Rather, Luke wants readers to see that both baptism and consciousness of the Spirit are requisite for full-bodied life in the divine realm.

Second Sunday after the Epiphany/Year C

1 Corinthians 12:1–11

Please see Pentecost Day/Year A for commentary on this passage.

Third Sunday after the Epiphany/Year C

1 Corinthians 12:12–31a

The long lection for today continues Paul's attempt to persuade the Corinthians who have high social standing in the community to yield their freedom to those of lower standing so the church can function authentically as the body of Christ. Commentators often speak of Paul's description of the church as a body (*soma*) as an analogy, metaphor, or figure of speech. However, people in antiquity spoke of communities as bodies in organic and not simply figurative terms. Community members are organically interrelated in the same way as the human body and its parts. Individuals represent the community, and individuals *are* part of the *body* of the community. The body is to fulfill its purpose; individuals and communities need to correct things that inhibit the body from enacting its purpose.[36] The body of Christ is to witness to the end of this world and the coming of the divine, and to provide an entry for Gentiles into the eschatological world.

When people are baptized and become aware of being a community animated by the Spirit, their individual bodies become a part of the corporate body of Christ (1 Cor. 12:12–13). They do not give up old identities—Jewish people are still Jewish people; Gentiles remain gentiles; slaves are still slaves; and the free are free—but they now relate with one another in a community that prefigures the differences-in-unity that will characterize the eschatological realm of God.

Paul describes the different parts of the human body in relationship with one another to show that people in the church with different gifts are responsible for one another (1 Cor. 12:14–26). By definition the various parts of the body are necessary to the body as a whole because *God* created the body and its parts (vv. 14–21).

In 12:22–26, Paul implicitly calls those of upper social standing to become healthy parts of the body of Christ by respecting those of lower strata. Indeed, the weaker parts of the body (referring both to delicate internal organs and to the people described in 8:7–12) are indispensable (10:22). The parts of the body *we* think are less honorable (genitalia) should be clothed with greater honor for *God* makes all members of the congregation share the same status in the body of Christ (10:23–24). The dissensions in the congregation, which mirror the distinctions of the social pyramid outside the church, have no place in the body of Christ (v. 25a). In this body, all people are to care for one another without regard for conventional social standing; in particular, the elites are to adjust their behavior to act for the benefit of those of lower status. Indeed, when the behavior of a few causes others to suffer, the entire body suffers; however, when one member is honored or treated with the respect due a member of the body, all rejoice (v. 26).

In 12:28–31 the apostle appears to say the church has its own hierarchy ("first apostles, second prophets. . . ."). However, Paul previously said that the apostles are of low status (2:6; 3:6–8, 18–19; 4:1–2, 9–12, 16–21), thus implying that the same things just said of the elite and nonelite (12:12–27) apply to apostles and all with gifts. The list in 12:28 is not the church's hierarchy but the apostle's humorous undermining of the notion of hierarchy. Apostles and others of low standing share the status of those on the upper side, so that all are one body with each part necessary and carrying out its own function.

Paul envisions the church as a body whose egalitarian and caring patterns of social relationship demonstrate God's alternative to the stratified and abusive relationships in the larger culture. The preacher might explore the degree to which the actual life of today's church either embodies Paul's vision or incorporates the same distortions of relationship that demonize the contemporary world.

Fourth Sunday after the Epiphany/Year C

1 Corinthians 13:1–13

In 1 Corinthians 13, the apostle draws deeply on Jewish tradition to suggest that Gentiles who speak in tongues (people who seek high social status) should recognize that, from God's perspective, their gift is low status, and that they should relate to others with love to build up community. The term "love" (*agape*) is seldom found in the Greek language until it appears in the Septuagint, where it is standard speech for God's love for Israel (e.g., Deut. 10:15) and for how people should live in covenantal community (e.g., Lev. 19:18). Apropos of Paul's discussion of the fragmentation of the Corinthian community, while *agape* includes the feeling of one for another, its fundamental meaning is acting for the good of another as a result of deciding to do so.

Paul urges the Corinthians (12:31) to aspire to a greater gift than the ones he just described: *agape* is a "more excellent way." ("Way" is a Jewish way of referring to conduct as in Ps. 1). The spiritual gifts discussed in 12:1–31—illustrated by speaking in tongues (alluding to those in the upper social strata), prophecy, understanding (knowledge), and faith—are a noisy gong or clanging cymbal without love (*agape*). Such gifts were used in the worship of idols that destroy community (1 Cor. 10:14–23; 12:2; Rom. 1:18–32). In 13:3, while some ancient manuscripts read "so that I may boast" (the wording adopted by the NRSV), other preferable manuscripts read "body to be burned." The latter is to be preferred because Paul alludes here to Jewish people martyred by fire because of faithfulness (e.g., 2 Macc. 7:5; 4 Macc. 6:26, 7:12). Expressing *agape* for the neighbor in community is the absolute norm for life in community.

In their lives together the Corinthians should manifest qualities of *agape* that the apostle identifies in 13:4–7, such as the positive values of patience, kindness, and rejoicing in truth. They should avoid envy, boasting, arrogance, insisting on one's own way, being irritable or resentful, and rejoicing in wrongdoing. While Paul does not say that each of these negative qualities directly corresponds to behavior in Corinth, they likely characterize the feelings that are fragmenting the community (for example, envy on the part of people in the lower social rung, as well as arrogance, boasting, and insisting on one's way on the part of people higher on the social pyramid).

The expression "all things" in 13:7 means "in all circumstances." The meaning of "bearing" (*stego*) is indicated by the occurrence of the same term in 9:12, where the apostle renounces his apostolic rights in support of community. The Corinthians are to act similarly. To "believe" (*pisteuo*) is to live faithfully. In the apocalyptic literature, hoping for (*elpizo*) all things is to look forward to the new world while recognizing that one must endure (*hupomeno*) in the difficult circumstances of the present until the apocalypse.

In 13:8–13, the apostle makes the decisive point that the practice of *agape* "remains," that is, will be a part of the divine realm forever (*1 En.* 49:1;

61:14) whereas the spiritual gifts will cease when the present age of history comes to an end (v. 8). In the present evil age, God provides the gifts to help people bear, believe, hope, and endure, but they provide only partial knowledge of God. Indeed, the relationship of the present gifts (and the status that comes with them) to the future world is similar to the comparison of a child with a mature adult, and to looking in a mirror (in antiquity, mirrors gave back imprecise images) versus seeing face to face. While faithfulness, hope, and love are essential aspects of the eschatological world (they "remain"), *agape* is the greatest and defines the content of the faithful life as well as that for which the community hopes. If the lofty Corinthians want to be a part of the eschatological world, they need to love now.

Fifth Sunday after the Epiphany/Year C

1 Corinthians 15:1–11

Please see Easter/Year B for commentary on this passage.

Sixth Sunday after the Epiphany/Year C

1 Corinthians 15:12–20

On the issues that prompt Paul to take up the resurrection, see our comments on the Fifth Sunday after the Epiphany/Year C. Resurrection is not an end in itself but represents participation in the impending divine realm of peace, love, abundance, reunion of Jewish and Gentile peoples, and eternal life. For that realm, God would give the faithful a resurrection body (see our comments on 1 Cor. 15:1–11). The resurrection of Jesus is the "first fruits" of this realm (15:20). Paul wants the Corinthians to use their current bodies faithfully so that God will give them resurrection bodies in the new age.

The educated of the upper class denied the resurrection of the dead (15:12). With others of their class, they have a negative view of the body and may believe that a life beyond death would not involve the body. They like the freedom to use their bodies to suit themselves in the present and do not like the idea of an embodied future. Paul now identifies six consequences of their denial with an eye towards prompting them to adopt the apostle's adaptation of a Jewish apocalyptic hope.

The first consequence is that if Christ is not raised from the dead, Paul's preaching and the Corinthians' faith is in vain, *kene* (15:14). The second consequence is that the apostles are "found to be misrepresenting God" (15:15). The word translated "misrepresent" is *pseudomartureo*, which is used in the Septuagint at Exodus 20:16 and Deuteronomy 5:20 for "bearing false witness" in a legal setting. False witnesses were to be exposed and possibly expelled from the community (Deut. 19:15–19; 1 Kgs. 21:5–19). Paul, then, is not only saying that he is a liar if Christ is not raised from the dead but that he stands condemned at the last judgment. Since he believes that his commission comes from God to preach Christ crucified and resurrected as the turning point of the ages, the lack of a resurrection would make God a liar and, consequently, untrustworthy.

A third consequence is that the Corinthians' faith is "futile" (15:17a). The term for "futile" [*mataios*] is not just a synonym for "in vain" [*kene*] of verse 14 but is often associated with idols and idolaters (Wis. 13:1; 15:8): therefore, those who deny the resurrection partake of idolatry. A fourth consequence is that if Jesus has not been raised, the Corinthians would still be in their sins, living in a world shaped by the results of sin—the world with its false values, injustice, exploitation, violence, and death (1 Cor. 15:17b). Here, release from sin is connected not with Jesus' death but with the resurrection. A fifth consequence is that those who have already died in Christ are simply dead and have no future (1 Cor. 15:18). The sixth consequence is that if we have hoped in Christ "for this life only" (and not for the resurrection), we are of all people most to be "pitied" [*eleeinos*] or, as the term could better be translated to catch the spirit of this consequence, "most miserable."

A preacher today is in an awkward position with respect to these issues. Most Christians speak about life continuing immediately after death in ways that are closer to the upper-class congregants (who are, according to Paul, theologically mistaken) than to the apocalyptic notion of resurrection of the dead. In truth, today's minister cannot *know* with confidence which view (if either) is true. Nevertheless, a preacher can still make Paul's deeper point. As one of us says frequently, our deeds "matter ultimately because they matter to the One who is ultimate," and this One calls us to live now through our bodies toward a world of love, abundance, justice, and respect for all. Although we do not have a blueprint of the future, we can trust God to manage the future in ways that are consistent with unconditional love.

Seventh Sunday after the Epiphany/Year C

1 Corinthians 15:35–38, 42–50

This lection continues Paul's address to the Corinthians described in our remarks on the two previous Sundays. The apostle pleads with the educated

Corinthians in the upper class who deprecate the idea of bodily resurrection to recognize the truth of this idea and its corollary—that to share the resurrected life of the coming new world, they must live their embodied lives now in community with the less educated on the lower social reaches.

The lesson for today answers the questions of 1 Corinthians 15:35 by describing the nature of the resurrection body, the body in which believers will live in God's realm. Paul assumes that those who are raised will have a material body: the apostle contrasts the present body that decays with the resurrection body that does not. Paul does not contrast a present material body with life as a nonmaterial self. The question is, "With *what kind of body* do they come?" Paul seeks to describe the resurrection body so attractively that the Corinthian elites will want to reshape their current behaviors in order to have a share in the world to come.

Paul's use of the seed and growing in verses 36–37 is a Jewish image used to describe the process of moving from one state to another changed state (*4 Ezra* 4:26–32; 5:48–49; 8:6; esp. 8:41–45; 9:17–22). When buried, the body is simply dead. However, on the day of resurrection the body is transformed in the same way that a grain of wheat sprouts and yields a stalk and a harvest that is dramatically different from the seed (vv. 36–37).

God gives each kind of seed (and plant) its own kind of body (15:38). The apostle illustrates this principle by reminding the readers that different kinds of creatures have different kinds of flesh—human beings, animals, birds, and fish. Another illustration comes from the astral world— there are different heavenly bodies with different kinds of glory—sun, moon, and stars (15:39–41). Each has the body God designs.

As there are different bodies among earthly and heavenly beings so the present human body differs from the future resurrection one (15:42–44). The present body dies—perishable, dishonorable, weak, and physical— terms indicating not only the characteristics of the body but also having social resonance, suggesting that at death the congregants who value high standing go to the bottom of the status ladder. By contrast, the faithful have resurrection bodies—imperishable, glorious, powerful, and spiritual —in other words, *unending* high status in a world of people who all share that state.

The difference between the "physical body" (*psukios*) and the "spiritual" (*pneumatikos*) is not a contrast between nonmaterial and material. We learn from 15:45–49 that the "physical body" is the self as determined— and buffeted—by the present evil age. Though the first Adam was a "living being" (*pseuxen zosan*, Gen. 2:7), Adam's *psuche* brought death (15:21– 22), a symbol for the brokenness after the fall, an existence that is "of the earth" where the powers corrupt and enslave, and is "dust" (*choikos*), a created substance that has no power of its own and that sometimes has negative associations (*4 Ezra* 7:31–32, 62–69). By contrast, Christ is from heaven, the sphere where all things take place as God desires. Furthermore, for apocalyptic theologians, the quality of life in heaven is a prototype for life in the coming eschatological age. In this passage, Paul implicitly puts a question to the Corinthians who deprecate the body: In the unending time after the apocalypse, he is asking, which image would you rather bear: the image of the person of the dust, or the glory of the one from heaven?

Eighth Sunday after the Epiphany/Year C

1 Corinthians 15:51–58

In 1 Corinthians 15:1–49, Paul stresses that people in the new age have resurrection bodies. The first part of 1 Corinthians 15:50, "What I am saying, brothers and sisters, is this," indicates that the lection for this week is the capstone of the appeal to the cultivated Corinthians that we have previously described. When the apostle says, "Flesh and blood cannot inherit the [realm] of God, nor does the perishable inherit the imperishable" (v. 50), the problem is not that the flesh and blood and the perishable are bodies but that they embody the present, broken age. Qualities contrary to the purposes of God are not included in the eschatological world.

Beginning with 15:51a, Paul describes what he thinks will happen at the apocalypse, when Jesus returns to end the present era of history and finally and fully manifest the divine realm. The word "mystery" here is a nearly technical term by which apocalyptic writers sometimes refer to the time line and events leading to (and including) the apocalypse. These things are mysterious in that only God knows their timing.

Paul thinks the apocalypse may occur before some of the readers of the letter die. Even if it does, all believers' bodies will be transformed into resurrection bodies in a single, dramatic moment. Paul joins some other apocalyptic visionaries in thinking that a trumpet will sound to signal the great moment of transformation (15:51b–53). The current body is "perishable" and "mortal," characteristics of the body in the present broken age, but God will make the resurrection body "imperishable" and "immortal" for life in the new world (vv. 53–54a).

For Paul, death is not simply a state of being but a superpower. In this spirit, Paul personifies death (15:54b–55). According to Paul, Isaiah 25:8

and Hosea 13:14 interpret the apocalyptic moment. Isaiah 25:8 is part of a vision of a banquet celebrating God's royal rule when death is devoured by God's strength. Paul changes "strength" from the Septuagintal original to "victory." In Hosea 13:1–13, God condemns Ephraim for idolatry. Paul follows the Septuagint's understanding of the difficult Hebrew of Hosea 13:14 as an assurance from God that the judgment is only temporary and that God will redeem Ephraim from death. In any event, the apostle alters the Septuagint text of Hosea 13:14 from "Where is your penalty, O death," to "'Where, O death, is your victory?" (v. 55) again because victory seems better to fit Paul's point.

The "sting" of death is sin. Sin here, as usual for Paul, is a power that enslaves and fractures the world. The word "sting" (*kentron*) is more vivid in Greek than in English as it refers to a goad—a wooden rod with a sharpened end or capped with a metal point—that was used either to poke an animal to keep it moving in a particular direction or as an instrument for controlling (by jabbing) and even torturing, human beings. Death uses sin to jab and hurt people. Sin is a power lesser than death that causes the world to be a chaos.

"The power of sin is the law" (v. 56). Paul does not here make a negative evaluation of torah. Since the Corinthian congregation is largely composed of Gentiles, Paul must draw on a Jewish tradition, little known to most modern Christians, that regarded the Gentiles as condemned because they did not honor the commandments of God (for example, *4 Ezra* 7:20–24).[37] Sin uses the law to place Gentiles in a situation of disobedience for which they will be painfully punished at the apocalypse.

Paul bursts out a theocentric exultation in 15:57: "Thanks be to *God*" (emphasis added). The victory, of course, is release from death (and its agent sin) and condemnation, as well as welcome into the renewed world. The death, resurrection, and return of Jesus Christ are means through which God accomplishes the victory. Consequently, the Corinthians are to live in relationship with others in the congregation as Paul has prescribed in this letter. For "your labor is not in vain" (15:58). Indeed, it results in a resurrection body in the realm of God.

Ninth Sunday after the Epiphany/Year C

Galatians 1:1–12

Paul wrote Galatians because some in the community had abandoned Paul's interpretation of the gospel and adopted "another gospel" brought by other missionaries. Some earlier scholars saw the others as Jews who taught that, to earn God's favor, the Galatians needed to abandon Christ and perform works demanded by the law. According to this earlier view, Paul wrote to save the Galatians from Judaism, a religion of works righteousness, legalism, and empty ceremony. Christianity has replaced Judaism.

However, based on fresh understandings of Judaism, and on evidence in Galatians itself, many scholars are moving from this negative caricature and, instead, are revising how to understand the other missionaries, Judaism, and Paul's statements about the law. Increasing numbers of contemporary scholars see the other missionaries as people *in the Jesus movement* who do advocate Jewish practices, but scholars are divided regarding their theological identity. Some see them as "Christian Jews" (though the term "Christian" was not in use in Paul's day). Other scholars view the other missionaries as *Gentiles* who believed they must perform "works of the law" to be saved. For reasons given at Galatians 2 and 3, we join this latter group of scholars. In this view, Paul objects not to Judaism or the law but to the *misinterpretation of the law* by the other missionaries.[38] Indeed, Paul's evaluation of Judaism and the law are positive, and the apostle sees the church as an extension of the mission of Israel adapted for Gentiles because of eschatological emergency created by the imminence of the apocalypse.

While the revised understanding have their greatest impact in the interpretation of Galatians 2 and 3, their impact reaches into today's lesson. At the beginning of ancient letters, a typical salutation indicated author, recipients, and greetings. Paul nuances this formula for theological purposes. In 1:1 he not only identifies himself as author but as apostle (one sent with a commission) and immediately sounds a key theme in this letter: he is an authoritative interpreter because his commission came not from human beings but from Jesus and God. In Galatians 1:13–17, Paul explains further that his commission is to preach to Gentiles. He strengthens his credentials by pointing out that he is not alone: others join him in the views expressed in the letter (1:2).

In connection with 1 Corinthians 1:1–9 (Second Sunday after the Epiphany/Year A), we point out that the designation "church" and the formula "grace and peace" suggest positive association between the church and Judaism (Gal. 1:2b–3). Such positive connection is reinforced by 1:4b, where Paul joins other Jewish apocalyptic theologians in believing that God will soon end the present evil age and replace it with new age of love and justice (e.g., *1 En.* 91:15–17; 2 Esd. 7:50). For Paul, the cosmic rulers who distort the present world fought the coming of the new age by putting Jesus to death. That death, however, became the occasion whereby God revealed the divine power to free people from their sins, that is, from the actions and thoughts committed under the influence of the cosmic powers that turn the present into a chaotic and broken realm (1:4). Indeed, the earlier statement that God raised Jesus from the dead indicates that Jesus' death and resurrection are signs that the apocalyptic transformation is at hand (1:1). In 1:5, Paul highlights the theocentric (and Jewish) character of his theology: glory for the role of Jesus Christ in the transformation of the world goes to God.

In 1:6–9, Paul states the main theme of the letter in simple but stringent terms. As noted previously, some in the community are turning to a "different gospel" brought into the community by other missionaries. As we learn from 1:15 and 5:8, "the one who called you in the grace of Christ" is God. By adopting the other so-called gospel, the Galatians "desert" the grace of Christ; the other interpretation of the gospel is confusing and a "perversion of the gospel of Christ" (1:6–7). While Christians today may hear "the grace of Christ" and "gospel of Christ" as focusing on the person of Christ, in the Pauline context such phrases envision Christ as the agent through whom God is effecting the regeneration of the world, a regeneration that will be complete only when Christ returns to destroy the present world and remake it (1 Cor. 15:20–28, 50–57).

Paul may use hyperbole in referring to "an angel from heaven" preaching "a gospel contrary to what we preached to you" (1:8). The other missionaries may have claimed their gospel did come from an angel. Even if it did, it would be misleading. But nevertheless Paul's response is very strong: Let the person who follows the alternative gospel be accursed. In Israel, a curse could result in death (Lev. 17:28–29; Deut. 7:26). For apocalyptically oriented writers, to be cursed could mean to be left out of the realm of God (Zech. 14:11; Rev. 22:3).

Paul's point in 1:10 was important to the Hellenistic age that valued sincerity and integrity in public speakers: he says he has not shaped his gospel to win human approval by admitting Gentiles as Gentiles—without initiating them into Judaism—into the community awaiting the eschaton. To do so to please people would be to deny his calling as an apostle of Christ. Ministers in our self-absorbed culture would do well to ponder the degree to which we "seek human approval" in our preaching.

Last Sunday after the Epiphany/Year C

Transfiguration Sunday

2 Corinthians 3:12–4:2

Paul wants the Corinthians to understand why they should follow his teaching and turn away from that of the super apostles (11:5; 12:11) who have visited Corinth since the writing of 1 Corinthians. They offer dramatic, immediate spiritual experience whereas Paul appears modest and offers a theology that begins with the cross as the paradigm of life as the Corinthians await the second coming. Further background for today's passage can be found in our discussion of 3:1–6 on the Eighth Sunday after the Epiphany/Year B.

In 2 Corinthians 3:7–11, Paul uses a typical rabbinic argument from the lesser (the theology and ministry of the super apostles) to the greater (Paul's own theology and ministry).[39] In line with our remarks about 3:6, the expressions "letters" and "stone tablets" in 3:7a refer to the super apostles' teaching that they receive mystical visions directly from God. This view is evidently based on a particular interpretation of Exodus 34:29–34 that uses Moses' ascent to the mountain to receive the commandments as the *model for their own mystical ascent* to receive visions that assure them they already participate in "glory" (Exod. 34:29–32). "Glory" for the super apostles is the immediate effervescent experience of visions that assure them of the divine presence but that ignore suffering as a part of the transition from the present brokenness to the world to come. Paul points out in 3:8–11, however, that their experience of glory is only temporary and will pass away, and when God will manifest the "greater glory" of verse 10 and "the permanent come in glory" of verse 11 after the second coming.

The super apostles claim that their gospel brings people glory while Paul's gospel is veiled; here the interpretation of Exodus 34:29–34 is at issue. For these other missionaries, the text presents a picture of the unveiled Moses "who speaks ecstatically after his vision on the mount with glory on his face."[40] We learn from 2 Corinthians 1:12, 17; 6:11–12; and 7:4 that the super apostles accuse Paul of vacillation and of speaking in obscurity. Figuratively speaking, they accuse Paul of speaking "with a veil over his face."

In 3:12–18, the apostle not only rebuts this charge but implies that the other missionaries have incorrectly used Exodus 34:29–34. *Paul* speaks "with great boldness" (*parresia*), that is, not veiled but frankly and publicly (3:12). The *super apostles* imitate Moses, but not in the way they think they do. According to Paul, they speak from *behind a veil*, preventing the community "from gazing at the end of the glory." In other words, they prevent the congregation from seeing clearly the nature of the coming realm of God beside which the glory so prized by the super apostles will fail (3:13). Therefore, the super apostles and those who follow them are "hardened" against the purposes of God in the same way as Pharaoh (3:14a).

In 3:15b Paul applies his reading of Exodus more specifically to the super apostles. "Indeed, to this very day, when they hear the reading of the old covenant, that same veil is still there." The phrase "old covenant" (*palaia diatheke*) does not appear elsewhere in ancient literature. Although Christians have often taken it in a derogatory way (i.e., old = outmoded), nothing in the context insists on this. Indeed, the ancients valued old things. Gaston translates "the ancient covenant,"[41] or we might think of it as "the ancestral covenant" in the sense of the covenant previously made known to the ancestors whose eschatological implications are only now (at the time of Paul) being revealed.

The super apostles and their devotees need to realize that "when one turns to the Lord, the veil is removed": that is, they come to a theology and understanding of ministry similar to Paul's (3:16). Since Moses dealt with God, and since Paul's theology is theocentric, "the Lord" here is probably God, who uses the Spirit to bring people to such insights (3:17a). Indeed, Pauline theology and ministry, with its emphasis on suffering, frees the Corinthians from the tyranny of seeking evermore high-voltage spiritual ecstasies of the kind prescribed by the false apostles.

Echoing 1 Corinthians 13, Paul reminds readers that their present experience is at best a mirror image of what will be. (In antiquity, mirrors were much less precise than today and presented only a vague picture of the self). However, even now they are in the process of being "transformed" (in Greek the word is "metamorphosized") for the final glory of the realm of God.

The reading for today ends with a statement of the implications of Paul's critique of the super apostles and the positive impact of Paul's own theology. Although Paul recognizes that the time until the apocalypse will be one of tribulation and suffering (including conflicts such as the one with the super apostles), Paul does not lose heart, nor does he resort to the same kinds of tricks as the super apostles—cunning and falsification (shrinking) of God's purposes. Regardless of the cost, the apostle will continue to speak openly (see especially 4:1–2).

Ash Wednesday/Years A, B, and C

2 Corinthians 5:20b-6:10

Please see Ash Wednesday/Year A for commentary on this passage.

First Sunday in Lent/Year C

Romans 10:8b–13

Please see Proper 14/Year A for our discussion of this passage.

Second Sunday in Lent/Year C

Philippians 3:17–4:1

Today's passage continues the line of thought begun in Philippians 2:1ff. and our discussion on Palm/Passion Sunday/Years A, B, and C. On the Fifth Sunday in Lent/Year A and on Proper 21/Year C Paul seeks for the community to develop a common mind with regard to faithful living, especially in the face of challenges from Gentile "dogs" whose message is distracting the congregation.

In Philippians 3:15, when Paul says, "Let those of us who are mature [*teleioi*] be of the same mind," he means, "Let those of us who understand that we are living at the turning of the ages, be of the same mind." By the "same mind" Paul means the mind of Christ Jesus shared in the community (2:1–11). The coming apocalypse should bring the community together. In this vein, Paul continues, "If you think differently about anything, this too God will reveal to you." The expression "will reveal" is the future tense of *apokalupto*, the root of "apocalypse." The congregation needs to "hold fast," to be ready (3:16). The person listening in Greek would hear a meaning connected to the pervading concern for the common life. The verb *stoicheo* can mean "remaining together" or "being in harmony with one another."

When the apostle exhorts the congregation to imitate him and others who live faithfully (3:17), he is not engaging in massive egotism. In antiquity, imitation was a conventional pattern of education, with no intimation of preoccupation or self-elevation (e.g., 4 Macc. 9:23; 13:9; *Let. Aris.* 188, 210, 280–81; *T. Ben.*; 3:1).

In 3:18–19, Paul returns to the theme of the misleading missionaries, elsewhere the "dogs." They are "enemies of the cross of Christ," that is, they work against the revelation of God's purposes through Christ (2:6–8) and the qualities of community life that should come from having "the same mind." When the apostle speaks of his tears (3:18), readers feel the depth of his care. Paul is especially anxious because he believes that the misleading teachers will fall under "destruction," *apoleia*, a notion often applied to the condemnation and to their eternal punishment (*1 En.* 98:10; 99:4; 106:15).

In an earlier era, commentators thought that when Paul says, "Their God is their belly," he refers to the misleading teachers' view that the congregation should follow Jewish food laws. However, Jewish eating customs were seldom (if ever) associated with the term "belly" (*koilia*). Romans 16:18 provides a satisfactory explanation where a similar expression refers to self-consuming appetites, a typical Gentile problem.

When the apostle reminds the hearers that "our citizenship [*politeuma*] is in heaven," (v. 20), he does not thereby say that the present age is unimportant. Paul takes up technical vocabulary from the *polis*, the community of the common good. *Politeuma* referred to citizenship and often designates a group of citizens of one state who were sent to colonize another area in behalf of the state of their citizenry. From this point of view, the congregation is a colony of the eschatological world in the midst of the present evil age.

Paul ends this section of the epistle with a touching statement of his feeling for the congregation, his longing for them to be a part of the world to come (4:1) and, congruently, his hope that they will not be destroyed.

Philippians 3:17–4:1 is read in the heart of the season of Lent. Given the fact that several of the readings from the gospels in Lent critique the Jewish community, the preacher has an opportunity through today's text to make it clear that the Jewish people are not "enemies of the cross of Christ." This passage is diametrically opposed to that distortion. According to Paul, Judaism shares with Christianity the anticipation that God will transform this world so that all things, including "enemies of God," live together according to God's purposes.

Third Sunday in Lent/Year C

1 Corinthians 10:1–13

This passage interprets the story of the exodus as a second example (after 1 Corinthians 9:1–27) illustrating the call of 1 Corinthians 8:1–13 for the wealthy to limit their freedom for the sake of the community. The fact that Paul refers to "*our* ancestors" (our italics) in 1 Corinthians 10:1 indicates that Paul assumes that key traditions of Israel should now shape the identity of the largely Gentile congregation at Corinth. Like other typologists in antiquity, Paul retells the ancient story with language that connects it to the present by saying that these ancestors were "baptized" [*baptizo*] into Moses in the cloud and the sea (Exod. 13:21–22; 14:22; Ps. 105:39; Wis. 19:7–8). For Paul here, baptism is a kind of experience of the exodus for the Corinthians (1 Cor. 10:2). In 10:3, the ancestors consumed "spiritual" (*pneumatikos*) food (Exod. 16:4, 35; Deut. 8:3; Ps. 78:24–25) and drink (Exod. 17:6; Num. 20:7–11; Ps. 78:15–16), thus having the same spirit-animated life as the Corinthians (1 Cor. 2:13, 15; 9:11; 12:1; 14:1), who eat a similar spiritual meal (10:16–22; 11:17–34). The story of the ancestors is the story of the Corinthians.

For Paul, the ancestors drank from Christ, the spiritual rock that followed the Israelites (10:4). Jewish tradition referred to a well that traveled with the Israelites (*Sukkah* 3.11), and Philo envisaged such a rock as wisdom (*Leg.* 2.86). Insofar as Paul's theology is theocentric (Christ reveals God), we can understand his allegorization of the rock and Christ as indicating that the same divine providence the Corinthians experience through Christ was present for the ancestors in the wilderness. Despite such dynamic experiences of providence, however, many ancestors sinned. God was not pleased (10:5), and many died in the wilderness (Num. 14:16–30; Ps. 78:30–31).

In Corinthians 10:6–13, Paul uses four themes from the exodus and wandering to warn the status-seeking members of the community to avoid the sins of the ancestors: First, the community should avoid idolatry (v. 7), the quintessential act of unfaithfulness in the Jewish tradition and a phenomenon that was problematic for the Corinthian community (5:10–11; 6:9; 8:1–13, 10:14–11:1). Second, the community should not indulge in "sexual immorality" (v. 8) or fornication (*porneia*), another problem in the Corinthian congregation (1 Cor. 5:1, 9, 11; 6:9, 12–20; 7:2ff.). Because of sexual immorality in the wilderness, Paul says that twenty-three thousand died by the plague in a single day (Num. 25:1–9). Third, they should not put Christ to the test (*peirazo*; 1 Cor. 10:9) as their ancestors did in the wilderness, some of whom were destroyed by serpents (Num. 21:1–6). Finally, Paul says in 10:10 that the community should not complain or murmur (*gogguzo*; e.g., Num. 14:1–4; 27; 17:1–7) because they were destroyed by "the destroyer," an avenging angel (Exod. 12:23; Wis. 18:20–25). Rather, the Corinthians need to learn from these examples or face condemnation at the end of history.

The text ends with three problematic motifs that require careful theological reflection. First, today's preacher will likely want to take issue with Paul's assertion that the events in the exodus (just reported) occurred *in order to* serve as an example for the Corinthians (10:11a; also 10:6). Paul's approach robs the exodus events of their own integrity. The sermon can help the congregation learn from the exodus events simply as examples. Second, relatively few people in the long-established denominations today share Paul's confidence that the end of the ages is at hand (10:11b). The preacher could help the congregation recognize that we do not need to share that belief to appreciate Paul's deeper point that we are called to account for our behavior and its consequences. Paul wants the readers to "stand," that is, to be faithful (10:12). Third, according to 10:13 the situation of the world is one of "testing" (*peirasmos*, related to *peiarzo* in 10:9). Paul here evokes the apocalyptic idea that immediately before the apocalypse, life's difficulties would increase as the principalities and powers dug in their heels to resist God's coming so that temptations to unfaithfulness increase. The preacher should indicate forcefully that *God* does not visit difficult experiences upon people. They arise simply from the fallen nature of the world. Paul's enduring point is that God is faithful, and the divine presence makes it possible for us to live through such experiences.

Fourth Sunday in Lent/Year C

2 Corinthians 5:16–21

Paul is here not setting out abstract theology but responding to the situation in Corinth (described in Propers 4–6/Year B) in which super apostles promulgated a message based on dramatic but momentary visionary experiences. Today's passage is a part of Paul's driving purpose in this part of 2 Corinthians: to reclaim the congregation for his gospel with its notion that present suffering is part of the tribulation preceding the apocalyptic cataclysm and the coming of the new world.

When Paul says, "We regard no one from a human point of view" (5:16), the phrase "human point of view" is *kata sarka* or "according to flesh." Flesh, for Paul, is life under the fractious domain of the principalities and unawareness of the apocalyptic moment. Before Paul recognized Christ as an agent of apocalypse, the apostle thought of him as only a participant in the broken sphere of flesh. As a result of encountering Christ, Paul now perceives all persons from the perspective of their readiness for the new age.

This idea is explicit in 5:17, which draws on the image of "new creation" from apocalypticism to describe the coming world (*1 En.* 45:4–5; 51:4–5; *2 Bar.* 32:6; 2 Esd. 5:45; 7:55). People who are "new creations" in the present embody the eschatological world.

In Paul's apocalyptic theology, "reconciliation" (*katallaso*) not only refers to overcoming a feeling of alienation; it also has a social overtone (5:18a). While the term "reconciliation" occurs seldom in ancient literature, it usually bespeaks restoration of property and relationships to their original purpose (Isa. 9:5; with God: 2 Macc. 1:5; 5:20; 7:33; 8:29). From this perspective we might think of "to himself" (*heautos* in the dative) as meaning "to God's purposes [for community]." The "ministry [*diakonia*] of reconciliation" (5:18b) is to let others know that the apocalyptic renewal is underway and is helping them form communities of mutuality that prefigure those of the eschaton.

Christ is God's agent who demonstrates God's reconciling purposes for "the world" (*ho cosmos*) in the season of the apocalypse (5:19a). For Paul, the "world" often means the fallen creation. When the apostle says that Christ does not "count their trespasses against them," the word "count" (*logizomai*) refers, as in *Testament of Zebulon* 9:7, to the verdict of the final judgment (per 2 Cor. 5:10), while Paul uses the word *paraptoma* for "trespasses" (rather than the more frequent *hamartia* for "sin"). A trespass is a willful act that violates God's design for community and creates the need for reconciliation, that is, restoration of community (Wis. 3:13; 10:1; *Pss. Sol.* 13:5).

God has now entrusted to Paul the "clay jar" of 4:7, the message that the reconciliation or restoration of the world is underway (5:19c). Now Paul and his companions are "ambassadors [*presbeuo*] for Christ," that is, envoys who are charged with carrying out a mission (5:20a). Paul appeals to the community that is fractured by the false gospel of the super apostles to take steps that lead to reconciliation (5:20b).

The reason for this appeal is that God "made [Christ] to be sin [*hamartia*] who knew no sin, so that in him we might become the righteousness of God" (5:21). For Paul, sin is one of the powers that rule the world. Paul's reference to Christ not knowing sin is to the preexistence of Christ in the heavenly world when he was not under the power of sin. However, God sent Christ into the world to know sin, in other words, to be put to death by the powers of this age (including sin), so that God could raise Christ and thereby demonstrate the righteousness of God.

The phrase "righteousness of God" indicates not only that God in Godself is righteous but also that God acts righteously. Righteousness (*dikaiosune*) refers to God's setting right all relationships in the eschatological world. When Paul says, "We might become the righteousness of God," he means that the presence of the church (a community whose right relationships embody those of the new age) is a sign that God's promise to "righteous" the world is true.

Fifth Sunday in Lent/Year C

Philippians 3:4b–14

Please see Proper 22 [27]/Year A for commentary on this passage.

Palm/Passion Sunday/Years A, B, and C

Philippians 2:5–11

Please see Palm/Passion Sunday/Year A for commentary on this passage.

Monday of Holy Week/Year C

Hebrews 9:11–15

Please see Monday in Holy Week/Year A for commentary on this passage.

Tuesday of Holy Week/Year C

1 Corinthians 1:18–31

Please see the Fourth Sunday after the Epiphany/Year A for commentary on this passage.

Wednesday of Holy Week/Year C

Hebrews 12:1–3

Please see Wednesday of Holy Week/Year A for commentary on this text.

Holy Thursday/Year C

Maundy Thursday

1 Corinthians 11:23–26

Please see Holy Thursday/Year A for commentary on this passage.

Good Friday/Year C

Hebrews 10:16–25

Please see Good Friday/Year A (alt) for commentary on this text.

Hebrews 4:14–16; 5:7–9

Please see Good Friday/Year A for commentary on this text.

Holy Saturday/Year C

1 Peter 4:1–8

Please see Holy Saturday/Year A for commentary on this passage.

Easter Day/Year C

1 Corinthians 15:19–26

Along with many other Jewish theologians in the Hellenistic Age (300 BCE to 200 CE), Paul is apocalyptic in orientation, believing that God was soon to end the present evil age with an apocalypse and replace this world with a new one in which all relationships and circumstances manifest God's desire for all to live in love, peace, mutual support, and abundance. Paul's distinctive view is that the death and resurrection of Jesus Christ were the definitive revelation that this great transformation was underway. The world to come would include the reunion of Jewish and Gentile peoples.

One of Paul's overarching goals in the writing of 1 Corinthians was to persuade the members of the community to use their bodies in ways that are consistent with God's purposes and will bring them into the world to come. The apostle uses 1 Corinthians 15 as a lure to the congregation. Paul hopes that, after being reminded that the faithful will (after the apocalypse) receive resurrection bodies for life in the eschatological age, they will want to be a part of that world and will bring their individual and collective behaviors into line with the divine purposes.

Most apocalyptic writers in antiquity envisioned a sequence of events from the present through the apocalypse to God's establishing of the new age. Today's lection is one of Paul's summaries of how he anticipates these things taking place. Another time line is found in 1 Thessalonians 4:16–5:5.

According to 1 Corinthians 15:19, the congregation and the apostle are "most to be pitied" if they have hoped in Christ "for this life only." For this life is the present, evil, and unredeemed age. To make things right, God needs to create a new world.

The writer reminds the community in 15:20 that Christ has been raised from the dead. Jewish apocalypticists expected that in the new world people would be raised and given transformed resurrection bodies. For Paul, the resurrection of Christ is a sign that the general resurrection and the apocalypse are just ahead. The need for resurrection and a new world came about because of Adam who, by disobeying God in the garden of Eden, caused God to curse the human family with death (1 Cor. 15:21; Gen. 3:7–17).

In the present age, all die, but God has begun to bring people alive and will complete this at the apocalypse. The resurrection of Christ is the "first fruit," the first sign that the new world is about to come into being (15:23a). When Christ returns from heaven with glory, those who belong to him will be raised (15:23a), and according to 1 Thessalonians 4:16–18, they will be united in the air.

When the apocalypse itself occurs, Jesus will "hand over the realm [NRSV: kingdom] to God," but only after Jesus has destroyed "every ruler and every authority and power" (v. 24), as well as death. The rulers, authorities, and powers were transhuman forces (such as the devil and demons) in the world who defied God's authority and sought to make the world their own domain. These forces could inhabit individuals and groups and cause them to deviate from God's desires. For Paul, death is not simply the end of life but is a personified superpower who actively works against God.

Paul's thoroughgoing theocentrism comes into bold relief in 15:27–28. Despite the centrality of Jesus in the apocalyptic denouement to history, Paul underscores his perception that Jesus is God's agent. True, the apostle turns to Psalm 8:6 to establish that "'God has put all things in subjection under his feet'" (v. 27), "subjection," in this instance, referring to the power to order all things as God desires. Yet, Paul continues that the psalm "does not include the one who put all things in subjection under him [Jesus]." When all things are subject to Jesus, then Jesus himself will be subjected to God.

Today's preacher and congregation may be hesitant to embrace particular aspects of Paul's vision of what will happen as this world ends and the new one begins. Indeed, some preachers and congregations do not believe that history will come to a formulaic apocalyptic end. Nevertheless, on Easter Day it may help many congregations for the preacher to remind them that, for Paul, the resurrection is not the goal of God's work. Rather, it is a sign that God's life-restoring power is not only at work in this world of death but is stronger than all other forces that would resist it. The hope of the second coming reminds the congregation that God is perpetually at work and never gives up, to help the world more fully embody God's purposes of love, peace, and justice.

Second Sunday of Easter/Year C

Revelation 1:4–8

Please see the Reign of Christ, Proper 29/Year B for commentary on this passage.

Third Sunday of Easter/Year C

Revelation 5:11–14

Introductory background on the book of Revelation is unfolded on the Reign of Christ/Year A. We note further that the apocalyptic writers believed that the present earthly existence is an evil age shot through with poverty, exploitation, violence, and death that God would soon destroy and, in its place, establish an unending reign of love, justice, abundance, and eternal life (the realm of God). The latter qualities already operate in heaven where realities and events function as prototypes of realities and events for the earth. Apocalyptic prophets or visionaries such as John were often transported into the heavenly world to assuring visions of God's power and victory over evil on which the community on earth could count. The prophet returned to earth to announce what had been revealed in order to encourage the community to endure (Rev. 1:9; 2:2, 19; 3:10; 13:10; 14:12). Because the victory was already established in heaven, the community could live through the present age knowing that its suffering is temporary.

In Revelation 4:1–11 John is transported to the heavenly world that he describes in figurative language. God sits on a throne (symbol of ruling power) at the center (*1 En.* 14:15–25; *2 Bar.* 22:1). Israel and the church (represented by the twenty-four elders around the throne) are in the circle of God's protection. Before the throne is a sea of glass, like crystal indicating that God calms the power of chaos (often represented in Jewish tradition by a large body of water; see *1 En.* 10:10–14). The throne is surrounded by four living creatures bespeaking the various realms of animate life. The elders and the creatures willingly serve God's purposes as indicated by their constant hymn acknowledging God's holiness and by the elders taking off their crowns and placing them before God. This vision depicts the way things are in heaven, which means that the community on earth can live in the confidence that this is the way things will be on earth. The community would also recognize the implicit contrast between Caesar's limited court (with its oppressive purposes) and God's cosmic rule.

In 5:1–10, the prophet sees God hand a scroll (a symbol indicating that God had planned history to come to a redemptive apocalyptic conclusion; *1 En.* 106:19; 2 Esd. 14:45–47) to Jesus who is here described as "the Lion of the tribe of Judah, the root of David" (Gen. 49:9–10; Isa. 11:1–11; 2 Esd. 12:31–32) who has conquered and can open the scroll. Jesus does not oppose Judaism but is in the line of leaders of Israel. The distinctive work of Jesus is not to establish a new religion but to serve as instrument of the apocalyptic transformation on behalf of the God of Israel. This vision figuratively interprets the meaning of Jesus: he is the powerful Lion of Judah through whom the power of God is expressed as a slaughtered lamb (Exod. 12:6). Jesus ordains the persecuted church a priestly community (in the manner of Judaism, Exod. 19:6) who "reign" by serving God.

Revelation 5:11–14 depicts the creatures of 4:1–11, along with many others, celebrating God's victory through Christ (5:11; cf. Dan. 7:10; *1 En.* 14:21–22,). To be "worthy" is to exercise power faithfully for God's purposes (v. 12). Every living creature joins in the song—"in heaven and on earth and under the earth and in the sea" (v. 13). While they celebrate the worthiness of Christ, their thanksgiving is directed first to the God of Israel—"'the one seated on the throne'"—and then to the Lamb who is God's trusted representative (v. 13b).

Caesarism is in the background. The empire encircled the Mediterranean, but it had limits. Although the empire included people from many tribes, languages, and nations, it did not embrace the heavenly multitudes nor the myriads of others (including the creatures of 5:13). Beside God's cosmic sovereignty, the Roman Empire pales and will soon end. God's court, by contrast, endures "forever and ever." The elders model how the community should respond to this mighty revelation: by worshiping. The hymns of the church join those of heaven in celebrating God's triumph. This vision is one of many that empowers the church towards faithfulness in the midst of its gritty and often painful existence.

Fourth Sunday of Easter/Year C

Revelation 7:9–17

The passage assigned for today continues the vision of heaven beginning in 4:1. A vision in heaven (often in symbolic language) is a prototype of what will occur on earth. The community can live through suffering on earth because they have seen God's mighty victory over evil and the transformation of the world into the divine realm.

The prophet sees two visions of huge numbers of people in the heavenly world. The first one, Revelation 7:1–8, declares that 144,000 were sealed "out of the tribes of the people Israel." The number twelve is a figurative way of speaking of Israel. In antiquity, multiplying by a thousand represented a vast number. The "seal" (*sphragizo*) is God's protection over Jewish people (Ezek. 9:4; *Pss. Sol.* 15:6–9). Commentators sometimes speak of these 144,000 as the new Israel, but such language is imported from later Christian theology. The text itself does not suggest that they are anything other than Jewish people who, as Jewish people, are part of the eschatological world.

The second vision, Revelation 7:9–17, is of "a great multitude that no one could count from every nation . . . standing before" God and Jesus.

These folk, who include Gentiles, wear white robes, symbols of faithfulness (Rev. 3:4; 6:11). After the Jewish people evicted the forces of Antiochus Epiphanes IV from the temple, they entered carrying palm branches that became symbols of deliverance (1 Macc. 13:51; 2 Macc. 10:7).

Those in the white robes cry out that salvation (*soteria*) comes from God and the Lamb. Salvation here is life in the postapocalyptic new world (2 Esd. 6:25; 8:39). They are joined by the heavenly beings who fall on their faces (a demonstration of awe) from 4:1–11 and worship (7:11–12; on 4:1–11, see the Third Sunday after Easter/Year C).

An elder asks John to identify the ones robed in white and their origin, but John affirms that the elder has the answer (7:13). Although the asking of this question seems peculiar to today's reader, interactions such as the one between John and the elder are stock constituents in heavenly journeys in apocalypses, and they affirm the reliability of the information conveyed (*1 En.* 18:14–15; 2 Esd. 10:44–48). The robed figures are "they who have come out of the great ordeal; they have washed their robes and made them white in the blood of the lamb" (7:14). The "great ordeal" (*he thlipsis he megale*) is the heightened time of suffering immediately prior to the apocalypse when the forces of evil intensify their evil behaviors to try to persuade the followers of God to renege on their faithfulness (Dan. 12:1; 2 Esd. 13:16–19; *2 Bar.* 27:1–15; Matt. 24:21; Mark 13:7). As on the Second Sunday after Easter/Year C, "blood" here refers to the death of Jesus as the occasion whereby God's power is demonstrated. A garment dipped in blood is normally stained, but God's power is so awesome that robes dipped in Jesus' blood are whitened (that is, people who trust God's apocalyptic activity in Christ are saved).

In the age of salvation, the faithful worship God day and night within the eschatological temple (Wis. 9:8; *T. Levi* 3:4; 5:1; 18:6; *2 Bar.* 4:3; Rev. 21:22). They are a community of priests in the Jewish model after all (Rev. 5:10). God "shelters" (*sknenoo*) or dwells with or pitches God's tent with them as God dwelt with and provided for Israel in the wilderness (Exod. 25:8; Lev. 23:43; 26:11; Ezek. 37:27; Zech. 14:16–18). Indeed, Revelation 7:16 draws directly from Isaiah 49:10 (a description of Israel returning from exile in a new exodus; cf. Isa. 4:2–6) to note that the quality of life in the age to come will be free of threats to blessing such as hunger, thirst, and scorching heat.

In a stunning image, John asserts that this condition results from the Lamb functioning as a shepherd (7:17). The power of God is such that the creature who requires care becomes the caregiver as a part of the great apocalyptic transformation. Even more dramatically, the Lamb, who was *slaughtered*, guides the community to the *springs of the water of life*—the water of life being an image for the irrepressible, primordial power of God to support life (Ps. 36:9; Isa. 49:10). In this renewed setting, God will wipe away every tear because the causes of sorrow and mourning will be gone (Isa. 25:8) (see on "mourning" on the Second Sunday after Easter/Year C).

Fifth Sunday of Easter/Year C

Revelation 21:1–6

Please see All Saints/Year B for commentary on this passage.

Sixth Sunday of Easter/Year C

Revelation 21:10; 21:22–22:5

In language tending toward the figurative, the prophet John uses the imagery of a city to describe life in the new age. Revelation 21:10, recollecting 21:1–5, reminds the congregation that today's reading, loaded with visual images, does not depict heaven as a distinct sphere to which people ascend after death but offers an imagistic interpretation of the changed social worlds of both heaven and earth after God melds them into one new realm after the apocalypse (Rev. 21:1; cf. 2 Esd 13:35–36; *2 Bar.* 4:2–7).

In 21:11–14, the prophet pictures the new community surrounded by a high wall, an ancient symbol of security because it keeps out marauders. Unlike many other cities' walls (which would have had just one or two gates, placed on the side that was the most defendable), this community is so secure that its wall has three gates on each side, and the gates are always open. The names of the twelve tribes of Israel are on the gates: the Jewish community is part of this new world, as is the church, represented by the names of the twelve apostles on the twelve foundations.

The city is measured (21:15–17), an action that denotes God's control over the events that take place in it. The city is foursquare (21:16), intimating that the community partakes of the sacred in ways similar to being in the Holy of Holies and the eschatological temple. In 21:17 we learn the wall is unusually high—144 cubits. The number twelve ($144 = 12 \times 12$) represents community and suggests that security is found in community living according to the sacred purposes of God. The NRSV obfuscates the symbolic meaning of the size of the city by translating "twelve thousand stadia" as "fifteen hundred miles." The community is unimaginably large by ancient Mediterranean standards. Although the city is gold, the gold itself is clear as glass, meaning that, like the sea of 4:6, it is has lost its power to corrupt and to turn life into a chaos of greed (21:21).

According to 21:22, the community has no temple. In line with Isaiah 60:19–20, the community is illuminated by the glory of God and by the Lamb (cf. Isa. 60:1; Zech. 14:7; *2 Bar.* 5:1–4; *Sib. Or.* 3:787; *T. Dan.* 5:12–14). (Presumably God destroyed the sun and moon—structures that supported life in the old age as in Mark 4:24–27.) The life of the community functions like that of Israel—as a "light," a community that embodies God's purposes. "The kings of the earth" and "the glory and honor of the nations" are Gentiles who bring their glory and treasure to the God of Israel and live consistently with the divine purposes (21:24–26; Isa. 60:4–17; 62:5–7). However, the new world is free from behaviors and attitudes (such as uncleanness, abomination, and falsehood) that undermine covenantal community.

The river of the water of life flows from the throne through the middle of the city (22:1–2a). As described in Ezekiel 37:1–12, this river transforms the desert into fruitfulness and freshens the Dead Sea, thus denoting that in the new world the forces that sustain blessing permeate all circumstances. The tree of life (another symbol of unrelenting life force and providence) grows on either side of the river. The generative power of the tree is revealed in that it bears twelve kinds of fruit and produces each month (*1 En.* 10:19; 25:4; *2 Esd.* 8:25). Jewish tradition often refers figuratively to characteristics of life as bearing fruit. This community's life is good fruit, for the leaves of the tree are for "the healing of the nations," that is, for replacing the destructive results of Rome's rule over the nations of the Mediterranean basin as well as the more general distortions of life caused by Gentile idolatry, injustice, and violence (cf. Ezek. 47:12).

This community no longer experiences the curses that marked life in the old age after the fall in Eden (Rev. 22:3; Gen. 3:14–19). The writer makes clear what is implied in 21:22. The throne openly in the center of the community, where they can see God's face, means that the community has unmediated access to the divine (*T. Zeb.* 9:8; *2 Esd.* 7:97–98). The inhabitants of the community are marked on their foreheads, in a manner of speaking, meaning that they know that they are permanently gathered into this community (*Pss. Sol.* 2:6). There is no night (a fearful time) here (Zech. 14:7), and the community goes on "forever and ever" (Dan. 7:18, 27).

Many Christian communities believe that they are to live in the present as signs of the future world that John poetically unfolds here. A preacher might help the congregation reflect on the degree to which their common life bespeaks the qualities of the new Jerusalem.

Ascension of the Lord/Years A, B, and C

Ephesians 1:15–23

Please see Ascension of the Lord/Year A for commentary on this passage.

Seventh Sunday of Easter/Year C

Revelation 22:12–14, 16–17, 20–21

In Revelation 22:8, John takes responsibility for being the prophet who received through an angel the vision of Jesus given to him by God (1:1–2) in the preceding chapters. However, even prophets transported to heaven are not infallible, and when John attempts to worship the angel (a creature) who mediated the vision, the angel corrects him with a fundamental affirmation of Judaism: worship God only (22:9). One purpose of preaching is to help the community discern whether it worships creator or creatures.

Many apocalyptic writers believed that centuries before, God had dictated how the world would end to writers who sealed the message in a book that would remain closed until the last days of history drew near. At the right time, God would open the book to be read so that people could prepare for the coming cataclysm. That explains "'Do not seal up the words of the prophecy of this book, for the time is near'" (22:10). In the meantime, the world will continue with the evil and filthy, and the righteous and holy, living in their respective ways.

Jesus says in 22:12 that he is returning "soon" (*taxu*). While it is impossible to know precisely what John meant by "soon," it is clear that the prophet meant "in the foreseeable future." John wants the short time to encourage the faithful to endure. Revelation 22:12b presupposes Jesus as judge of the cosmos at the end of history, condemning some and welcoming others into the New Jerusalem (19:11–20:3; 20:7–15). On 22:13 ("I am the Alpha and the Omega"), see the Second Sunday after Easter/Year C.

Revelation 22:14 is an apocalyptic beatitude in which to be "blessed" (*makarios*) is to be included in the realm of God (Dan. 12:12; 4 Macc. 17:18). While 22:14b refers to "washing in blood," the use of "blood" here is figurative, as in 7:14 where the author called attention to the awesome power of God to take that which normally stains (blood) and use it for cleansing (see the Fourth Sunday after Easter/Year C). Such folk are welcome at the tree of life of 22:2–3 (Fifth Sunday of Easter/Year C). However, persons who think and act in ways that derogate the God of Israel and that destroy God's purposes for community are excluded (22:15). Gentiles typically practiced sorcery, fornication, murder, and idolatry. The new Jerusalem is populated and operated according to traditional Jewish covenantal values.

As in 1:1, Jesus is identified as a source of the vision narrated in this last book of the Bible (22:16). The author underscores Jesus' Jewish identity by calling him "root and descendant of David." The image of the "bright morning star" is also a traditional Jewish designation for a leader in community (Num. 24:17). Jesus governs the new age in accord with traditional Jewish patterns.

Just as the heavenly angel called John to "come up here" and see the vision of the future (with its consequences for the present in 4:1), so the writer invites the reader to behold that vision in the pages of this book and to respond in kind (22:17). The writer hopes that such readers will turn away from the futility and destructiveness of idolatry, especially as expressed through the Roman Empire, and remain in the church awaiting the final manifestation of the eschatological world. The time has come to spread the message (22:10–11). The "Spirit" spoke through prophets such as John in the community (the bride, per 21:9). All who hear become prophets and carry the message (22:17c). The thirsty are those who yearn for the coming of the new eon when all circumstances and relationships will take place in the way God intends (Matt. 5:6).

Revelation 22:18–19 is a stern warning. While some Christians apply it to the whole Bible, it is clear that by "the prophecy of this book," John means the book of Revelation. People who add to or take away from its message will fall under the plagues that the vision describes on evildoers (especially Rome) and will be excluded from the tree of life and the holy city. Preachers need to handle this aspect of the text carefully. Rome collapsed long ago; Jesus has not returned; and evil continues unabated. Furthermore, many preachers subscribe to theological worldviews that are not apocalyptic. In fact, when thinking about Revelation's specific implications, many preachers "add to" and "take away" from the details of the book. Nevertheless, beneath John's first-century language is an abiding point: faithfulness to the God of Israel in every time and place is a matter of death and life.

Day of Pentecost/Year C

Romans 8:14–17

Please see Trinity Sunday/Year B for commentary on this passage.

Trinity Sunday/Year C

Romans 5:1–5

Please see the Third Sunday of Lent/Year A for commentary on this passage.

Proper 4 [9]/Year C

Galatians 1:1–12

Please see the Ninth Sunday after the Epiphany/Year C for commentary on this passage.

Proper 5 [10]/Year C

Galatians 1:11–24

Some in Galatia may have said that Paul shaped his message to win human approval (Gal. 1:10) and that his gospel was not from God but "of human origin" (1:11), for the apostle begins today's lection with a dramatic statement that his gospel is not of human origin (*kata anthropon*; v. 11): he did not receive (*paralambano*) it from a human source nor was he taught it (*didasko*, a term sometimes used of formal processes of transmitting tradition). Rather, Paul's message came through a "revelation of Jesus Christ." The word "revelation," *apokalupsis*, suggests that the gospel has world-shaping power whose character comes from the apocalypse. The content of the revelation is God's work in Christ to restore the world as Paul specifies in 1:15–16.

Paul does not regret the earlier part of his still Jewish (Pharisaic) life but does regret his persecuting the church (1:13–14). Religious groups could discipline their members, so by "persecuting" Paul likely meant imposing synagogue discipline (2 Cor. 12:24) in the hope it would "destroy" the church. Paul does not give the reason for discipline, but it was usually employed when someone violated God's purposes and needed to live more faithfully.

In 1:13–14, the apostle emphasizes the exceptional qualities of his earlier life. Jewish sources commend Jewish zealousness (*zelotes*) in behalf of tradition (1 Macc. 2:24–26, 50–54, 58; 4 Macc. 16:20; 18:12), and if the other missionaries are Gentiles who took up Jewish practices as adults, then Paul's language undermines their authority as interpreters of Judaism: "*my* earlier life in Judaism," "among *my* people," "*my* ancestors" (italics added).

Until the last forty years, commentaries routinely spoke of the "conversion" of Paul, which can suggest leaving one religion (Judaism) for another (Christianity). Paul, however, uses the prophets in verses 15–16a to say he was *called* from one arena of the God of Israel (disciplining violators) to another arena (preaching to Gentiles). He was not called to preach to Jewish people or to dissuade them from honoring their traditions. There is no reason to think that Jewish people affiliated with the eschatological community stopped practicing Judaism.

In verses 15–16a, Paul draws from two prophets to interpret his call. Like Jeremiah (1:5), God set Paul apart in the womb to be a prophet to the Gentiles. God called Deutero-Isaiah to be a "light to the Gentiles" so "salvation could reach to the end of the earth." (Isa. 49:1–7). By preaching to Gentiles, Paul continues the work of such prophets.

Judaism had long testified to God for the benefit of Gentiles (Gen. 12:1–3). It was a Jewish hope that God would gather Gentiles into the age to come (*1 En.* 10:18–22; *Sib. Or.* 3:767–95; *T. Naph.* 8:3), and occasional Jewish sources report Gentiles coming to God apart from circumcision (Josephus, *Ag. Ap.* 2.282). The distinct element in Paul is that the turning point of the ages is revealed through Christ and that Gentiles as Gentiles can prepare for the new world through the church. In other letters (especially Romans), Paul does exhort Gentiles to respect Judaism and to adopt many Jewish values and behaviors. He does not state why Gentiles need not convert, but the best explanation we can offer is that many Jewish customs (such as circumcision) were intended to help the community maintain its identity and remain faithful amidst cultures that were often inimical to the purposes of the God of Israel. Now, with the apocalypse around the corner, such long-term identity markers would not be needed. The mission of the church was to introduce Gentiles to the God and values of Israel and serve as an emergency shelter for Gentiles (sponsored by Judaism) in the gathering apocalyptic crisis. Paul did not plan to establish an alternative religion for Gentiles that would last centuries.

From 1:16b through 24, Paul recounts his travel itinerary after his call. He does this for three reasons: First, it establishes the fact (important for 2:1–21) that Paul was recognized early by the Jerusalem church and had a long-standing relationship with that pivotal community. Second, it reinforces Paul's claim that he did not receive his gospel from a human source. Third, it demonstrates that the churches in Judea approved of Paul. Indeed, "they glorified God because of me." This suggests to the Galatians that Paul bore the stamp of approval of central congregations in the Jesus movement who were Jewish in character.

Proper 6 [11]/Year C

Galatians 2:15–21

Many Christians have interpreted Galatians as sponsoring a negative view of the law and proclaiming the superiority of Christ to the law and the church to Judaism. This interpretation has been influential in the church, but we join a growing community of scholars in rejecting it and claiming, instead, that Paul is correcting a misuse of the law by Gentiles who as adults adopted aspects of the law on the basis of false reasoning. Preachers sometimes refer to Paul's gospel as "law-free." This expression casts a shadow on the law even when none is intended because it intimates that it is good to be free of the law. We speak simply of Paul's gospel, meaning that it is the good news of God's provision for Gentiles *as* Gentiles as short-term preparation for the imminent return of Christ.

In 1:13–24, Paul recalls his call to preach to the Gentiles and emphasizes that the Jerusalem church recognized him. In 2:1–10, he reports a meeting in Jerusalem that confirmed Peter as leading the mission to the circumcised, and Paul as entrusted with the gospel to the uncircumcised. They shook the "right hand of fellowship [*koinonia*]," thereby sealing an official "partnership" (*koinonia*) in which the two groups affirmed each other's missions. The Jerusalem congregation asked only that Paul "remember the poor" in Jerusalem by taking up a collection, which Paul did (on *koinonia* and the collection, see Thanksgiving/Year A and Proper 8/Year B).

In 2:11–14, Paul recollects Peter's visit to Antioch as an negative example for the Galatians. Peter ate as a Gentile with Gentiles until a group arrived from the Jerusalem congregation, at which time Peter and others began to follow Jewish eating practices. Paul castigates Peter for inconsistent behavior, but Paul does not criticize Jewish food customs. Paul's point is that Peter's behavior prior to the arrival of the Jerusalem contingent was good enough for Peter then, and it is good enough for the Gentiles now. Strikingly, given our reconstruction of the other missionaries, Paul speaks of compelling the "Gentiles to live like Jews" (*ioudaizo*). In first-century usage, the latter "is used of Gentiles who take up wholly or in part the Jewish way of life without thoroughgoing conviction of heart."[42]

In the crucial passage 2:15–16, Paul contrasts those who are "Jews by birth" with "Gentile sinners." Jewish people know God via the covenant and are, therefore, justified (*dikaioo*, made righteous, that is, in right relationship with God and others, especially in preparation for the apocalypse). Gentiles who worship idols violate God's intentions for human community and are condemned. Yet a person (*anthropos*, which here may refer to "a Gentile") is justified "not by works of the law but through faith in Jesus Christ." The phrase "works of the law" [*ta erga tou nomou*] does not occur in Jewish literature and here "refers to the adoption of selected Jewish practices on the part of Gentiles and their attempt to impose them upon others as means of self-justification."[43] Such Gentiles misunderstand the law, for in Judaism obedience does not *earn* justification but is a joyous response to it. Gentiles are justified by the faithfulness [*pistos*] of Jesus Christ who mediates to them the grace of God.

In 2:17–18, Paul refers to the "effort to be justified in Christ" by which he means living in right relationship with Gentiles in the eschatological fellowship of the church (as Peter did in Antioch, 2:14). In doing this Paul and his companions were "found to be sinners," that is, closely identified with Gentiles. But that does not make Christ "a servant of sin" any more than Paul is a transgressor by virtue of now building up the church that he formerly tried to tear down (2:18). To the contrary, Christ created a community through which Gentiles serve God and are reconciled with Jewish people.

Christians have often taken 2:19 to mean that Paul died to torah, but a more nuanced understanding of "law" yields a different perception. Many people in first-century Judaism understood the word "law" to function in multiple ways, two of which surface here.[44] For Israel, the Torah (which included the commandments and the ancestral narratives) revealed the covenant and how to live in response and pointed to the final redemption at the apocalypse. Gentiles had access to the law but stood condemned when they turned to idols and violated covenantal values (2 Esd. 7:20–24). For Gentiles the law functioned negatively to condemn. In 2:19 Paul says, "For through the law I died to the law," or to the condemnation awaiting him by virtue of identification with Gentiles. For the Torah (as Paul makes clear in 3:6–18) teaches that God will justify Gentiles.

Now, Paul lives "to God" in the sense of witnessing in joyous response to God's redemptive work (2:19b). Paul has been "crucified with Christ" by way of having suffered under the principalities and powers for witnesses to the coming of the cosmic transformation (2:19c). Given Paul's apocalyptic orientation, when he says that "Christ . . . lives in me" and "the life I now live in the flesh I live by faith in the Son of God" (or better, "in faithfulness through the agency of the Son of God"), the reference is to the risen Christ manifesting qualities of the eschatological world through Paul. Paul's ministry to the Gentiles is a demonstration of the faithfulness of God in the present and in the eschaton (2:20). These insights pave the way for a better translation of 2:21 as the culmination of this line of thought: "I do not nullify the grace of God [carrying out the Gentile mission] since through Torah is the righteousness of God [made known], consequently Christ died as a free gift."[45]

Proper 7 [12]/Year C

Galatians 3:23–29

In ancient Judaism, the word "law" (*nomos*) functioned in several ways, two of which are important for today. (1) It often bespoke the Torah, that is, the gracious story of creation and the formative experiences of Israel—especially the revelation of the faithfulness of God and the gracious gift of the covenant—as well as the commandments as God's instructions in faithful living. (2) Another use of "law" pertained directly to the Gentiles. In the Hellenistic age, as a part of the identification of torah with wisdom (which is available to all people), some Jewish theologians came to think that through wisdom-containing-torah, the Gentiles had access to the knowledge of the sovereignty of the God of Israel and to the values that God wanted people to live. When Gentiles disregarded these matters, they brought condemnation upon themselves through perverse social relationships, both now (Rom. 1:18–32) and at the apocalyptic judgment:

> Let many perish who are now living, rather than that the law of God that is set before them be disregarded! For the Lord strictly commanded those who came into the world, when they came, what they should do to live, and what they should observe to avoid punishment. Nevertheless, they were not obedient, and spoke against him;
>
> they devised for themselves vain thoughts,
>   and proposed to themselves wicked frauds;
> they even declared that the Most High does not exist,
>   and they ignored [God's] ways.
> They scorned [God's] law,
>   and denied [God's] covenants;
> they have been unfaithful to [God's] statutes,
>   and have not performed [God's] works.
>
> (2 Esd. 7:20–24)

On this view, the law functions to condemn Gentiles.[46]

Because Paul writes Galatians to a Gentile congregation, his medita-
tions on the law in this letter focus on how the law relates to Gentiles.
While Paul does ponder the relationship of torah to law-as-condemna-
tion-of-Gentiles, in Galatians 3:23–24, "law" operates in the second sense
mentioned above, that is, as means of condemnation. Furthermore, in
Judaism the word "faith" [*pistos*] did not so much mean intellectual belief
or trust (with a human being as actor) as much as it did "faithfulness"
(often with God as stated or implied actor). The Gentiles were "under
condemnation" until the faithfulness of God was revealed to them through
Jesus Christ. The word "disciplinarian" translates *paidagogos*, a person in
ancient culture who was in charge of children in the household and who
often used harsh methods. Paul's "we" in this passage is his own identification with Gentiles and not a universal "we."

Now that the Gentiles are aware of the faithfulness of the God of Israel
(the one true and universal God) for them through Jesus Christ, they are
freed from the harsh life under the *paidagogos*, which results in immediate
social chaos (as in Rom. 1:18–32) and in fear of the final judgment (Gal.
2:25–26). The Galatian Gentiles are "children of God" in company with
Israel—beloved, instructed in the way of life that God desires for all, and
prepared for the final judgment. By graciously gathering Gentiles in the
household through Jesus Christ, God proves faithful to the promises that
God made to Abraham and Sarah (Gal. 3:6–18; Rom. 3:27–4:25). Such a
faithful God can be trusted in all things.

In antiquity clothing often represented identity. In 3:27 Paul uses the
image of changing clothing ("putting on Christ") as a symbol of the fundamental change that occurs to Gentiles in baptism. They go not only
from serving idols to serving the living God but also from the social world
of the present evil age with its abusive hierarchies into the eschatological
community of the church, in which the fractious divisions of the old age
are replaced by relationships of mutuality and acceptance (3:28). Because
the church lives on this side of the apocalypse and its members do not yet
live in resurrection bodies (1 Cor. 15:35–57), elements of their present
identities continue: men go on being men, and women, women. Presumably slaves continue as slaves and free people, as free, and, of course, Jewish people continue in that identity and Gentiles, as Gentiles. However,
insofar as their life in the church goes, they relate with one another as an
egalitarian community of the new age. Their life in the church now should
prefigure how God intends for all people to live together in the world to
come. In this respect, the Gentiles are, indeed, offspring of Abraham and
Sarah and heirs of the promise.

Proper 8 [13]/Year C

Galatians 5:1, 13–25

The term "freedom" (*eleutheria*) was especially significant in Paul's day given Roman hierarchical society, in which the few in the upper rungs wielded power over those below and a significant number of people in the lower classes were enslaved. Paul further believed the universe was populated by demon-like "elemental spirits" (Gal. 4:1–11) or "principalities and powers" (Eph. 6:12), who, in league with Satan, enslaved people and turned them and the world against God's purposes. Paul's affirmation "For freedom Christ has set us free" (v. 1) is therefore quite powerful, especially since the social relationships of the congregation are to embody the egalitarian qualities of the eschatological world (Gal. 3:27–28).

Paul's affirmation is powerful in another way. The congregation is to "stand firm" and not to "submit again to a yoke of slavery" (v. 1). Many Christians take Paul to refer to freedom from torah since Galatians 4:21–31 deals with those who desire to be "under the law" and 5:2–12 focuses on circumcision. However, Paul does not object to torah (or to Jewish people living in its light) but to an interpretation by other missionaries who grew up as Gentiles and in adulthood came to the mistaken belief that they needed to adopt elements of Jewish practice (such as circumcision) to win God's love (see Propers 4, 5, 6, and 7/Year C). That such folk did not convert fully to Judaism is clear in 5:3 when Paul says that since they practice circumcision, they are "obliged to obey the entire law."

The phrase "under the law" (4:21) occurs in Paul in reference to such *Gentiles* who thought and lived like the other missionaries.[47] Indeed, Paul used the word "law" in at least two senses—(1) as "torah" in the sense of the covenant and how to live in covenantal community but also (2) in reference to Gentiles standing condemned at the last judgment (for further discussion, see Propers 6 and 7/Year C). In 4:21–31, Paul shows that torah (in line with the first understanding of law just given) teaches that God planned a day when Gentiles as Gentiles would come into covenantal community in the present and the eschaton. Through Christ, God is keeping that promise. Consequently, the Gentiles are free from both the misguided attempt to justify themselves by playing Jewish and from condemnation at the judgment.

In 5:13–25, Paul describes the life of freedom. To be free is not simply to have the opportunity to be self-indulgent (*en sarki* = live in the realm of the flesh) but through love (*agape*) to be slaves (*doulos*) of one another. This "slavery" is not the hierarchical imposition of one will arbitrarily upon another but is mutual submission to one another's needs to know fullness of life. In living as God wants—in covenantal community—we discover real freedom.

That Paul is in no way against torah is evident in 5:14, where he sums up the purpose of Gentile life through the church as *fulfilling torah* by citing a passage from the Septuagint: "For the whole law is summed up in a single commandment, 'You shall love your neighbor as yourself'" (see Lev. 19:18). The Gentiles are obedient to torah by practicing the core Jewish value of neighbor-love. The Jewish character of Paul's theme here is reinforced by the fact that other Jewish leaders in the same period, such as Rabbi Hillel, encapsulated Jewish life similarly. Thus, for Paul, when Gentiles come to the God of Israel through the church, they *are* to live by essential Jewish values but are not to misinterpret or misuse Jewish life (as do the other missionaries).

Galatians 5:16–25 contrasts life in two realms—flesh and Spirit. For Paul, the flesh (*sarkos*) is not simply the material or bodily realm but is life unresponsive to the presence and purposes of God. Paul lists representative qualities of the flesh in 5:19–21, many of which are associated with idolatrous Gentile life. In 5:21b, Paul bracingly says that "those who do such things will not inherit the realm of God," in other words, will not be saved in the world to come.

By "Spirit" Paul means life animated by the Spirit that prompts responsiveness to the love and purposes of God. The receipt of the Spirit is the firstfruit, down payment, or guarantee of life in the divine realm. The fruit of the Spirit, then, is life in the present that manifests qualities of the life to come through such things as are mentioned in 5:22–23a, which are qualities of life in the new age. There is no condemnation (law in the second sense of understanding above) for people who live in these ways (5:23b). Indeed, for Gentiles in Christ, the power of the realm of the flesh has been crucified. They are *free from* corrupting powers and desires of the flesh and are *free for* living even now according to the Spirit.

Proper 9 [14]/Year C

Galatians 6:(1–6), 7–16

Paul now invites the Galatians to put into practice in the congregation the qualities of life suggested in 5:13–25 (esp. 5:14, 22–26) as necessary in relationships. Paul addresses the Galatians as "brothers" (including sisters; NRSV: "friends"), thus empowering his instructions with the powerful family bonds of antiquity. If someone in the congregation engages in a transgression (*paraptoma*, violation of God's purposes), those with the Spirit should take steps to help them restore (*katartizo*, help them get back in line with the purposes of community life) the transgressors gently (6:1).

In 6:2, recalling 5:13–14, the members of the community are to "bear one another's burdens, and in this way you will fulfill the law [*torah*] of Christ." As we have noticed throughout Galatians, the work and law of Christ is not opposed to Judaism but adapts Judaism for Gentiles. In this context to "bear one another's burdens" (*allelon ta bare bastazete*) means to help restore others to community especially when their behavior causes suffering (a dimension of *baros*) to themselves or the congregation.

A Pharisaic spirit lies behind Galatians 6:3–4, for the Pharisees were noted in antiquity for practicing self-criticism. Though some in Galatia (who have followed the teaching of the other missionaries?) deceive themselves with their own mistaken views, the apostle admonishes the Galatians to "test" (*dokimazo*) their own work to determine the degree to which they are living by qualities of the new age and helping others do so. By stating that "all must carry their own loads," Paul means that each person is obliged to tend to the community. An aspect of carrying one's load is helping provide for the teacher in community (6:6).

In 6:7a Paul forcefully urges the Galatians not to be deceived (*planao*), that is, "Do not wander from the ways of God," presumably in the manner of the false gospel of the other missionaries. "Wandering" is typical Gentile behavior (Wis. 12:24) and brings about condemnation. For "God is not mocked" (*mukterizo*): one may deceive in the present, but when the judgment day comes, you will reap what you sow. This principle is very important because, as we saw a similar saying in connection with Thanksgiving/Year A, all people (including believers) reap what they sow (6:7b), a statement that following the gospel of the other missionaries (and otherwise scorning God's ways) results in eschatological judgment (6:8–9).

Galatians 6:10 epitomizes a Jewish understanding of responsibility to others. The Gentiles are not to place limits on their care for others but are to work "for the good of all" to witness to the love of the God of Israel for all, remembering the "family of faith."

Implying that he dictated the earlier part of the letter to a scribe, Paul writes the last lines in large letters in his own hand (6:11). The apostle ends the letter with a last critique of the other missionaries, accusing them of encouraging the Gentiles to be circumcised so the missionaries can "make a good showing [*euprosopoeo*, to put forth a good face] in the flesh" (v. 12). The identity of these others as Gentiles who came lately to Jewish practices based on misunderstandings of Jewish life surfaces as Paul points out that even though they want the Gentiles in Galatia to boast about their flesh (being circumcised), the missionaries "do not themselves obey the law" (6:13).

In verse 14, the apostle asserts that he does not want to boast (exult) about anything except the cross of Christ "by which the world has been crucified to me, and I to the world." Paul often uses the word "world" (*kosmos*) to refer to the world as fallen creation, the broken home of the present evil age that God will soon end. However, as far as Paul is concerned, the corrupt and enslaving qualities of the world no longer have power over Paul. He is dead to that aspect of existence ("crucified to me, and I to the world"). Paul is living in the present as an agent of the "new creation," the regenerated world that will be manifest in its fullness only after the return of Jesus. Because that realm anticipates the reunion of Jewish and Gentile peoples, Paul can say, "neither circumcision or uncircumcision is anything" (v. 15). As a faithful Jewish person, Paul closes by wishing peace and mercy upon the Gentile Galatians and upon the Israel of God.

Proper 10 [15]/Year C

Colossians 1:1–14

Today's reading falls into three parts: a greeting (vv. 1–2), a thanksgiving for the Colossians (vv. 3–8), and a prayer for them (vv. 9–14).

The greeting is "Grace to you and peace from God our Father" (v. 2). "Peace" (*shalom*) is the standard Jewish greeting; it is typical of Paul's greetings to his congregations (see Rom. 1:7). Paul "and Timothy our brother" send this greeting "to the saints and faithful brothers and sisters in Christ" (v. 1). The metaphors "brothers and sisters" indicate that Paul's was a shared ministry, not one exercised in top-down fashion. All are "in Christ," that is, included in the community, the "body" of Christ. The brothers and sisters "in Colossae" are Gentiles, as Paul makes clear in 1:21, 27; 2:13; and 3:7. Scholars debate whether Paul or one of his later students wrote Colossians; Paul is nonetheless the claimed author, and we refer to him in this sense.

Paul thanks God (vv. 3–8) for the faith and love of the Colossians and the "hope laid up for you in heaven" (v. 5), the familiar faith-hope-love triad (see 1 Cor. 13). The thanksgiving lets us know that Paul was not the missionary who brought the gospel to the Colossians. Rather, they "learned [it] from Epaphras, our beloved fellow servant" (*doulos*, slave; v. 7), who "is a faithful minister [*diakonos*, servant and emissary] of Christ on your behalf." That Epaphras is a slave (see also 4:12) is important to the community, which doubtless had slaves in its membership. Note that it was a slave who led the Colossians to understand "the grace of God" (v. 6). It was Epaphras who informed Paul and Timothy of "your love in the Spirit" (v. 8). Paul did not found the community; Epaphras did. Paul is unknown personally to the Colossians and is now off the scene; the letter is concerned to establish his authority among the Colossians to back up the teaching that follows; he is an apostle "by the will of God" (v. 1).

When the church later began to use the word "catholic" or "ecumenical" to describe itself, the meaning of "catholic" included all the socioeconomic levels of society, from slaves at the bottom to the well-to-do at the top. A slave in the world could be a leader in the church, as was Epaphras. The most radical thing the early church did was what it did not do: replicate the oppressive structures of the world in its own life. Hence it could function as a "light to the world" of an alternative way of life. We get a glimpse of that in Paul's thanksgiving for the faithfulness of the Colossians.

In Colossians, Paul is concerned to help the community resist attempts by some group or movement to "take you captive through philosophy and vain deceit" (2:8), teachings and practices that contradict the gospel that Epaphras taught the Colossians. To set the stage for that discussion (2:8–23), Paul's prayer for the Colossians (1:9–14) is that they "may be filled with the knowledge of God's will in all spiritual wisdom and understanding" (v. 9). The faith, love, and hope of the community are based on an understanding of the grace of God (v. 6) that the letter sees as endangered by the ideas and practices proposed by those whom, in its view, would lead the Colossians astray.

Hence Paul prays that they may be filled with knowledge, spiritual wisdom, and understanding. These are essential if the Colossians are to "lead lives [*peripateo*, walk] worthy of the Lord" (v. 10). At stake are their way of life, which lives out their ideas, and their ideas, which are given flesh in their way of life. Paul asks God to empower them to "endure everything with patience" (v. 11) and thus overcome their difficulties. The church always needs this prayer; it is as pertinent now as it was then.

Proper 11 [16]/Year C

Colossians 1:15–28

An example of a wisdom hymn or saying in Judaism regarding Woman Wisdom reads, "She is a reflection of eternal light, a spotless mirror of the working of God, and an image of his goodness" (Wis. 7:26); and Wisdom herself claims, "Before the ages, in the beginning, he created me" (Sir. 24:9). Verses 15–20 of today's reading quote a Christ hymn that was developed from the Wisdom tradition of Israel in its hymns to Woman Wisdom, Sophia. The church expressed its faith in the language of Israel's Scriptures.

Christ is the "image [*eikon*] of the invisible [*aoratos*] God" (v. 15). *Eikon* connotes agency; it does not mean that Christ is God. That God is invisible and hence discloses Godself to be known is basic Jewish piety. Verse 15 shows the difficulty of the concept of the "image of God." How can the "invisible" be "imaged?" The revelation of God does not reduce God's mystery; it invites us to be in awe of it. That Christ is "the firstborn of all creation" is not the language of Nicaea; it points to the preeminence of Christ over "all things" that were created "in him" (vv. 15–16). Verse 15 recalls Genesis 1:27: "So God created humankind in his image." Christ as the image of God reveals not only God to us but humankind as well; who we are given and called to be is made known to us in Christ.

Note that "in him all things [*ta panta*] . . . were created, things visible and invisible, whether thrones or dominions or rulers or powers" (v. 16). Whether such "rulers" are visible (earthly) or invisible (heavenly), God and Christ have dominion over them. Neither Satan (should one believe in Satan) nor Caesar, creatures themselves, has the final say over any other creature. There is no ultimate reason to fear them. The passive language of "were created" and "have been created" indicates that God does the creating "through him and for him." God creates us with an end in view— "for him" in the sense that the goal of creation, its consummation in perfection, is made known in Christ.

Christ as the image of God has a cosmic function: in him "all things hold together," and he is "the head of the body, the church" (v. 17). In antiquity the "body" could serve as a metaphor for the individual, the community, the state, and the universe. The universe and the church find their center in Christ. The church is not its own center; rather its center is Christ as well as the least of these, and the universe is the scope of its concern. "All the fullness of God" dwelt in Christ and through him God "reconcile[d] to himself all things" (vv. 19–20). The utterly universal scope of salvation is here portrayed as already accomplished!

Verses 21–23 make clear that this universal reconciliation includes the Colossians: "You who were once estranged and hostile in mind . . . he has now reconciled in his fleshly body through death" (see Eph. 2:1–12). This describes the past of these Gentiles (v. 27) as well as "how great among the Gentiles are the riches of the glory of this mystery, which is Christ in you, the hope of glory" (v. 27). But Christ (and Paul his emissary) intend to present the Colossians "holy and blameless and irreproachable before him" (v. 22). The Colossians were more than strangers to God—they were "hostile in mind, doing evil deeds." The language connotes spirited antagonism to God. But the Gentiles were reconciled through the hearing of the gospel, of which Paul is a servant (v. 23).

Colossians 1:24–2:5 concentrates on the authority of Paul. He "suffers" on behalf of the Colossians, completes in his sufferings what was "lacking in Christ's afflictions for the sake of . . . the church" (v. 24) and was commissioned by God to make God's word fully known to the Colossians ("for you," v. 25). Paul disclosed the mystery of God's setting-right of the Gentiles to the Colossians. Hence his subsequent arguments against those who would "condemn you [the Colossians] in matters of food and drink or of observing festivals, new moons, or sabbaths" (2:16) can be trusted.

Proper 12 [17]/Year C

Colossians 2:6–15, (16–19)

Today's reading focuses on Jesus Christ—who he is and what God has done for us in him (v. 12). Colossians addresses its readers, "As you therefore have received Christ Jesus the Lord, continue to live [*peripateo*] your lives in him" (v. 6). "You" means "you Gentiles," to whom Colossians is addressed (1:27). *Peripateo* means "to walk," as the people Israel and the early church talked of how we are to live the life to which God calls us. Verse 7 spells out what it means to "walk" in him: be "rooted in him," "built up in him," "established in the faith," and let your thanksgiving (*eucharistia*) be heartfelt.

The attitude of thanksgiving urged in verse 7 anticipates the discussion of grace in verses 8–15. The appropriate response to grace is gratitude, not a sense of superiority to others but sheer gratefulness. This point bears repeating, as we regularly forget it.

In verse 8, Colossians begins its repudiation of the teachings and practices by which it assumes the Colossians are tempted: "See to it that no one takes you captive through philosophy and empty deceit, according to human tradition." Scholars are perplexed about just who the opponents are who foster the teachings and practices described in verses 16–23. They have variously been identified as a local kind of Judaism, Cynicism, Gnosticism, mystery religion (mystery religion terminology is used in 2:18), or Stoicism.

Preachers would be well advised to avoid making their interpretations of the passage dependent on an attempt to identify the source of the teachings and practices that Colossians rejects. In his undisputed letters, Paul indicates that his greatest opposition came from fellow missionaries who disagreed with him. That may also have been the case in Colossae.

Colossians urges its readers to pay no attention to the "elemental spirits of the universe" (v. 8), a phrase that also perplexes scholars, but to remember what Christ has done for them. They are to remember their baptisms: "In him also you were circumcised with a spiritual circumcision, by putting off the body of the flesh in the circumcision of Christ; when you were buried with him in baptism, you were also raised with him through faith in the power of God, who raised him from the dead" (vv. 11–12). Baptism and circumcision are counterparts of each other. "Putting off the body of flesh" metaphorically refers to casting aside our "old" selves—when we "were once estranged and hostile in mind, doing evil deeds" (1:21)—and putting on the "new" persons who can live in the new and transformed way of love for the neighbor and for God.

Verse 13 says to the Colossian Gentiles, "When you were dead in trespasses and the uncircumcision of your flesh, God made you alive together with him." The lack of circumcision of the Colossians signaled their estrangement from God. God, however, graciously "set right" their relationship with God and "forgave us all our trespasses, erasing the record that stood against us with its legal demands" (vv. 13–14). God deals with Gentiles by mercy; hence thanksgiving is appropriate. The Torah did not demand that Gentiles be circumcised. We do not know who might have asked it of the Colossians.

Paul began this discussion with an affirmation of Christ as the one in whom "the whole fullness of deity dwells bodily, and you have come to fullness in him" (v. 9). As God "dwelled" among Israel, so God "dwells" in Jesus of Nazareth. This christological affirmation serves to refute the counterfeit claims that the Colossians need to attend to the "worship of angels" or "dwell on visions" (v. 18). All that can be known of God they already know in Jesus Christ.

Proper 13 [18]/Year C

Colossians 3:1–11

In today's reading verses 1–4 proclaim the transformed life of believers in Christ since they have died to their old selves and been raised to newness of life in him. Verses 5–11 describe the guiding moral principles of this new life. Please see Easter Day/Year A for our discussion of verses 1–4; here we will deal with verses 5–11.

To this point Colossians has discussed how the Colossians once lived (1:21–23) before they received the mercy of Christ, and how they should not live, even if they are tempted to do so (2:8–23). Now it turns to how believers in Christ should live. Colossians is deeply concerned with the grace of God, but never to the neglect of how believers in Christ should "walk" (*peripateo*) the way of life.

Because they "have died" (3:3) to their old selves, the Colossians are urged to "put to death, therefore, whatever in you is earthly: fornication [*porneia*], impurity [*akatharsia*], passion [*pathos*], evil desire [*epithymia*], and greed (which is idolatry)" (v. 5). The theme is that each believer has been drastically transformed: "you . . . have clothed yourselves with the new self, which is being renewed in knowledge according to the image of its creator" (vv. 9–10). The list of sins in verse 5 has to do with sex, except for greed, which of all of these, is singled out as "idolatry." This is particularly significant in our time when an insatiable hunger for money is at the bottom of the many financial scandals that make the headlines in the business section of the newspaper.

Referring to how the Colossians once lived, verses 7–8 comment, "These are the ways you also once followed, when you were living that life. But now you must get rid of all such things—anger, wrath, malice, slander, and abusive language from your mouth." Anger and wrath refer to emotions and malice to an injurious purpose. "Abusive language" (*blasphemia*) has to do with libeling or slandering another person. Verse 9 also deals with sins of talk: "Do not lie to one another." Lying about one another and to one another are both condemned. Talking is the most frequent thing we do; we need to be responsible in how we use language. Ephesians argued that we should not lie about one another because "we are members of one another" (4:25). Colossians argues the point from baptism: because "you have stripped off the old self with its practices" (v. 9). We are reminded that how we talk is as important as anything else that we do. We should talk in ways appropriate to who we are—people transformed by the grace of God. And we should be aware of how our language can be abusive of others.

Verses 10–11 make it clear that the theme is the renewal of all members of the community. You have been renewed, and "in that renewal there is no longer Greek and Jew, circumcised and uncircumcised, barbarian, Scythian, slave and free; but Christ is all and in all." "Greek and Jew, circumcised and uncircumcised" means that the ethnic divisions that structured the Greek and Roman world were jettisoned. There is to be no looking down on other people because they are different from us. Rather, that very difference is to be celebrated as enriching the community. Nor was the hierarchical relation of free people and slaves to have any place in the community of believers, although Colossians urged slaves to "obey your earthly masters" (3:22). Oddly, Colossians does not say "no longer male and female" (Gal. 3:28), perhaps because it later claims that wives should "be subject to your husbands" (3:18). On these two points, Colossians, for whatever reason, reverts to a conventional Hellenistic outlook and steps back from the proclamation of freedom in Galatians 5:1.

Proper 14 [19]/Year C

Hebrews 11:1–3, 8–16

The paragraph of Hebrews immediately prior to this reading, which provides its context, is not in the lectionary. There Hebrews calls on its readers not to "shrink back" and be lost but to endure in faith and be saved (10:36, 39). In today's reading Hebrews praises the faith that sustained the heroes of Israelite tradition.

Verses 1–2 offer a definition of faith: "the assurance [*hypostasis*] of things hoped for, the conviction [*elegchos*] of things not seen." The term translated "assurance" more likely means the "reality" of things hoped for; and the translation "conviction" is better rendered "proof." The Reformers began interpreting these terms in their way of understanding faith, but that does not seem to have been Hebrews's meaning. For Hebrews, the "reality" of things hoped for refers to the eternally real heavenly temple to which Jesus has gained access on behalf of all believers.

"Things hoped for" and "things not seen" have different referents for Hebrews. "Things hoped for" refers to the future eschaton. The author has just finished quoting, from the Septuagint, Habakkuk 2:3–4: "For yet 'in a very little while, the one who is coming . . . will not delay'" (10:37). "Things not seen" refers to God who is invisible (11:27) and to eternal realities, such as the platonically real eternal sanctuary. "Things hoped for" are not visible because they have not yet happened; "things unseen" are not visible because they are not objects of sense perception.

Verse 2 introduces the main theme of the chapter: the extraordinary examples of faith found among our biblical "ancestors" (*presbuteroi*, "elders") who found "approval" by faith. "Elders" was a standard Jewish way of referring to trustworthy bearers of the tradition of faith. In chapter 11, Hebrews names and praises many of them.

Verse 3 further unpacks faith's awareness of things unseen by referring to the creation: "By faith we understand that the worlds were prepared by the word of God, so that what is seen was made from things that are not visible." We do not see God's creation of the universe; we apprehend it in faith. Verse 3 functions ontologically to make the claim that faith is grounded on a basic insight into the very nature of reality. Faith understands that the world itself depends on the power and love of God.

Verses 8–12 highlight the faith of Abraham and Sarah. Faith enables Abraham to obey (v. 8) and to endure (see vv. 9–10, where Abraham persists because he "looked forward" to things hoped for). Jewish writers often appealed to Abraham as a paradigm of faith: "Abraham was the great father of a multitude of nations, and no one has been found like him in glory" (Sir. 44:19). Abraham's goal was a "place," which for Hebrews is no longer Canaan but "the city that has foundations, whose architect and builder is God" (v. 10). This is the new Jerusalem, but unlike in Revelation 21, it does not come down from heaven to earth; instead it is a heavenly reality. Verse 11 in the Greek gives Sarah a more active role in the story than does the NRSV translation, saying that "by faith Sarah received power for conception even beyond time of age" (our translation).

Verses 13–16 make the point that the elders, like Moses outside the promised land, could only scan the horizon for a sight of their hoped-for goal. They remained wanderers seeking a homeland. This homeland is now guaranteed to them because "God is not ashamed to be called their God; indeed, he has prepared a city for them" (v. 16). Jesus Christ leads faithful Israel home.

Proper 15 [20]/Year C

Hebrews 11:29–12:2

Please see Wednesday of Holy Week/Year A for commentary on this passage.

Proper 16 [21]/Year C

Hebrews 12:18–29

Verses 18–24 continue the paranesis that began in 12:1. Hebrews has urged its readers to "pursue peace with everyone and the holiness without which no one will see the Lord" (12:14). Pursuing peace was a *mitzvah* among Jews: "Hillel says: 'Be disciples of Aaron, loving peace and pursuing grace, loving people and drawing them near to the Torah.'"[48]

Here Hebrews provides more reasons to reinforce the appeal to pursue peace.

Our author does this by contrasting Mount Zion, to which "you have come" (v. 22) with Sinai. Sinai is not explicitly mentioned, but Hebrews's description of the place to which its readers "have not come" (v. 18) is one of "blazing fire, and darkness, and gloom, and a tempest." Deuteronomy 4:11 says of Sinai, which the Israelites approached, "The mountain was blazing up to the very heavens, shrouded in dark clouds." Hebrews describes the Israelites as fearful (asking that not another word be spoken to them by God), unable to endure the commandment that "any who touch the mountain shall be put to death" (Exod. 19:12). Even Moses shakes with fear.

Unlike Sinai, which was "something that can be touched" (v. 18), "Mount Zion and . . . the city of the living God" (v. 22), which Jesus' followers approach, is in "the heavenly Jerusalem" (v. 22). Partly what is in play here is Hebrews's platonism: anything spiritual is "better" than its physical counterpart. The heavenly Mount Zion is a joyous and not a fearful place, where there are "innumerable angels in festal gathering" (v. 22). Also the "firstborn who are enrolled in heaven" (v. 23), human beings, are there. They are the faithful followers of Jesus, the "firstborn" whom God brought into the world (1:6). "God the judge of all" is on the spiritual Mount Zion; note that God here is not a judge who inspires dread but a God who makes perfect the righteous (v. 23). And finally, Jesus is present, who made possible entry to the new Jerusalem, who mediated a "new covenant," and whose spilled blood is "better" than Abel's. Abel's blood still speaks; he stands in the long line of faithful Israelites extolled in chapter 11. Christ's blood is a better sacrifice than Abel's, not one that negates Abel's sacrifice.

Verses 25–29 are a concluding warning to readers of Hebrews. They open, in a striking shift of tone, on a threatening note. Hebrews regularly alternates between the contrasting tones of joy and menace, with apparently little awareness that this can be something of a mixed message. "See that you do not refuse the one who is speaking; for if they did not escape when they refused the one who warned them on earth, how much less will we escape if we reject the one who warns from heaven!" (v. 25). The joy of the preceding paragraph has quickly dissipated. Here Hebrews's contrast of the old and the new leaves us with the new covenant being more intimidating than the old.

Verse 26 presents a quotation from Haggai 2:6–7: "For thus says the LORD of hosts: Once again, in a little while, I will shake the heavens and the earth and the sea and the dry land; and I will shake the nations, so that the treasure of all nations shall come, and I will fill this house with splendor." Haggai's text has to do with all the Gentiles worshiping God in the temple; Hebrews cites only the first part of it and turns it into a prophecy of an eschatological shaking of the foundations.

In Hebrews's eschatology, what is shaken will be removed (v. 27); only what is eternal and unshakable will remain. And that is the "kingdom that cannot be shaken" (v. 28), established by God, the heavenly Jerusalem to which Jesus has gained access for us. Hebrews does not look forward to a transformation of this world, its renewal, but to the realm of eternity.

Proper 17 [22]/Year C

Hebrews 13:1–8, 15–16

In this concluding chapter, the author instructs the community on matters of behavior (13:1–19), until the blessing (vv. 20–21) and a final appeal (vv. 22–25).

Verses 1–6 constitute a series of paired exhortations. The first (in vv. 1–2) urges the community: "Let mutual love [*philadelphia*] continue. Do not neglect to show hospitality to strangers." *Philadelphia* was frequently used by the early church to talk about how we should love one another (see 1 Thess. 4:9; Rom. 12:10); "mutual love" appropriately translates it. The theme is an age-old biblical motif: we are to love the stranger as ourselves, recognizing that we are different from each other and loving each other's difference. So Hebrews immediately links mutual love with showing hospitality to strangers and alludes to the biblical stories in which by doing so "some have entertained angels without knowing it." Abraham and Sarah in their tent by the oaks of Mamre (Gen.18:1–15) are the prototypical biblical example of the virtue of hospitality.

Verse 3 presents the second pair: "Remember those who are in prison, as though you were in prison with them; those who are being tortured, as though you yourselves were being tortured." Hebrews had earlier commended the community for its "compassion for those who were in prison" (10:34). And the reference to torture recalls the "sufferings . . . abuse and persecution" that the community endured (10:32–33). The emphasis on mutuality remains: remember these things as though they are happening to you. We may assume that the author refers to members of the community who are in prison or being tortured, but our interpretation of these verses should include all who are in prison or tortured anywhere.

The third set of exhortations deals with sex: honor marriage and keep it undefiled, and God will take care of adulterers and fornicators (v. 4).

This is not just another in a string of ad hoc pieces of advice, unrelated to what has gone before. It is one example of what mutual love means: we cannot be members of one another and steal each others' wives and husbands. The fourth set of exhortations deals with money: "Keep your lives free from the love of money, and be content with what you have" (v. 5). We are urged not to be rapacious, to be "without love of money," *aphilarguros*. Instead, "be content with what you have." Today, when greed seems to know absolutely no limits, it is timely to suggest that everybody should have enough and that nobody should have too much.

Hebrews grounds these moral proposals on two biblical citations, God's promise never to forsake us and the claim that the Lord is our helper and we need not be afraid (vv. 5–6). The first articulates the notion of God's faithfulness; the second quotes Psalm 118:6: "With the Lord on my side, I do not fear. What can mortals do to me?" Each verse appeals to YHWH's steadfast love.

Verse 7 urges the community, "Remember your leaders." We know nothing about these leaders except that they did the one thing that leaders of the church are called to do: they "spoke the word of God to you."

Then says Hebrews, "Jesus Christ is the same yesterday and today and forever" (v. 8). The point is the constancy of Christ, not some metaphysical speculation about his immutability. We are to be strengthened by grace, not by odd and strange teachings (v. 9). Verses 15–16 conclude the reading urging us to offer continually a sacrifice of praise to God with all our lives, as verse 16 indicates: by doing good and sharing what we have.

Proper 18 [23]/Year C

Philemon 1–21

Slavery in antiquity was brutal, but it differed from slavery in the Americas. A chief difference was that ethnicity played no role in antiquity; under certain circumstances slaves could earn freedom or otherwise be freed; some people voluntarily became indentured slaves to improve their economic circumstances; slaves could expect manumission by age thirty. Nevertheless, slavery was harsh, and freedom was valued.

Jewish people, like others in antiquity, practiced slavery. However, because they had been freed from slavery in Egypt, Jewish people were uncomfortable with slavery, as revealed in those laws that limited them in enslaving one another: they held fewer slaves than others, and torah mandated more humane treatment of slaves. The undesirability of slavery is indicated in the decree that slaves be freed in the Jubilee (Exod. 20:10; 21:1–11, 26–27; Lev. 25:39–46; Deut. 5:14; 15:12–18; Sir. 7:20–21; 33:31–33; cf. 33:25–30). God's people would not be enslaved in the new age (2 Esd. 12:34). Jewish criticism of slavery and impulses towards freedom underlie Paul's words to Philemon.

Typical of letters of the time, Philemon begins (1:1–3) with sender, recipient, and greeting. Paul's description of himself as a prisoner (probably under house arrest) is simple information but also evokes sympathy for the letter as whole. (v. 1). Although the letter speaks directly to Philemon, it is addressed to the house church. This means that Philemon's relationship with Onesimus is a community concern. On the formula "grace and peace" see the Second Sunday after Epiphany/Year A.

In verses 4–7 Paul uses the thanksgiving paragraph (another typical part of the Hellenistic letter) to help Philemon recognize that welcoming (and freeing?) Onesimus would not only be consistent with Philemon's "love for the saints" and "refreshing" the saints (*hagioi*, "holy ones", a term taken from the Septuagint and evoking continuity between Judaism and the church), but would be a piece of "all the good we may do for Christ."

It is not entirely clear why Philemon's slave, Onesimus, went to Paul. Earlier scholarship thought Onesimus ran away in search of freedom and was, therefore, a fugitive. Some recent scholars think that Onesimus was in a difficult situation with Philemon and took advantage of a provision in Roman law whereby a slave could seek mediation from a third party—Paul, who would be attractive for such a role because of his close relationship with Philemon.[49]

In verses 8–9, Paul reminds Philemon that there are important reasons he could impose on Philemon to carry out the latter's duty. However, the apostle appeals instead to a love (*agape*) that goes beyond emotion to include acting in covenantal faithfulness. Indeed, according to verse 10, Paul has become Onesimus's father, making them immediate kin, which means that how Philemon responds to Onesimus is also a response to Paul. Because God is the "father" of the congregation (v. 3), all within it are related. This fact implies that Philemon and Onesimus are also kin in the eschatological family, and that Philemon is obligated to welcome Onesimus as a kinsperson, as becomes clear in verse 16.

Such is the bond between Onesimus and Paul that in sending Onesimus back to Philemon, Paul is sending his own heart (the heart = the self, v. 12). While Paul would like to keep Onesimus, Paul sends Onesimus to Philemon with the implication that in so doing, Paul is giving up his own (adopted) son for Philemon's sake. Paul thus respects Philemon's freedom in deciding how to receive Onesimus while Paul demonstrates what he hopes Philemon will do.

While the letter can be read otherwise, it seems to us that Paul urges Philemon to free Onesimus. Paul hopes Onesimus and Philemon will be together "forever" (*aiovos*), perhaps referring to the divine realm (v. 15). Paul hopes that Philemon will relate with Onesimus "no longer as a slave" but "as a beloved brother," that is, as a member of the same household (v. 16). Indeed, Paul hopes that Philemon will welcome Onesimus as Philemon would welcome Paul and regard him as a "partner" (*koinos*, v. 17). While the word "welcome" (*proslambano*) can apply to acts of hospitality (providing lodging, food, safety, and companionship), Paul uses it in Romans 15:7 of the coming together of Jewish and Gentile peoples as part of the new age, and it appears in the Septuagint to describe God's welcoming (and covenantal faithfulness) to Israel (1 Kgs. 12:22; Ps. 17:6; 26:10; 64:4; 72:25). Philemon should receive Onesimus as God receives Israel.

In verses 18–19 Paul may allude to the difficulty that prompted Onesimus to come to him. Onesimus may have "wronged" Philemon by mishandling funds (or by doing something that damaged Philemon's life). Setting a further example (and modeling love), Paul agrees to make restitution.

By welcoming Onesimus, Philemon can actually minister to Paul, for such a welcome would refresh Paul's own heart. Acts of faithfulness often have community-wide consequences.

Proper 19 [24]/Year C

1 Timothy 1:12–17

Earlier in chapter 1, Paul or the author writing in his name describes the situation in Ephesus to which this letter to Timothy is a response. (Many scholars argue that the Pastoral Epistles are pseudonymous. Nonetheless, taking them seriously as Scripture will yield many significant insights). Paul charges Timothy with instructing "certain people not to teach any different doctrine" (v. 3), particularly not to busy themselves "with myths and endless genealogies" (v. 4) and to avoid being "teachers of the law" (v. 7). We do not know what myths or genealogies are at issue, because we are not told. "Teachers of the law" are probably not Jews, as the author identifies himself (as Paul always did) as "a teacher of the Gentiles" (2: 7); the implied audience that would have heard Timothy read his letter of commission is Gentile.

Today's reading is Paul's self-description as one whose life had been transformed by the grace of God in Christ. It is best read as part of Paul's opening argument against the opponents in Ephesus, their mythologizing of faith, and their teaching of the law, which, according to Paul, they do not understand (1:8–11).

Paul begins (v. 12) by giving thanks to Christ for empowering him and judging him faithful (*pistos*); elsewhere Paul also describes himself as faithful (1 Cor. 7:25). Christ "appointed me to his service" (*diakonian*, v. 12). His language here is that of being called to service, not that of being converted. It coheres with Galatians 1: 15: "But when God, who had set me apart before I was born and called me through his grace, was pleased to reveal his son to me, so that I might proclaim him among the Gentiles."

Paul continues, describing himself as having been "a blasphemer, a persecutor, and a man of violence [*hybristes*]" (v. 13). Nowhere else does Paul use the noun "blasphemer," but he does describe himself as having persecuted the church (Gal. 1:13; 1 Cor. 15:9; Phil. 3:6). "Violence" would be better translated as "filled with hubris; arrogance." Nonetheless, Paul "received mercy" because he had acted ignorantly. Paul is the oppressor who became an apostle, by the mercy of God, a point that we should remember at those moments when we are most angry at oppressors—it is not outside the range of possibility that they, too, might be transformed by God's grace.

God's grace "overflowed" (*huperpleonazein*, more than abounded) for Paul with Jesus Christ's faithfulness and love. God's grace is profligate, a fact that never ceases to amaze Paul. He later claims that God "desires everyone to be saved" (2:4); the vision in 2:1–7 is remarkably expansive and suggests that 1 Timothy should be accorded more attention than it typically receives. We are struck that for Paul faithfulness and love are who Jesus Christ is, and they are what we are to become—persons with "a pure heart, a good conscience, and sincere faith" (1:5)—traits that are to constitute us as persons as they do Christ and that are available to us by God's grace.

Christ "came into the world to save sinners" (v. 15), of whom Paul considers himself the chief. Verse 16 needs to be read carefully: Paul is an "example" for those who come to faith in Christ not because of who Paul is but because Paul's merciful treatment demonstrates how the grace of God can effectively transform the rest of us. To "believe" in Christ here means to trust, to place one's confidence in God's activity in Christ; we should not give it the tight definition of affirmation of a creed.

The reading ends with praise of "the only God [*mono theo*]," recalling the Shema Israel, and which will be repeated in 2:5: "There is one God."

Proper 20 [25]/Year C

1 Timothy 2:1–7

Please see Thanksgiving/Year B for commentary on this passage.

Proper 21 [26]/Year C

1 Timothy 6:6–19

Today's reading falls into two parts; verses 6–10 are part of a longer discussion (vv. 6:2b–10) of "the love of money" (v. 10), and verses 11–19 constitute Paul's concluding statement to Timothy.

"There is great gain [*porismos*] in godliness" (v. 6) says Paul. *Porismos* was widely used to talk of a significant gain of money; Paul here is using it ironically because the gain that he wants to recommend is of a different order. There is great gain in godliness "combined with contentment [*autarkeia*]." *Autarkeia* has to do with self-sufficiency, and Paul recommends it elsewhere: "God is able to provide you with every blessing in abundance, so that by always having enough [*autarkeia*] of everything, you may share abundantly in every good work" (2 Cor. 9:8). Quoting a piece of proverbial wisdom (v. 7; see Job 1:21), Paul suggests that "if we have food and clothing, we will be content with these" (v. 8).

Paul here deals with "those who want to be rich" (v. 9); in verses 17–19 he will address "those who in the present age are rich." What prompts these remarks is the fact that some are "bereft of the truth, imagining that godliness is a means of gain" (6:5). The specific problem is that some poorer members of the community, envious of the more well-to-do members (for example, some owned slaves, as shown in 6:1–2), are using their roles in the *ekklesia* for profit. Paul had earlier argued that anyone aspiring to exercise oversight of the community should not be "a lover of money" (3:3). The rabbis, too, cautioned against the misuse of religious office: "Rabbi Zadok says: 'Do not make [Torah-teachings] a crown in which to glorify yourself or a spade with which to dig.'"[50]

In verses 9–10, Paul lays stress on the spurious security that wealth promises: "Those who want to be rich fall into temptation and are trapped by many senseless and harmful desires that plunge people into ruin and destruction." One cannot avoid hearing echoes of Jesus' teaching: "Do not store up for yourselves treasures on earth, where moth and rust consume and where thieves break in and steal; but store up for yourselves treasures in heaven." (Matt. 5:19–20). Those who are "rich in good works" (1 Tim. 6:18), similarly are "storing up for themselves the treasure of a good foundation for the future, so that they may take hold of the life that really is life," that is, the life of God.

It is the "love of money," *philarguria*, more than the having of it, that is called into question. Those who have "in the present age" are no more to "set their hopes on the uncertainty of riches" (6:17) than are those who do not. But, placing their hope in God, they are to be "generous, and ready to share." On the other hand, "love of money" connotes a kind of concern that confuses what is proximate, relative, and uncertain with what is ultimate and true; it places faith in an idol and hence leads to destruction. Money is a good servant but a poor master.

Sandwiched between the discussions of money in 6–10 and 17–19 are Paul's other instructions to Timothy in verses 11–16. The center of the discussion is in verses 13–14: "I charge you to keep the commandment [*entole*] without spot or blame until the manifestation of our Lord Jesus Christ." The commandment is the content of the entire letter—Paul's instructions to Timothy, particularly the *telos*, aim, of the commandment which is "love that comes from a pure heart, a good conscience, and sincere faith" (1:5).

Paul reassures Timothy that God will bring about the "manifestation of our Lord Jesus Christ," his second coming, "at the right time," and ends on praise of God who is "the King of kings and Lord of lords" (v. 15). On this note, Paul undercuts the claims to divinity of those kings for whom the letter has advised the community to pray (2:2).

Proper 22 [27]/Year C

2 Timothy 1:1–14

Second Timothy is an intensely personal letter from the author, presumably Paul, to Timothy, his representative (see Proper 19/Year C).

In the greeting (vv. 1–2), Paul presents himself as an apostle "of Christ Jesus by the will of God" (v. 1). Paul's apostleship is not something to which he was elected by popular demand but by God's calling of him through Jesus Christ. And it is for a purpose: spreading the good news of the "promise of life that is in Christ Jesus" (v. 1). Toward the end of the letter, Paul writes, "The Lord stood by me and gave me strength, so that through me the message might be fully proclaimed and all the Gentiles might hear it" (4:17). As in his other letters, Paul identifies himself as apostle to the Gentiles.

Paul's address of Timothy as "my beloved [*agapetos*] child" (see 1 Cor. 4:17) establishes the personal nature of the letter, all of which is directly addressed to Timothy.

The theme of verses 3–7 is memory—Paul's memory and his reminder to Timothy of the meaning of faith, with the purpose of encouraging Timothy to "rekindle the gift of God that is within you" (v. 6). Paul begins by thanking God "whom I worship with a clear conscience, as my ancestors did" (v. 3). Paul's ancestors, of course, were Jewish, not Gentile and not followers of Jesus. That Paul was loyal to his Jewish identity agrees with what he says of himself elsewhere (Rom. 9:1–5; 2 Cor. 3:4–5) and also functions to remind Timothy of his forebears in faith—"your grandmother Lois and your mother Eunice" (v. 5), who were also Jewish. Note that Timothy learned faith from two women. Urging Timothy to embrace the same kind of loyalty, Paul reminds him of their faith and entreats him to "rekindle the gift of God that is within you" (v. 6).

Why Paul felt it necessary to do so is explained in verses 6–7: "For God did not give us a spirit of power and of cowardice, but rather a spirit of power and of love and of self-discipline." Love, like self-discipline, is a quality of the life of faithful people. As verses 8–14 will make clear, Paul apparently feels that Timothy is "ashamed" of Paul who is, after all, in prison (vv. 15–18), a situation in the honor-shame culture of the Roman Empire that would typically bring shame upon the prisoner. Paul mentions those "who have turned away from me" (v. 15).

So he says to Timothy, "Do not be ashamed, then, of the testimony about our Lord or of me his prisoner" (v. 8). Instead, Paul invites Timothy to "join with me in suffering for the gospel, relying on the power of God" (v. 8), that is, as God empowers him to do so. It is God who "saved" and "called" both Paul and Timothy; they were not saved by their own "works," that is, endeavors. "Works" here has nothing to do with "works of the law"; Paul refers to human effort as such.

Then follows an intriguing sentence: "This grace was given to us in Christ Jesus before the ages began, but it has now been revealed through the appearing of our Savior Christ Jesus" (vv. 9–10; compare Rom. 8:28–30). Grace *was given* . . . "before the ages began," declares Paul, and what was long ago given has latterly been disclosed. God did not wait until Jesus Christ's appearance to give grace. What Paul exactly meant, we do not know, but the gracious disposition of God to God's creatures seems always to have been the case; our good fortune is that because of God's self-disclosure we know this.

Notice also (v. 10), that although Paul's gospel is one of crucifixion and resurrection, he does not focus on death but on life: Christ "abolished death and brought life and immortality to light through the gospel."

Paul is "not ashamed," because he was appointed "a herald and an apostle and a teacher" of this gospel (v. 11), and because he knows whom he trusts. Hence, he urges Timothy, in the face of opposition, to "hold to the standard of sound teaching" and to "guard the good treasure entrusted to you" (vv. 13–14).

Proper 23 [28]/Year C

2 Timothy 2:8–15

Paul began his letter urging Timothy to remember the faith of his mother and grandmother and now urges him to "remember Jesus Christ, raised from the dead, a descendant of David—that is my gospel, for which I suffer hardship, even to the point of being chained like a criminal" (vv. 8–9). Paul had asked Timothy to hold to the "faith and love that are in Christ Jesus" (1:13). It is Christ's faithfulness that Paul wants Timothy to remember. Paul is obviously concerned that Timothy remain faithful in spite of the "distressing times" (3:1) that he says "will come" but that, also, are already present in Timothy's community (3:1–9).

Paul is not urging on Timothy an existential if occasional moment of penetrating recall, but a persisting memory that will help Timothy persevere in the face of contrary teaching, such as that of "Hymenaeus and Philetus, who have swerved from the truth by claiming that the resurrection has already taken place" (2:17–18). This claim has not to do with the resurrection of Jesus but with the general resurrection in the eschaton, the claim that we already live in resurrected bodies, which can express itself either in moral asceticism or hedonistic indulgence (we do not know which might have been the case).

Paul makes clear the hardships that he is undergoing, having been arrested ("chained like a criminal," v. 9). It is this that might have led Timothy to be "ashamed" of Paul (1:8). To be in chains for being an apostle was not necessarily a cause for shame in Greco-Roman society, but being imprisoned as a criminal was. The only other "criminals" (*kakourgos*, "evildoer") mentioned in the Second Testament are the two men crucified alongside Jesus (Luke 23:32). However, "the word of God is not chained" (2:9). Martin Luther's "theology of the cross" is helpful here:

God's self-disclosure occurs in situations that apparently deny the glory and power of God—a weak baby in a manger, a crucifixion, an imprisonment. We have it "in clay jars, so that it may be clear that this extraordinary power belongs to God and does not come from us" (2 Cor. 4:7).

Clearly, Paul offers Jesus as an example for Timothy to remember and to try to duplicate. Timothy's ministry will be measured not by its success but by its faithfulness to the good news (v. 8) that has been passed on to him from Paul: "Proclaim the message; be persistent whether the time is favorable or unfavorable" (4:2).

Verse 11 reads, in the NRSV, "The saying is sure." The Greek, *pistos ho logos*, might be better translated as "the word is faithful." Paul regularly speaks of God's *pistos*, faithfulness, as of Christ's or God's faithfulness. If God is faithful, God's word made known in Christ is faithful. Because he has just (2:9) spoken of "the word of God," *ho logos tou theou*, it is God's word of which he speaks in 2:11. That word, for Paul, is definitively disclosed in the crucifixion and resurrection of Jesus Christ: "If we have died with him, we will also live with him; if we endure, we will also reign with him" (v. 11). Paul speaks elsewhere of believing that we will live with Christ (Rom. 6:8). Notice the word "endure." It is this idea that Paul wants to inculcate in Timothy: a spirit of endurance in a situation that can tempt Timothy to turn away, both from Paul and from his gospel.

Verses 12b and 13 present what appears to be, on the surface, a mixed message. First, "if we deny him, he will also deny us." Affirming or denying Jesus seems to be a quid pro quo—God will treat us precisely as we deserve. But verse 13 counters with "If we are faithless, he remains faithful—for he cannot deny himself." What he cannot deny is "the faith and love that are in Christ Jesus" (1:13) and that make him who he is.

The reading concludes in verses 14–15 with a further admonition to "remember these things," to work constructively and not destructively in the community, to rightly interpret the gospel, and not to be ashamed of it or of Paul.

Proper 24 [29]/Year C

2 Timothy 3:14–4:5

Today's reading starts in the middle of a paragraph where we find Paul reminding Timothy to "continue in what you have learned and firmly believed, knowing from whom you learned it" (3:14). He learned it from his mother Lois and his grandmother Eunice (1:5), and has before him the examples of Jesus (2:8–13) and Paul himself (3:10–11). Paul's intensely personal letter to Timothy has throughout one concern: to advise Timothy to stay true to the faith that has been passed on to him.

Hence, in verses 14–17 Paul reminds Timothy of yet another resource to keep him faithful—the Scriptures. He begins, in verse 14, by urging Timothy to "continue [*mene*, stay, abide] in what you have learned and firmly believed [*epistothes*]" and reminds him of those "from whom you learned it." "Firmly believed" could be translated "have come to trust." Lois, Eunice, and Paul are those from whom Timothy learned.

Then we have two verses (15–16) in which Paul calls Timothy's attention to the "sacred writings [*hiera grammata*]" or "scripture [*graphe*, writings]." "All scripture," says Paul, "is inspired by God [*theopneustos*, God-breathed] and is useful for teaching." These two verses have often been ripped from their context and used to rationalize a claim to biblical inerrancy that cannot be supported by the text. In the first place, there was at the time no such thing as the Second Testament (it was officially canonized at councils of the church in Hippo, North Africa, in 393 CE and Carthage in 397 CE). Second, the writings of the Tanakh, an acronym derived from the letters T (for Torah), N (Neviim, prophets), and K (Ketuvim, writings), or the Septuagint (the Greek translation of the Tanakh), were themselves fluid at this time, constituting a loose collection. Third, Christians do not find the Scriptures inspired because they claim to be so. Many other texts make the same claim, but we do not conclude that, therefore, they must be. Rather, Christians find the Scriptures inspiring; they find that in faithful wrestling with them the word of God to which the Scriptures attest sometimes penetrates the heart.

Paul's point is that the sacred writings can "instruct [*sophisai*] you" (v. 15), make you wise, about the meaning of salvation. To this end they are "useful," *ophelimos*, profitable. Paul's point is not theoretical (about the nature of the Scriptures) but practical: by study of them one can be "proficient, equipped for every good work" (v. 16). They are, as they were for Israel, "a lamp to my feet and a light to my path" (Ps. 119:105).

In 4:1–5, we find the last statement in 2 Timothy in which Paul urges Timothy to remain faithful: "In the presence of God and of Christ Jesus," in light of his coming parousia, "I solemnly urge you: proclaim the message; be persistent whether the time is favorable or unfavorable [*eukairos akairos*, the time is propitious or not propitious]" (vv. 1–2). Whatever the circumstances, regardless of its popularity or lack thereof, tell the truth. This includes convincing, denying, and encouraging, and doing it all by patiently teaching (denying is important—if we deny nothing, that is only because we stand for nothing and, hence, nothing can contradict it).

There will be a time, says Paul, when people "having itching ears . . . will accumulate for themselves teachers to suit their own desires" (v. 3). Every pastor understands this point. Paul's counsel is that the gospel of God, the incredibly good news of God's grace lovingly offered to each and all and God's command that justice be done to each and all, is the one word that the church is given and called to make known. As for you, says Paul, "carry out your ministry fully" (v. 5).

Proper 25 [30]/Year C

2 Timothy 4:6–8, 16–18

After urging Timothy to "proclaim the message . . . whether the time is favorable or unfavorable," Paul makes his last request, which follows the first three verses of today's reading: "Do your best to come to me soon" (4:9). He wants to ascertain that Timothy is not afraid to come to him (1:7), not ashamed of him (1:8) for being "chained like a criminal" (2:9). So he begins by describing what he senses is the end of his life: "As for me, I am already being poured out [*spendomai*] as a libation, and the time [*kairos*] of my departure has come" (v. 6). Associations with liquid offerings in the temple are unmistakable; it is Paul's life that is being "poured out." *Kairos* is a time that is right for something to happen; Paul sees this time as the period in which his departure has arrived.

Then in verse 7 Paul shifts to athletic metaphors, which he has used before in 2 Timothy (2:5) and elsewhere: "So I do not run aimlessly, nor do I box as though beating the air; but I punish my body and enslave it, so that after proclaiming to others I myself should not be disqualified" (1 Cor. 9:26). Hellenistic moral philosophers used athletic metaphors to talk about the spiritual discipline of the morally transformed life (good athletes are remarkably self-disciplined). And Paul did think that grace transformed human lives, as his own was transformed.

He says of himself here, "I have fought the good fight [*kalon agona*], I have finished the race [*dromon*], I have kept the faith [*pistin*]" (v. 7). In verse 7, Paul regards these efforts as having arrived at their conclusion; he has fought, has finished his struggles on behalf of the good news. Yet they are not over; he does not speak in the simple past tense but in the perfect tense; the effort persists even in the face of its anticipated end. It is a struggle (*agon*) and a marathon (*dromon*); it takes a lifetime and will for us as well. Paul "has kept the faith" in the face of opposition, which in his own letters comes mainly from his fellow missionaries who disagree with him.

Doing all these things, for Paul, requires reliance on God's grace and strengthening, but that does not mean that it is easy.

What remains for Paul is "the crown [*stephanos*] of righteousness, which the Lord, the righteous judge, will give me on that day, and not only to me but to all who have longed for his appearing" (v. 8). *Stephanos* is also an athletic metaphor; it is the garland of laurels that was awarded as the "gold medal" to the winner of an athletic contest. The Lord who will give the garland to Paul "on that day" is Jesus, of whom Paul spoke in 4:1 as the one "who is to judge the living and the dead." Lest we encourage fear of Jesus as judge, it is helpful to remember that for Paul we are to be judged by the one who died out of love for us.

Today's reading resumes in verse 16 with Paul's commenting, "At my first defense no one came to my support, but all deserted me." Since he mentioned in 4:11, "Luke is with me," verse 16 may not mean that he was utterly abandoned but that he was not supported in his case with the authorities. He prays that the Lord will not count it against them, using the passive voice, as often, in speaking of the Lord.

Verse 17 reminds us of the purpose of Paul's mission: the Lord strengthened him "so that through [him] the message might be fully proclaimed and all the Gentiles might hear it." Paul consistently presents himself as the apostle to the Gentiles.

He ends on a note of promise and praise: the Lord will save him for the kingdom; may God be glorified forever.

Proper 26 [31]/Year C

2 Thessalonians 1:1–4, 11–12

Scholars are divided on whether 2 Thessalonians was written by Paul or by one of Paul's followers in the apostle's name. The preacher who inclines towards the latter could help the congregation understand that in antiquity such a practice was not considered misrepresentation. Under the umbrella of "pseudepigraphy," disciples of a teacher saw themselves applying their teacher's thoughts to new situations. Regardless of who wrote it, encounters with such texts have been instructive for the church across centuries.

Whatever a preacher decides about authorship, the situation in the congregation at Thessalonica has changed. When Paul wrote 1 Thessalonians, the congregation was dispirited, so Paul held out Jesus' apocalyptic return as a lure and encouragement to more vital and faithful living (see Propers 27–28/Year A). Perhaps 1 Thessalonians had greater success than Paul intended, so to speak, because by the time of 2 Thessalonians, apocalyptic fervor had seized the community. The author seeks to help the community recognize that the apocalypse may be farther ahead of them than they think and that, to prepare for it, they need to live and witness faithfully in the present.

This short epistle begins with formal elements found in letters in antiquity: author, recipients, and greeting (1 Thess. 1:1–2). The remarks that we made on Proper 27/Year A, interpret how the writer expected the recipients to understand these matters.

The thanksgiving paragraph (another formal element of the Hellenistic letter) gives thanks to God for the congregation and sets out the main themes of the letter (1:3–12). In verses 3–4, the author intends to create receptive dispositions by complementing the community on their growth in faithfulness. If the author was familiar with 1 Thessalonians, these lines are a progress report: members have taken increased responsibility for encouraging one another in the way Paul suggested. The congregation is enduring, a word that in apocalyptic circles means not only "hang on" but witness faithfully amidst "persecutions" (*diogmos*) and "afflictions" (*thlipsis*)—terms associated with intensified suffering of the last days (Matt. 13:21; 24:9; Mark 13:19, 24; Rom. 8:35).

The lectionary does not appoint 1:5–10 for today. While omitting these verses eases the preacher's task, it misses the point of 2 Thessalonians 1:3–12 and also bypasses an important opportunity to wrestle with a text whose theology may be troubling.

The sufferings of 1:4 are the "evidence" (*endeigm*) of the "righteous judgment of God," a notion in apocalyptic theology that God will call the evil to account and fully manifest the eschatological realm of God. The congregation's endurance through suffering prepares them for the realm (1:5). God will repay with affliction (*thlipsis*, 1:4) those who afflict and will give relief (*anesis*) to those who have been afflicted in the present. Such themes permeate: the faithful are welcomed into the divine realm while the unfaithful are punished, sometimes by the means whereby they caused suffering (*1 En.* 1:3–9; 38:1–6; 2 Esd. 7:26–44; *2 Bar.* 82:1–83:23; Wis. 11:15–16; Rom. 1:18–32).

This affliction and relief take place in connection with the apocalypse described in 1:7b–8a. This passage uses stock apocalyptic imagery to depict Jesus coming with an armada of angel warriors in flaming fire to inflict vengeance on unconverted Gentiles ("those who do not know God") and those in the church who do not "obey our Lord Jesus Christ" (1:8). Fire is a traditional symbol of judgment (Isa. 66:15; Jer. 10:25; Mal.

3:19; 2 Esd. 14:23; *Sib. Or.* 3:80–90). The term "obey" (*pekoe*) signals that Jesus is a kind of rabbi who helps the Gentiles know and live according to the God of Israel.

According to 1:9, unregenerate Gentiles and the unfaithful from within the church will suffer the punishment of "eternal destruction" (*oletheros aionios*) and be "separated from the presence of the Lord and from [God's] glory" (glory = the new world that God is bringing about). The earlier reference to fire combined with the reference to eternal destruction suggests that the writer shares the view of some other apocalypticists that the wicked would burn in fire (2 Esd. 7:35–44; *2 Bar.* 44:15; 48:39; *3 Bar.* 4:16; *Sib. Or.* 4:23; 4 Macc. 12:12). This view was not universal in Jewish circles. Some Jewish theologians envisioned fire as temporary and for the purpose of purgation (Mal. 3:2–4). Some others did not envision a final judgment, much less eternal punishment. On this matter as on so many others, Judaism in antiquity was pluralistic.

At the same time, the saints (*hagioi*, "holy ones," Gentiles and Jews who have lived the holy or faithful life as God instructed) glorify God. To help the Thessalonians be among the saints on that great day, the author asks God to empower the Gentile congregation toward faithfulness. Such living glorifies the name of Jesus Christ now in prefiguration for the eschatological glorification at the apocalypse.

The preacher needs to help the congregation sort through the degree to which they believe in (1) a single apocalyptic moment in which God ends the present age and completes the manifestation of the new one, (2) a single moment of judgment in which all people stand before the cosmic judge, and (3) an eternal punishment (perhaps by fire) of the wicked. To respond to such questions the preacher must draw on the deepest sources of theological reflection.

Proper 27 [32]/Year C

2 Thessalonians 2:1–5, 13–17

Different apocalyptic theologians offered different projections of the series of events by which the current age would come to a close and God would bring the full manifestation of the renewed world. Today's text recounts the author's interpretation of these events for the purpose of encouraging the Gentile Thessalonian congregation to recognize that such events are not imminent and that the community needs to live now by avoiding complicity with lawlessness.

The author cautions readers against being "too quickly shaken in mind or alarmed," thinking the "day of the Lord is already here" (*enistemi*) (2:1–2). A prophet ("spirit," 1 Thess. 5:19–22 Third Sunday of Advent/Year B), or a preacher or teacher ("word"), may have mistakenly said that the day of the Lord is at hand. Or the community may have misinterpreted 1 Thessalonians on this point ("or by letter, as though from us"). This misinformation illustrates the importance of "testing everything" (1 Thess. 5:19–22).

The community needs to be wary of being "deceived" (2:3), a verb that Job uses of how idolatry works (31:27). Before Jesus returns, a rebellion (*apostasia*, apostasy) will occur. Jewish literature sometimes uses the word "rebellion" of Gentiles who flagrantly violate God's desires (1 Macc. 2:15; Sir. 36:12). The rebellion will be led by "the lawless one" whose designation—lawless (*anomia*)—sometime describes Gentile existence (Wis. 5:7, 23; 15:17; 17:2; 2 Macc. 8:17; 3 Macc. 1:27; *Pss. Sol.* 17:11, 18). The "lawless one" lives in violation of torah by making idols and acting contrary to God's purposes.

It is small wonder that the lawless one is heading for the destruction described in 1:7–9 since the lawless one commits idolatry by exalting "himself above every so-called god or object of worship," taking a "seat in the temple [*vaos*] of God, and declaring himself to be God" (1:4). Since prophets give similar descriptions of idolatrous leaders (primarily Gentiles) who destroy covenantal community by authorizing personal and social behavior that is exploitative and destructive (Isa. 14:13–14; Ezek. 28:1–10; Dan. 11:35–36), the writer may have in mind a person who exercises political muscle that permits lawlessness. Other writers expected such figures as part of the tribulation—the increase of chaos in the last days of the old age (Mark 13:6, 21; Rev. 13:13–14).

It is tempting to report that the letter writer is here making a theological critique of the Roman Empire and the emperor, since the description of the lawless one in 2:9 is similar to one of Roman religion in Revelation 13:11–15. However, the text does not contain enough clues to support that identification (or any other) with confidence. Nevertheless, the preacher could help the congregation reflect on figures and movements in our world that are "lawless" and that turn life into chaos. In view of 1:6, such forces will be destroyed by the very lawlessness (violation of covenantal living) they encourage.

The lawless one must be fully revealed before Jesus returns, but that revelation has not taken place yet. The congregation should not be overwrought with the future. They have the "first fruits for salvation through sanctification by the Spirit," that is, manifestations of the Spirit that empower them to live as sanctified people (2:13). A better rendering of *hagiasmos*, sanctification, would be "becoming holy," for the latter communicates that the Gentiles are joining Israel in the covenantal life to demonstrate how God wants all people to live.

God called the Thessalonian community to the holy life so that they can join the group giving glory to God (and avoid eternal destruction) when Jesus returns (1:11–12; 2:14). The way forward is for the congregation to "hold fast to the traditions that you were taught by us" (2:15). We have seen abundant evidence in this letter and in 1 Thessalonians that these traditions include many key concepts and practices of Judaism. The Gentiles live faithfully now and prepare for the apocalypse by living according to important Jewish values.

Proper 28 [33]/Year C

2 Thessalonians 3:6–13

Today's lection illustrates why the congregation at Thessalonica needs to reframe its perception concerning the timing of the apocalypse from expecting Jesus to return immediately to recognizing that while the cataclysm may be on the horizon (and getting closer), all the events have not happened that must occur before the end. Some people in the community, mesmerized by the prospect of Jesus' immediate return, have neglected some of the responsibilities of the faithful life. Today's reading names some of these lapses and, in the spirit of 1 Thessalonians, encourages the readers to resume covenantal behavior with respect to their roles in the community.

The writer states the problem straightforwardly in 3:6: some believers are "living in idleness" (*ataktos*). In connection with 1 Thessalonians 5:14, we follow scholars who adopt an alternate meaning of "disorderly," since that seems better to fit the context of the first letter. In view of 2 Thessalonians 3:7–11, "idleness" fits the context here. Some congregants thought the apocalypse was so close that they quit working and waited.

The Thessalonian idlers do not live according to the Jewish traditions that the apostles taught them (2:6b). Jewish tradition saw several problems with idleness. First, because they did not work, idlers had limited resources and were in danger of suffering hunger and other conditions that threatened God's will for blessing (Prov. 6:6–11; 19:15; Tob. 4:13). Second, idlers could easily drift into evil (Wis. 13:13; Sir. 22:1–2; 33:26–30). The idler thus does not fulfill the purpose of human life, which is to help all things work together as God intends (Gen. 1:26–27). Third, to provide for the idlers the community used resources that could have gone to better purposes. By contrast, working generates materials for life and blessing for one's household and that of the community (Ps. 128:2; Prov. 31:27; Ecc. 11:6). It keeps one focused on the good and distracts from evil (Sir. 24:22; 33:28–30).

The author instructs the congregation to imitate the apostles (vv. 7, 9). We discuss imitation as an important motif in Hellenistic education in connection with Proper 24/Year A. The apostles' work in Thessalonica was the epitome of the opposite of idleness as they worked to provide their own resources and were faithful to God's purpose for them to witness to the Gentiles and build up community. The writer reminds the Thessalonians that the apostles paid for the bread that they ate in Thessalonica and worked night and day to support themselves, thus not depriving anyone of resources (2 Thess. 3:8–9; 1 Thess. 2:9–12). According to the author, those who are unwilling to work should not eat, that is, the community should not provide for them (3:10).

Some in the community exemplify the dangers of idleness mentioned above by becoming "mere busybodies [*periergazomai*], not doing any work" (3:11). The author does not reveal the exact nature of the busybodies' activities, but typically they meddle in matters that are beyond them (Sir. 3:23) and that frustrate God's purposes (*Let Aris* 3:315), as, for example, by entering into inappropriate sexual liaisons (Sir. 41:22).

The authors state forcefully that idlers and busybodies are to "do their work quietly and to earn their own living" (v. 12), for by so doing, they are fulfilling God's purposes ("doing what is right," v. 13). However, if the community sees the idlers not obeying the apostolic instruction the community is to "have nothing to do with them, so that they may be ashamed" (v. 14). The community is not to excommunicate the idlers but is to warn them as "unbelievers." This command and the earlier one to deny food to the idlers (3:10) are not simply punishments but function in the manner of a covenantal curse that is designed to prompt a change of behavior. These actions are pastoral strategies to motivate the idlers and busybodies to become responsible members of the community (Deut. 30:15–20) and thereby be among the saints on the great day of glory (2 Thess. 1:9–10).

Reign of Christ (Proper 29 [34])/Year C

Colossians 1:11–20

Verses 11–14 of today's reading are part of Paul's prayer of intercession for the Colossians. Verses 15–20 are a christological hymn that Paul quotes and adapts for the purposes of writing to the Colossians.

Paul is concerned that the Colossians might be led astray by inappropriate teachings and practices (2:8–23). In his prayer, Paul speaks as much to the Colossians as to God, preparing the ground for his later arguments against "philosophy and empty deceit" and "self-abasement and worship of angels" (2:8, 18). He does this first by asking the Colossians to remember their baptism(s): "giving thanks to the Father, who has enabled you to share in the inheritance of the saints in the light. He has rescued us from the power of darkness and transferred us into the kingdom of his beloved Son" (1:12–13). He is saying to the Colossians, Remember who you were and who you now are. You once dwelled in darkness; you now live in the light.

Colossians addresses itself to Gentiles (1:27) "who were once estranged and hostile in mind, doing evil deeds" (1:21; compare Eph. 2:11–12). Jesus Christ has "reconciled [you Gentiles] in his fleshly body through death, so as to present you holy and blameless . . . before him" (1:22). The proviso in all this, however, is that the Colossians will have to live in such a way that their lives bear witness to their transformed status: "So if you have been raised with Christ, seek the things that are above" (3:1). Grace calls forth ethics; ethics is empowered by grace.

Verses 15–20 are a wisdom Christology hymn (others are Phil. 2:6–11; Heb. 1:2b–4; John 1:1–15). The importance of the personification of wisdom as Woman Wisdom in the Scriptures of Israel cannot be overemphasized. Proverbs 1–9 emphasizes the role of Woman Wisdom in creation, providence, and moral instruction. Hers is an authoritative and revelatory voice, "that of Woman Wisdom, who is teacher, sage, Queen of Heaven, the child of God, and the mediator between heaven and earth."[51] Wisdom comes to be a way of talking about torah (in Sirach the two are identified) and then in the Gospels and christological hymns Wisdom comes to be a way of talking about Jesus. Sirach says of Wisdom, "Put your neck under her yoke, and let your souls receive instruction" (51:26). Matthew's Jesus says, "Take my yoke upon you, and learn from me; for I am gentle and humble in heart" (11:29). Here Jesus speaks as Wisdom incarnate. Jesus' followers came to speak of him as the incarnate Logos of God because *logos* was what happened to wisdom (*chokmah*) when Jews began to speak Greek instead of Hebrew.

Remembering that verses 15–20 are a wisdom hymn will help Christians see them in their context in Colossians; Christ as the "image [*eikon*] of the invisible God, the firstborn of all creation" is God's agent of creation who takes precedence over all creation. The language is that of wisdom Christology, not of Nicaea. It is on a trajectory toward Nicaea but far from arrival there in Colossians.

That "all things have been created through him and for him" (v. 15) means not only that all things once were created but that all things remain in existence now as created both through and "for" Christ. There is a hint of later Augustinian platonism here—all things have been created "towards God," for reconciliation with God.

We comment further on verses 15–20 on Proper 11/Year C.

All Saints/Year C

Ephesians 1:11–23

Please see the Second Sunday after Christmas Day/Year A for commentary on this passage.

Thanksgiving Day/ Years A, B, and C

Philippians 4:4–9

Please see Proper 23/Year A for commentary on this passage.

Notes

Introduction

1. William Barclay, *The Letter to the Romans*, rev. ed., The Daily Study Bible Series (Philadelphia: Westminster Press, 1975), 64.
2. —— *The Letters to the Galatians and Ephesians*, rev. ed., The Daily Study Bible Series (Philadelphia: Westminster Press, 1975), 30.
3. Ernst Käsemann, "Paul and Israel," in *New Testament Questions of Today*, trans. W. J. Montague (Philadelphia: Fortress Press, 1969), 186.
4. Ibid., 185; emphasis ours.
5. Lester Dean, "The Problem of a Jew Talking About Paul," in *Bursting the Bonds*, ed. Leonard Swidler, John Eron Lewis, Gerard Sloyan, and Lester Dean (Maryknoll, NY: Orbis Books, 1990), 129.
6. C. G. Montefiore, *Judaism and St. Paul* (London: Max Goschen, 1914), 29–30.
7. C. G. Montefiore and H. Loewe, eds., *A Rabbinic Anthology* (New York: Schocken Books, 1974), 236–37.
8. H. J. Schoeps, *Paul: The Theology of the Apostle in the Light of Jewish Religious History* (Philadelphia: Westminster Press, 1961), 213.
9. Matthew Black, *Romans* (London: Marshall, Morgan & Scott, 1973), 47.
10. Charles Y. Glock and Rodney Stark, *Christian Beliefs and Anti-Semitism* (New York: Harper & Row, 1966); Rodney Stark, Bruce D. Foster, Charles Y. Glock, and Harold E. Quinley, *Wayward Shepherds: Prejudice & the Protestant Clergy* (New York: Harper & Row, 1971).
11. Clark M. Williamson, *When Jews and Christians Meet* (St. Louis: CBP Press, 1989), 44–45, 48, 51; *A Guest in the House of Israel: Post-Holocaust Church Theology* (Louisville, KY: Westminster/John Knox Press, 1993), 245–46.
12. With acknowledgments to Calvin L. Porter, "A New Paradigm for Reading Romans," *Encounter* 39 (Summer 1978): 257–72.
13. Krister Stendahl made these points in *Paul Among Jews and Gentiles* (Philadelphia: Fortress Press, 1976), 7–10.
14. Lloyd Gaston, *Paul and the Torah* (Vancouver: University of British Columbia Press, 1987), 14.

253

15. See Clark M. Williamson and Ronald J. Allen, *The Teaching Minister* (Louisville, KY: Westminster/John Knox Press, 1991), 21–25.

Commentary

1. Krister Stendahl, *Final Account: Paul's Letter to the Romans* (Minneapolis: Fortress Press, 1995), 16–17.
2. *Yalkut* on Pss. 5 and 92, cited in C. G. Montefiore and H. Loewe, *A Rabbinic Anthology* (New York: Schocken Books, 1972), 236–37.
3. Pamela Eisenbaum, "Paul as the New Abraham," in *Paul and Politics*, ed. Richard A. Horsley (Harrisburg, PA: Trinity Press International, 2000), 133.
4. Gustaf Aulen, *The Faith of the Christian Church* (Philadelphia: Fortress Press, 1960), 218.
5. Ibid.
6. Dale B. Martin, *The Corinthian Body* (New Haven, CT: Yale University Press, 1985), 87–92.
7. M. T. Hooker, "*PISTIS CHRISTOU,*" *New Testament Studies* 35 (1989): 321–42.
8. Lloyd Gaston, *Paul and the Torah* (Vancouver: University of British Columbia Press, 1987), 116–34.
9. Markus Barth, "Was Paul an Anti-Semite?" *Journal of Ecumenical Studies* 5, no. 1 (1968): 85.
10. Peter Richardson, "Augustan-era Synagogues in Rome," in *Judaism and Christianity in First-Century Rome*, ed. Karl P. Donfried and Peter Richardson (Grand Rapids: Wm. B. Eerdmans Publishing Co., 1998), 19.
11. Martin Luther's *The Freedom of a Christian* is a fine articulation of Paul's understanding of freedom; it can be found in John Dillenberger, ed., *Martin Luther: Selections from His Writings* (Garden City, NY: Doubleday & Co., 1961), 42–85.
12. N. T. Wright, "Paul's Gospel and Caesar's Empire," in Horsley, ed., *Paul and Politics*, 172.
13. Martin Buber, *On Zion*, trans. Stanley Goodman (New York: Schocken Books, 1973).
14. Stendahl, *Final Account*, 35; John Gager, *The Origins of Anti-Semitism* (New York: Oxford University Press, 1983), 223–25.
15. E. P. Sanders, *Paul and Palestinian Judaism* (London: SCM Press, 1977), 47, 427.
16. Jon D. Levenson, *Sinai and Zion* (San Francisco: Harper & Row, 1985), 77.
17. John Chrysostom, "Homily I Against the Jews," in *Jews and Christians in Antioch*, ed. Wayne A. Meeks and Robert Wilken (Missoula, MT: Scholars Press, 1978), 85–104.
18. Beverly Roberts Gaventa, *First and Second Thessalonians*, Interpretation: A Bible Commentary for Preaching and Teaching (Louisville, KY: Westminster John Knox Press, 1998), 24.
19. Ibid., 80–83.
20. Gaston, *Paul and the Torah*, 29–30.
21. Dale B. Martin, *The Corinthian Body* (New Haven, CT: Yale University Press, 1995), 174–75.
22. Gaston, *Paul and the Torah*, 29–31.
23. Stanley K. Stowers, *A Rereading of Romans* (New Haven, CT: Yale University Press, 1994), 135–37.
24. Ibid., 46–52.
25. In much of what follows, we are indebted to Gaston, *Paul and the Torah*, 151–68, though at points we offer our own nuances of difference.

26. Ibid., 154–55.

27. Ibid., 166.

28. Martin, *Corinthian Body*, 104–22.

29. Jacob Neusner, *Torah from Our Sages*: Pirke Avot (Dallas: Rossel Books, 1983), 2:4.

30. Stendahl, *Final Account*, 31.

31. Michael Wyschogrod, *The Body of Faith: God and the People Israel* (Northvale, NJ: Jason Aronson, Inc., 1996), 256.

32. Geza Vermes, *Jesus the Jew* (New York: Macmillan, 1973), 114, 210–13.

33. See Don S. Browning, *The Moral Context of Pastoral Care* (Philadelphia: Westminster Press, 1976).

34. S. R. F. Price, "Rituals and Power," in *Paul and Empire*, ed. Richard A. Horsley (Harrisburg, PA: Trinity Press International, 1997), 62.

35. Clark M. Williamson and Ronald J. Allen, *The Teaching Minister* (Louisville, KY: Westminster/John Knox Press, 1991).

36. Adapting from Martin, *Corinthian Body*, 15–21, 37; on the broader notion of body see Jon L. Berquist, *Controlling Corporeality: The Body and the Household in Ancient Israel* (New Brunswick, NJ: Rutgers University Press, 2002).

37. Gaston, *Paul and the Torah*, 25–29.

38. Aspects of this view are found in a number of scholars, but it is particularly accessible in Gaston, *Paul and the Torah*, 80, 90, 109, and in John G. Gager, *Reinventing Paul* (Oxford: Oxford University Press, 2000), 77–100. We have also been instructed greatly by J. Louis Martyn, *Galatians*. Anchor Bible (New York: Doubleday, 1997).

39. Our interpretation of this passage largely follows Gaston, *Paul and the Torah*, 151–68.

40. Ibid., 163.

41. Ibid., 164.

42. Martyn, *Galatians*, 236, 245.

43. Gaston, *Paul and the Torah*, 25.

44. Ibid., 71.

45. Adapted from ibid., 66.

46. Ibid., 27–28.

47. Ibid., 29–30.

48. Neusner, *Torah from Our Sages*, 1:12.

49. Here and in other places in discussing Philemon, we are indebted to S. Scott Bartchy, "Philemon, Epistle To," in *The Anchor Bible Dictionary*, ed. David Noel Freedman, et al. (Garden City: Doubleday, 1992) 5: 307–08.

50. Neusner, *Torah from Our Sages*, 4.5.

51. Leo Perdue, *Wisdom and Creation* (Nashville: Abingdon Press, 1994), 78.

Reference List of Ancient Jewish Sources in English Translation

Ahikar, trans. J. M. Lindenberger. In *The Old Testament Pseudepigrapha*, ed. James H. Charlesworth (Garden City, NY: Doubleday, 1983), vol. 2.

Babylonian Talmud, ed. Rabbi Dr. I. Epstein (London: Soncino Press, 1938).

Charlesworth, James H., ed. *The Old Testament Pseudepigrapha: Apocalyptic Literature and Testaments* (Garden City, NY: Doubleday, 1983), vol. 1.

Dead Sea Scrolls Translated, The, trans. Florentino Garcia Martinez (Grand Rapids: Wm. B. Eerdmans Publishing Co., 1996).

Fathers According to Rabbi Nathan, The, trans. Judah Goldin. Yale Judaica Series (New Haven, CT: Yale University Press, 1955).

Jerusalem Talmud. In *The Talmud of the Land of Israel: An Academic Commentary to the Second, Third and Fourth Divisions*, ed. Jacob Neusner. University of South Florida Academic Commentary Series (Atlanta: Scholars Press, 1988).

Josephus. *Against Apion*, trans. H. St. J. Thackeray. Loeb Classical Library (Cambridge: Harvard University Press, 1926).

———. *The Antiquities of the Jews*, trans. H. St. J. Thackeray, Ralph Marcus, Allen Wikgren, and Louis H. Feldman. Loeb Classical Library (Cambridge, MA: Harvard University Press, 1926–1965).

———. *The Jewish Wars*, trans. H. St. J. Thackeray. Loeb Classical Library (Cambridge, MA: Harvard University Press, 1927).

Midrash on Psalms, The, trans. William G. Braude. Yale Judaica Series. (New Haven, CT: Yale University Press, 1959).

Midrash Rabbah, trans. H. Freedmand and M. Simon (London: Soncino Press, 1939), 13 vols.

Mishnah, The, trans. Herbert Danby (London: Oxford University Press, 1933).

Odes of Solomon, trans. James H. Charlesworth. In *The Old Testament Pseudepigrapha*, ed. James H. Charlesworth (Garden City: Doubleday, 1983), vol. 2.

Philo. "On Husbandry." In *Philo*, trans. F. H. Colson and G. H. Whitaker. Loeb Classical Library (Cambridge, MA: Harvard University Press, 1930), vol. 3.

———. "Allegorical Interpretation." In *Philo*, trans. F. H. Colson and G. H. Whitaker. Loeb Classical Library (Cambridge, MA: Harvard University Press, 1930), vol. 3.

————. "On Abraham." In *Philo*, trans. F. H. Colson and G. H. Whitaker. Loeb Classical Library (Cambridge, MA: Harvard University Press, 1935), vol. 6.

————. "On Creation." In *Philo*, trans. F. H. Colson and G. H. Whitaker. Loeb Classical Library (Cambridge, MA: Harvard University Press, 1929), vol. 1.

————. "On Dreams." In *Philo*, trans. F. H. Colson and G. H. Whitaker. Loeb Classical Library (Cambridge: Harvard University Press, 1934), vol. 5.

————. "On Drunkenness." In *Philo*, trans. F. H. Colson and G. H. Whitaker. Loeb Classical Library (Cambridge, MA: Harvard University Press, 1930), vol. 3.

————. "On Flight and Finding." In *Philo*, trans. F. H. Colson and G. H. Whitaker. Loeb Classical Library (Cambridge, MA: Harvard University Press, 1934), vol. 5.

————. "On Noah's Work as Planter." In *Philo*, trans. F. H. Colson and G. H. Whitaker. Loeb Classical Library (Cambridge, MA: Harvard University Press, 1930), vol. 3.

————. "On the Migration of Abraham." In *Philo*, trans. F. H. Colson and G. H. Whitaker. Loeb Classical Library (Cambridge, MA: Harvard University Press, 1932), vol. 4.

————. "On the Special Laws." In *Philo*, trans. F. H. Colson and G. H. Whitaker. Loeb Classical Library (Cambridge, MA: Harvard University Press, 1939), vol. 7.

————. "On the Giants." In *Philo*, trans. F. H. Colson. Loeb Classical Library (Cambridge, MA: Harvard University Press, 1927), vol. 2.

————. "On the Posterity and Exile of Cain," In *Philo*, trans. F. H. Colson. Loeb Classical Library (Cambridge, MA: Harvard University Press, 1927), vol. 2.

————. "On the Virtues," In *Philo*, trans. F. H. Colson. Loeb Classical Library (Cambridge, MA: Harvard University Press, 1938), vol. 8.

————. "On Noah's Work as Planter." In *Philo*, trans. F. H. Colson and G. H. Whitaker. Loeb Classical Library (Cambridge, MA: Harvard University Press, 1930), vol. 3.

————. "Questions and Answers on Genesis." In *Philo Supplement*, trans. Ralph Marcus. Loeb Classical Library (Cambridge, MA: Harvard University Press, 1953).

————. "On the Unchangeableness of God." In *Philo*, trans. F. H. Colson and G. H. Whitaker. Loeb Classical Library (Cambridge, MA: Harvard University Press, 1930).

————. "The Embassy to Gaius." In *Philo*, trans. F. H. Colson and G. H. Whitaker. Loeb Classical Library (Cambridge, MA: Harvard University Press, 1930).

"Psalms of Solomon, The," trans. R. B. Wright. *The Old Testament Pseudepigrapha*, edited by James H. Charlesworth (Garden City, NY: Doubleday, 1983), vol. 2.

Sifra: An Analytical Translation, trans. Jacob Neusner. Brown Judaica Series (Atlanta: Scholars Press, 1988).

Sifre Deuteronomy, trans. Reuven Hammer. Yale Judaica Series (New Haven, CT: Yale University Press, 1986).

Sibylline Oracles, trans. John H. Collings. In *The Old Testament Pseudepigrapha*, ed. James H. Charlesworth (Garden City: Doubleday, 1983), vol. 1.

Testament of Reuben in "Testaments of the Twelve Patriarchs," trans. H. C. Kee. In *The Old Testament Pseudepigrapha: Apocalyptic Literature and Testaments*, ed. James H. Charlesworth (Garden City, NY: Doubleday, 1983), vol. 1.

Testament of Simeon in "Testaments of the Twelve Patriarchs," trans. H. C. Kee. In *The Old Testament Pseudepigrapha: Apocalyptic Literature and Testaments*, ed. James H. Charlesworth (Garden City, NY: Doubleday, 1983), vol. 1.

Testament of Levi in "Testaments of the Twelve Patriarchs," trans. H. C. Kee. In *The Old Testament Pseudepigrapha: Apocalyptic Literature and Testaments*, ed. James H. Charlesworth (Garden City, NY.: Doubleday, 1983), vol. 1.

Testament of Judah in "Testaments of the Twelve Patriarchs," trans. H. C. Kee. In *The Old Testament Pseudepigrapha: Apocalyptic Literature and Testaments*, ed. James H. Charlesworth (Garden City, NY: Doubleday, 1983), vol. 1.

Testament of Issachar in "Testaments of the Twelve Patriarchs," trans. H. C. Kee. In *The Old Testament Pseudepigrapha: Apocalyptic Literature and Testaments*, ed. James H. Charlesworth (Garden City, NY: Doubleday, 1983), vol. 1.

Testament of Zebulon in "Testaments of the Twelve Patriarchs," trans. H. C. Kee. In *The Old Testament Pseudepigrapha: Apocalyptic Literature and Testaments*, ed. James H. Charlesworth (Garden City, NY: Doubleday, 1983), vol. 1.

Testament of Dan in "Testaments of the Twelve Patriarchs," trans. H. C. Kee. In *The Old Testament Pseudepigrapha: Apocalyptic Literature and Testaments*, ed. James H. Charlesworth (Garden City, NY: Doubleday, 1983), vol. 1.

Testament of Naphtali in "Testaments of the Twelve Patriarchs," trans. H. C. Kee. In *The Old Testament Pseudepigrapha: Apocalyptic Literature and Testaments*, ed. James H. Charlesworth (Garden City, NY: Doubleday, 1983), vol. 1.

Testament of Gad in "Testaments of the Twelve Patriarchs," trans. H. C. Kee. In *The Old Testament Pseudepigrapha: Apocalyptic Literature and Testaments*, ed. James H. Charlesworth (Garden City, NY.: Doubleday, 1983), vol. 1.

Testament of Asher in "Testaments of the Twelve Patriarchs," trans. H. C. Kee. In *The Old Testament Pseudepigrapha: Apocalyptic Literature and Testaments*, ed. James H. Charlesworth (Garden City, NY: Doubleday, 1983), vol. 1.

Testament of Job, trans. R. P. Spittler. In *The Old Testament Pseudepigrapha: Apocalyptic Literature and Testaments*, ed. James H. Charlesworth (Garden City, NY: Doubleday, 1983), vol. 1.

Testament of Joseph in "Testaments of the Twelve Patriarchs," trans. H. C. Kee. In *The Old Testament Pseudepigrapha: Apocalyptic Literature and Testaments*, ed. James H. Charlesworth (Garden City, NY: Doubleday, 1983), vol. 1.

Testament of Benjamin in "Testaments of the Twelve Patriarchs," trans. H. C. Kee. In *The Old Testament Pseudepigrapha: Apocalyptic Literature and Testaments*, ed. James H. Charlesworth (Garden City, NY: Doubleday, 1983), vol. 1.

Torah from Our Sages: Pirke Avot, trans. Jacob Neusner (Dallas: Rossel Books, 1984).

Tosefta: Translated from the Hebrew, trans. Jacob Neusner (New York: KTAV, 1977–80), 6 vols.

Bibliography

Aulen, Gustaf. *The Faith of the Christian Church*. Philadelphia: Fortress Press, 1960.

Barth, Markus. "Was Paul an Anti-Semite?" *Journal of Ecumenical Studies* 5, no. 1 (1968): 78–104.

Berquist, Jon L. *Controlling Corporeality: The Body and the Household in Ancient Egypt*. New Brunswick: Rutgers University Press, 2002.

Black, Matthew. *Romans*. London: Marshall, Morgan & Scott, 1973.

Browning, Don S. *The Moral Context of Pastoral Care*. Philadelphia: Westminster Press, 1976.

Buber, Martin. *On Zion*. Translated by Stanley Goodman. New York: Schocken Books, 1973.

Davies, Alan T., ed. *Anti-Semitism and the Foundations of Christianity*. New York: Paulist Press, 1979.

Dillenberger, John, ed. *Martin Luther: Selections from His Writings*. Garden City, NY: Doubleday, 1961.

Donfried, Karl P., and Richardson, Peter. *Judaism and Christianity in First-Century Rome*. Grand Rapids: Wm. B. Eerdmans Publishing Co., 1998.

Gager, John. *The Origins of Anti-Semitism*. New York: Oxford University Press, 1983.

Gager, John. *Reinventing Paul*. Oxford: Oxford University Press, 2000.

Gaston, Lloyd. *Paul and the Torah*. Vancouver: University of British Columbia Press, 1987.

Gaventa, Beverly Roberts. *First and Second Thessalonians*: Interpretation: A Bible Commentary for Preaching and Teaching. Louisville, KY: Westminster John Knox Press, 1998.

Glock, Charles Y. and Stark, Rodney. *Christian Beliefs and Anti-Semitism*. New York: Harper & Row, 1966.

Glock, Charles Y., Rodney Stark, Bruce D. Foster, and Harold E. Quinley. *Wayward Shepherds: Prejudice & the Protestant Clergy*. New York: Harper & Row, 1971.

Hooker, M. T. "*PISTIS CHRISTOU*." *New Testament Studies* 35 (1989), 321–42.

Horsley, Richard A., ed. *Paul and Empire*. Harrisburg, PA: Trinity Press International, 1997.

———. *Paul and Politics*. Harrisburg, PA: Trinity Press International, 2000.

Kasemann, Ernst. *New Testament Questions of Today*. Translated by W. J. Montague. Philadelphia: Fortress Press, 1969.

Levenson, Jon. *Sinai and Zion*. San Francisco: Harper & Row, 1985.

Martin, Dale B. *The Corinthian Body*. New Haven, CT: Yale University Press, 1995.

Martyn, J. Louis. *Galatians*. Anchor Bible. New York: Doubleday, 1997.

Meeks, Wayne A., and Robert Wilken. *Jews and Christians in Antioch*. Missoula, MT: Scholars Press, 1978.

Montefiore, C. G. *Judaism and St. Paul*. London: Max Goschen, 1914.

Montefiore, C. G. and H. Loewe, eds. *A Rabbinic Anthology*. New York: Schocken Books, 1974.

Perdue, Leo. *Wisdom and Creation*. Nashville: Abingdon Press, 1994.

Porter, Calvin L. "A New Paradigm for Reading Romans." *Encounter* 39 (Summer 1978): 257–72.

Sanders, E. P. *Paul and Palestinian Judaism*. London: SCM Press, 1977.

Schoeps, H. J. *Paul: The Theology of the Apostle in the Light of Jewish Religious History*. Philadelphia: Westminster Press, 1961.

Stendahl, Krister. *Final Account: Paul's Letter to the Romans*. Minneapolis: Fortress Press, 1995.

———. *Paul Among Jews and Gentiles*. Philadelphia: Fortress Press, 1976.

Stowers, Stanley K. *A Rereading of Romans*. New Haven, CT: Yale University Press, 1994.

Vermes, Geza. *Jesus the Jew*. New York: Macmillan, 1973.

Williamson, Clark M. *A Guest in the House of Israel: Post-Holocaust Church Theology*. Louisville, KY: Westminster/John Knox Press, 1993.

Williamson, Clark M. and Ronald J. Allen. *The Teaching Minister*. Louisville, KY: Westminster/John Knox Press, 1991.

Williamson, Clark M. *When Jews and Christians Meet*. St. Louis: CBP Press, 1989.

Wyschogrod, Michael. *The Body of Faith: God and the People Israel*. Northvale, NJ: Aronson, Inc., 1996.

Index of Passages in Canonical Order